SETTLING THE POP SCORE

For my late parents, Grace and Harold Hawkins

Settling the Pop Score

Pop texts and identity politics

STAN HAWKINS

Ashgate

Published by
Ashgate Publishing Limited
Gower House
Croft Road
Aldershot
Hants GU11 3HR
England

Ashgate Publishing Company
131 Main Street
Burlington, VT 05401–5600 USA

Ashgate website: http://www.ashgate.com

British Library Cataloguing in Publication Data
Hawkins, Stan
  Settling the pop score : pop texts and identity politics. -
(Ashgate popular and folk music series)
  1. Popular music - History and criticism 2. Identity
(Psychology)
  I. Title
  781.6'4

Library of Congress Cataloging-in-Publication Data
Hawkins, Stan.
  Settling the pop score : pop texts and identity politics / Stan Hawkins.
      p. cm. -- (Ashgate popular and folk music series)
  Includes bibliographical references, discography, and index.
  ISBN 0-7546-0351-2
      1. Popular music--Social aspects. 2. Gender identity in music. 3. Sex in music. 4.
  Musical analysis. 5. Musicology. I. Title. II. Series.

  ML3918.P67 H39 2001
  782.42164--dc21   2001033361

ISBN 0 7546 0351 2 (Hbk)
ISBN 0 7546 0352 0 (Pbk)

This book is printed on acid free paper.
Typeset in Times New Roman by Q3 Bookwork, Loughborough.
Printed and bound by T.J. International Ltd., Padstow, Cornwall.

Contents

General Editor's Preface

The upheaval that occurred in musicology during the last two decades of the twentieth century has created a new urgency for the study of popular music alongside the development of new critical and theoretical models. A relativistic outlook has replaced the universal perspective of modernism (the international ambitions of the 12-note style); the grand narrative of the evolution and dissolution of tonality has been challenged, and emphasis has shifted to cultural context, reception and subject position. Together, these have conspired to eat away at the status of canonical composers and categories of high and low in music. A need has arisen, also, to recognize and address the emergence of crossovers, mixed and new genres, to engage in debates concerning the vexed problem of what constitutes authenticity in music and to offer a critique of musical practice as the product of free, individual expression.

Popular musicology is now a vital and exciting area of scholarship, and the Ashgate Popular and Folk Music series aims to present the best research in the field. Authors will be concerned with locating musical practices, values and meanings in cultural context, and may draw upon methodologies and theories developed in cultural studies, semiotics, poststructuralism, psychology and sociology. The series will focus on popular musics of the twentieth and twenty-first centuries. It is designed to embrace the world's popular musics from Acid Jazz to Zydeco, whether high tech or low tech, commercial or non-commercial, contemporary or traditional.

Professor Derek B. Scott
Chair of Music
University of Salford

Visit Project Pop: http://www.salford.ac.uk/FDTLpop/welcome.htm

List of Music Examples, Figures and Tables

Examples

Figures

Tables

Copyright Acknowledgements

Preface and Acknowledgements

The year was 1985. I recall the rise of Madonna and her domination of MTV with her teasing video, 'Like a Virgin', and her performance being anything but. This was also the same year that Prince was breaking through into mainstream pop. Many adored him in his self-indulgent film, *Purple Rain*, while others were bewildered, shocked, and repulsed. Then there were the Pet Shop Boys – weird, ironic and definitely gloomy, their identities captured through the dazzling sounds of the Fairlight CMI and Hi-NRG, camped-up disco riffs. Everyone seemed to love the Eurythmics and their brassy gender bending songs, even if Annie Lennox appeared to parade around as a social worker. And, in the same year, dressed in a large, pink blouse with crystal necklace, singing, 'Heaven Knows I'm Miserable Now' on BBC's *Top of the Pops*, the misery of the decade – the underside of the consumer boom – was captured by Manchester's favourite son, Steven Morrissey.

Throughout the 1980s and into the 1990s there was a scrambling of musical vocabularies which threw together a diversity of cultures, identities, and sexualities. Over the years, as part of the generation growing up with this pop celebrity culture, I have gradually worked out that music not only affects our identities but also shapes them. This book is one of several recent texts to pursue the interpretation of popular music within a broad, interdisciplinary framework. On a related front, it explores the functions of pop music on a constantly shifting social plane where the appropriation of musical styles and idioms raise larger questions about contemporary Western cultures.

Through an appraisal of selected case-studies from the early 1980s onwards, my purpose is to suggest various approaches for the analysis of pop artists and their music. Central to my enquiry is the question of what these musicians and their texts have signified for me during the last two decades of the twentieth century. Because reading music on the part of the musicologist instates so many definitions that foreclose agreed-upon dialogic structures and concepts, I have clung to the belief that meanings are also derived from our personal understandings of our social contexts. This would certainly imply that the process of musical interpretation needs to explore how meanings are instituted and relinquished according to the practices that constitute them. In all the discussions presented, an underlying thread concerns the general idea that a politics of identity can be approached through interpreting aspects of compositional design, sonic gesture, and musical structure alongside matters relating to the various components of nationality, race, age, ethnicity, sexuality, and gender. In this light, notions of authorial identity and the problems associated with musicological criticism form a most critical basis for my work. Given that dialogic exchanges of meaning flow through never ending streams of signification, my project has been to consider how musical meaning resides in social values and discursively rated strategies. Indeed, musical expression in pop texts not only produces but also reflects the trends in consumption which are commonly based around paradoxical notions of authenticity. At any rate, it would seem to be in the appeal of different kinds of musical affect that the motivation behind our preferences for musical forms and styles rests.

Much of my work is informed by an emergent musicological paradigm that deals with the formalist questions of music analysis alongside the more inter-textual discursive theorisations of musical expression. The frequent use of the term 'popular musicology', which I knowingly use at my own peril, is intended to signify the potential for a more critical approach to a musicology that favours the serious consideration of how the structures and codes of sound produce meaning in popular music. An important dimension of my thinking has taken place in relation to the reconsideration of musicology as both a scholarly and practical enterprise. I am currently working with a group of progressive musicologists (notably, all of whom are also musicians) on a new Internet journal, *Popular Musicology Online*, that seeks to bring scholarly and practical experience into productive dialogue on questions of the music's text and context.

Those of us who have grown up with pop and gone on to study and teach it within music departments around the world know that there is a general intellectual tendency to retreat from the idea that commercial production and consumption can be aligned to artistic authenticity, let alone serious musicological inquiry. These troublesome perspectives continue to pose a set of problematics in both musicology and music education, and have thus had a direct bearing on my reasoning for selecting the highly profiled commercial artists covered in this book. For a growing number of music scholars, the barriers between high and low art forms in music have already been eroded – a process which started in the early 1970s with the systematic dismantling of modernist meta-narratives. Yet, somewhat curiously, today one still encounters the essentialist assumptions that have underpinned the ideological foundations of musicology since the nineteenth century. I am referring to a set of attitudes and beliefs that are underpinned by the Western canon which, unfortunately, tend to collide with popular music studies – one of the most broadly based areas of study concerned with the pleasures, vulgarities and delights of consumerism that drive so-called mass music.

Concentrating predominantly on artists within a British and North American context, most of this book is concerned with how they have effected changes within western popular music during the past few decades. Since my main task is to tackle some of the challenges facing textual analysis, I have limited myself to a relatively small repertoire of musical examples in order to facilitate a more in-depth examination. In chapters 2–6, my discussions are presented in the form of case studies which provide me with a platform to probe a range of methodologies that uncover musical codes in relationship to a plurality of meanings. These five chapters make reference to specific song recordings often in association with other forms of medium – videos, film, interviews, album cover shots, and live concerts. Of course, the advantage of choosing such well known pop artists is that the reader should have little difficulty in accessing the material under discussion in any good record store or library. Although it should not be impossible to follow the thread of most of my discussions without the aid of the original examples, it is however recommended that the reader have recordings on hand if the details of some of the analyses are to be followed closely.

While the studies in this book cannot purport to be anything more than personal, the questions dealt with are drawn from my experience as a musician, student, and teacher working in several university music departments since the mid-1970s. I am indebted to the cohorts of popular music students who I have been fortunate enough to teach and supervise since establishing courses in popular music at the School of Media, Music and Performance, Salford University, Manchester, England, in 1987, and at the Department of Music and Theatre, Oslo University, Norway, from 1995 onwards. I owe a debt to many of my former colleagues at Salford University who encouraged me, sometimes against all odds, to establish a research base in the form of the Popular Music Research Unit (PMRU), in particular Jonty Stockdale, Derek Scott, Sheila Whiteley, and Steve Sweeney-Turner. Thanks also go to my musicologist colleagues at Oslo University for all their support and encouragement, and moreover for affording me the necessary academic stimulation for productive research – an element vital to a thriving music department such as ours. In the same breath, my gratitude goes to the Faculty of Arts, Oslo University, which has continuously supported me generously in all my applications for research work. Very special thanks go to my recent cohorts of Norwegian graduate students who have always participated enthusiastically in my popular music seminars and lectures. In particular, pioneering dissertations in a broad range of aspects of popular musicology have been delivered by my postgraduate students: Bengt Olav Hansen, Elisabet Davidsen, Torbjørn Rodal, Arne Brunvoll, Harald Sandø, Odd Turleiv Furnes, Espen Eriksen, Solveig Christensen, Knut Bjørnar Oppsahl, Elisabeth Anvik, Erik Strandberg, Vidar Holm, Vegard Schow, Håvard Gravdal, and Kyrre Tromm Lindvig. Suffice to say, amongst the key academics working in the interdisciplinary field of popular music studies, a number deserve mention as they stand out as invaluable sources of critical inspiration (direct and indirect) during the eight years it has taken to write this book.

I especially want to acknowledge the influence of the output of work by Sheila Whiteley, John Richardson, Simon Frith, Richard Middleton, Philip Tagg, David Brackett, Dai Griffiths, Peter Wicke, Lucy Green, Allan Moore, Robynn Stilwell, Andy Bennett, Lutgard Mutsaers, Steve Sweeney-Turner, Robert Burnett, Rob Walser, Portia Maultsby, Maria Marquise, Anahid Kassabian and Will Straw. In addition, many other IASPM friends and associates also deserve a heartfelt thanks for their encouragement and, at times, necessary hard critique ever since I became a member of the organisation, not least during my time as UK Chair from 1991 to 1993. Most recently, my position as representative of the Norwegian branch of IASPM-Norden continues to offer me the opportunity, both in a Scandinavian and international context, for contact with the many scholars who work within the broader discipline of popular music studies.

On a personal level I owe a great deal to close life-long friends for helpful comments, lively discussions, and provocative arguments surrounding the issues of musicianship, performance, and taste; I thank Jackie, Tim, Dezi, Lynne, Tom, Martin, Vera and Karsten, Geir, Andreas, Gisela, Bjarne, Nunu, and Adrian. My thanks also go to Paul Jackson of the BBC and André Viervoll for assisting me with copyright and transcription matters, which, as all of us working in the field know, can plague the task of writing a text book from beginning to end. At the level of the production work and editing of this book, my gratitude goes to Jeanne Brady, Huw Jones and the staff of Ashgate, in particular Rachel Lynch, Claire Annals and Ruth Peters. In addition, assistance in meeting some of the costs of this publication was generously provided by the Research Council of Norway to whom I am most grateful.

Perhaps my staunchest critic and supporter remains Derek Scott, editor of this Ashgate series, whose belief in my work from the outset has helped motivate me in attempting to address many of the musicological problematics of popular music. His distinguished scholarship in sociomusicology, his musical breadth and critical outlook, has been a driving force behind the completion of this project. And, finally, without the encouragement of my closest ones, Grace, Harold, Carmen and Tina Hawkins, through sad and joyous times, this book would never have been realised. My most deep-felt gratitude goes to them.

Chapter 1

Settling the Pop Score . . .

Introduction

Reading pop texts is about rethinking the musical assumptions that engender
the analytic approaches to Western music. Recently, numerous frameworks for
accommodating the analysis of pop within musicology have been forthcoming,
as musicologists engaged in popular music scholarship[1] have set out to demonstrate how music-theoretical approaches need to be modified to accommodate
music produced by the media. The historical causes for these recent changes
have been debated extensively, and generally speaking are linked to problems
involving our music education traditions. Philip Brett has insisted that the
acquisition of musical skills traditionally takes place in Western music institutions through a 'tacit understanding of the superiority' of the musical canon
through which 'the "masterwork" ideology is first and most effectively
instilled' (1994: 14). A sense of musical abstraction is experienced at the
outset through harmony courses and ear training programmes where music
students are confronted with analysing and setting four-part chorale settings of
J.S. Bach. Seldom aware of the social or historical backgrounds to these
harmonic arrangements, the music student learns the rules of technical correctness, and so the way is paved towards a working understanding of formal
construction and ideological supposition.

Yet, paradoxically, what most students enrolled on music degree
programmes listen, dance and respond to in their spare time remains by and
large well outside the lecture theatre and classroom. Few music curricula focus
on the differences in performance practices from one music culture to the next.
With the emphasis so often on abstraction, music analysis often renders
musical meaning void of any social and emotional effects. Furthermore, far too
often questions of meaning presume that the music speaks for itself.

Theoretically, the scientific objectivity afforded to the internal structures and
architectonic levels of music can easily rule out the possibility of creative criticism.[2] Yet, in spite of a general scepticism on the part of the critical scholar to
the ideologically-laden scientific legitimisation of conventional approaches,
there is a general recognition of the need to draw on aspects of music theory
through reformulation. Certainly, reappropriations of formalistic views of
music and a move towards creative hermeneutics (that renounce ideas of
mastery) have begun to offer scholars new ways for approaching music
analysis.[3] The reader will note that throughout this book my use of the word
analysing is interchangeable with the term *reading,* which I deliberately

employ to designate a move between focusing on the structures of music alone and the broader contexts within which the music is located.

In a general sense, my aim is to address a number of tensions that arise out of music-analytical application by turning to a more hermeneutic position in my readings of pop texts from the 1980s and 1990s. To this end, I set out to concentrate on the music produced by artists of my generation born towards the end of the 1950s and early 1960s – indeed the first pop icons of the MTV boom, a period greatly impacted by the visual spectacle of the pop video. Accordingly, all the artists studied in this book are products of the MTV phenomenon in one way or another.

One central issue needs to be raised at this point, namely that which concerns what pop music is. Always shaped by social, political and cultural conditions, pop is about patterns in consumption and production. Seen in a historical light, some have declared that pop stylistically evolved out of what Simon Frith terms the total 'fragmentation of rock' at the end of the 1970s. In contrast to the early 1970s, when rock reached its height as an authentic mode of expression, pop music only really came to age in the 1980s when, as Frith recalls, it emerged for the first time as a 'term of praise'. In considering this from a sociological perspective, it is significant that research into 1980s pop was based on different premises from rock: 'The meaning of music was itself up for grabs and rock criticism no longer meant playing each new release in its tradition, describing its provenance, codifying sounds in terms of accustomed social codes' (Frith 1988: 5).

The issue here is that lineages of styles and genres transport with them sets of assumptions. This is rife in writings on popular music where descriptions and discussions promote and legitimise certain trends discriminately. In much music journalism, one finds a tendency to privilege one genre of music over the next. This commonly occurs on the basis of commercial production, which is seen to negate the authenticity (read: quality) of specific musical styles and trends (see Hamm 1995). Yet, there seems little worse than the poor arguments that attempt to negotiate the authenticity of one style at the expense of another.

All too often the kind of thinking I am referring to encircles the intricate problematics of definition. Like the overarching categories of world music, pop-rock, folk, funk and jazz, pop, as a term in itself, is often applied loosely to refer to that broad expanse of music that has undergone industrialisation and commercialisation. Alone, the interchangeability of the terms 'rock' and 'pop' highlights the constraints of narratives that embrace countless definitions of popular music (Moore 1993). Of course the distinctions linked to categorisation are not only tied up in the degree of control that artists and fans have over their music, but also in the problems music critics have with clarification. A case in point, as Steven Feld has indicated, is Frith's employment of the word pop where 'what he [Frith] typically means is "rock" and, more specifically, the internationally marketed American- and western European-derived rock of the last thirty-five years' (Keil and Feld 1994: 261). Feld argues that processes of stylistic identification are linked to a range of debatable historical and cultural positions predicated upon complex and often contradictory debates surrounding the issue of what pop is.

Undoubtedly, the hurdle one faces in determining what pop actually signifies creates numerous sets of arguments and debates. One only needs to glance at the recent spate of textbooks on popular music to appreciate the full extent of this. From one perspective, Robert Burnett's call (1996) for a broader definition provides us with a helpful starting point. He insists that by reaching fans through its selection, pop music becomes *self-defined*: it is identifiable through the nature of its distribution, consumption and content. Yet, this alone is not enough to distinguish commercial pop from other music genres. Clearly, questions of production and consumption are strong reminders that categorisation through the authentication of one style over the next continually compounds the task of definition. The fact is that pop music is about shifting levels of styles, texts, genres and responses, and how these engender feelings. And, on a broader scale, what pop signifies is ultimately wrapped up in our readings of musical effect through the choice of language. But what about the question of defining pop styles?

Since identifying musical style can be positioned very differently from one individual to the next, there will always be limitations to our definitions. Whatever position one decides to take, however, musical styles are ideologically grounded in aesthetic preferences, and it is this that determines our tastes. Given this, the task of selecting methods for reading musical texts might be best directed towards what Philip Tagg has called for: an analysis that 'acts as a basis for understanding "*what* is being communicated" and "*how*" (1982: 65). Most importantly then, the task of interpreting pop is an interdisciplinary task that deals with the relationship between music and social mediation. It is one that includes taking into account the consideration of the sounds in their relation to us as individuals. And, thus, my purpose in this book is to explore the issue of what pop signifies in terms of its communicative function.

Grounding aesthetic and ideological values

Shifts in the world markets during the latter part of the twentieth century rapidly gave way to large-scale modes of production that profoundly affected the music industry. The result of all this was that pop music would confirm, resist and subvert dominant values within the context of the dominant Anglo-American market. In fact, the pleasures derived from experiencing music through the acts of dancing, concert-going and purchasing – not to forget the ongoing everyday wrangles over taste – would create the basis for social interaction and exchange of knowledge amongst entire generations of young people.

During the post-war period, *rebellion* and *modernity* were two interlinked concepts in shaping an ideology that quickly legitimised certain musical trends. For example, by the late 1970s, African American-influenced styles such as funk, soul and disco were more in demand than progressive rock and firmly embedded in a changing mainstream of popular music produced by artists such as George Clinton, James Brown, Isaac Hayes, and Sly and the Family Stone. But, entering the international scene from another direction, it was the music without conventional instrumentalists, indeed that which presented new forms of artistic virtuosity – the New Pop of the 1980s – which signalled the MTV shake-up in popular music.[4]

What forms the backdrop to the studies presented in this book is the significant period of development from 1983 onwards when music production became completely restructured. Described by Paul Théberge as a 'watershed in the history of popular music' (1997: 5), this era signified a moment of tremendous change in marketing and patterns of consumption. The advent of MIDI (Musical Instrument Digital Interface) and digital electronics ushered in a new generation of instruments and software important for expanding styles and concepts in production. For the musician and producer during this period, the sound possibilities arising from these new modes of technical reproduction would redefine compositional thinking.[5] In this way, digital technology instantly became an inspiration for processing compositional ideas and approaching sounds and effects in new ways.

Notwithstanding the general challenges of tracing its stylistic developments, the analysis of pop music when situated within the discipline of musicology has not been without its problems. One reason for this is that traditional musicology has generally considered popular music to exist well outside its discipline, belonging more to the sociological domain (see Middleton 1990, 2000; Frith 1996).[6] When the primary textual analysis of pop or rock texts is undertaken, there is easily a tendency to prioritise procedures aligned to traditional music analysis. Naturally, the results of such scholarship have sparked off much debate and controversy in the broader field of popular music studies. A good example of the causes for this is borne out by the recent spate of Schenkerian rock studies undertaken by North American musicologists, such as Walter Everett (2000), Lori Burns (2000), and John Covach (1998, 2000). Hardly radical in their formalist approaches to analysing the primary text, such studies have nevertheless succeeded in igniting debates around the approach to popular musicology (on both sides of the Atlantic). Indeed, Everett's bold assertion that most pop and rock music conforms to Schenkerian methods of tonal working seems the kind of proposition intended to evoke harsh retort. Yet, despite the general scepticism towards Everett's formalistic approaches, it is evident that all popular music scholars come to terms at some point with the practice of conventional analytic procedures, even if it is to reject them as a basis for structural analysis.

The problems surrounding approaches to popular musicology also offer an insight into assumptions still surrounding the question of aesthetic preference in the academy (Frith 1996; Cook 1998; McClary 2000). As a result of their own conventional predispositions, many music pedagogues continue to exist in a social vacuum worlds apart from the majority of their students and pupils. How music is experienced, enjoyed, or performed by the majority of young people studying music is seldom acknowledged or taken seriously. Let alone is it fully grasped that teaching with the use of pop examples might be a useful way for approaching music analysis through interrelated subjects. In his argument for teaching pop in the classroom, Andrew Goodwin has gone as far as proclaiming pop music as 'simply the best tool for teaching theory that one can imagine' (Goodwin 1997: 47). To a large extent this is borne out by my experience of teaching on undergraduate and postgraduate courses in popular music over the past 15 years, where an interdisciplinary approach to music has proven an invigorating vehicle for developing a critical approach to studying all musical genres through compositional techniques. Possibly the most defining quality of exploring pop texts and measuring their signification is, after all, in learning how to view things differently and critically. Like all forms of human expression, the *musically popular* seems to denote something truly remarkable, namely, that special event or moment in performance that alters our ways of sensing things and, thus, our identities in a contemporary social setting.

By the early 1980s, musicological research in popular music had started to increase, providing the necessary stimulus for generating a corpus of work in this field (Middleton 1990, 2000). This period also witnessed the launch of the international journal *Popular Music*, and the establishment of the International Association for the Study of Popular Music (IASPM) in 1981, which initially attracted more sociologists and cultural theorists than musicologists. Significantly, it was the interdisciplinary nature of the IASPM that would prove in later years to have a profound effect on the development of popular musicology. Though we cannot ignore the pioneering work of musicologists in the 1960s and 1970s, such as Charles Hamm and Wilfred Mellers,[7] it was not until the next generation of musicologists – Richard Middleton, John Shepherd, Gino Stefani and Philip Tagg – that the way was paved for musicology to enter the field of popular music studies.

In a general sense, research into popular music during the early 1980s was influenced by the overarching meta-narratives of modernism that focused on class struggle, democratisation and the social conditions of the period (see Hamm 1995). If we frame this further, the Anglo-American media's influence in the 1980s was manifested through a boom in newspaper and magazine publishing – a result of Reaganite and Thatcherite free-market policies

– which targeted the political objective to construct the nation through theories of the market. Curiously enough, it was under such social conditions that a style culture emerged with a generation of writers who understood little about social issues (see Frith and Savage 1997). Certainly, the effect of this was to ideologise educational authority to the point that the so-called experts were swiftly replaced by men and women 'whose cultural expertise [was] not measured by any scholarly credentials, but in straightforward tests of political correctness'. Modes of argument soon started changing in the 1980s as 'common sense' became a celebration of anti-intellectualism, and cultural studies emerged as a 'spawning ground for eighties style journalism' (Frith and Savage 1997: 12). In this light, it is not difficult to appreciate the reactions of modernist-oriented music departments to proposals of incorporating the popular and folk within general music courses.

Notably, it was during this same period that a number of musicologists within the academy began pushing for more critical approaches within music criticism. This move was greatly prompted by Joseph Kerman's hermeneutic position. In emphasising the link between music analysis and ideology, he claimed:

> I do not think we will understand analysis and the important role it plays in today's music-academic scene on logical, intellectual, or purely technical grounds. We will need to understand something of its underlying ideology, and this in turn will require some consideration of its historical context [Kerman 1980: 314].

It has been widely acknowledged that Kerman's insight into the role of analysis denotes a special landmark in the discipline of musicology. In adopting a more critical approach, he insisted that enquiring into music in new, heuristic ways could provide a vastly increased analytical power for addressing a range of diverse genres and discourses. This clearly paved the ideological way forward for the eventual accommodation of popular music within the academy. In effect, Kerman succeeded in exposing the constrictions of formalist analysis (as applied to the canon) by challenging the idealism of aesthetics and stressing the need for further development in musicology.

This meant that by the end of the twentieth century the way had been cleared for what Hamm described as 'the first generation of writers whose awareness and consciousness has been shaped by the fragmented, non-hierarchical postmodern world' (1995: 37). For the first time the meta-narratives that had intellectualised music were now under scrutiny by those wishing to focus on the destabilising issues of deconstruction and *différance*. French post-structuralism quickly spawned a generation of writers keen to dismantle the truths and norms that had universalised Western musicological practice.[8] Thus, by the 1990s poststructuralist approaches abounded in the academy as deconstructing aesthetic criticism meant that accommodating the Other could be accessed right across the humanities.[9] For the popular musicologist then, music's autonomy could now be subjected to a hermeneutics of indeterminacy, which would provide exciting new ways of dealing with music criticism (Tagg 1982; Shepherd 1982; Small 1987; Middleton 1990; Moore 1993; Scott 2000).

Now a general problem commonly encountered in scholarly books on musicology is located in the tendency to focus more on the intricacies of theoretical debate than to attempt the interpretation of music. I have therefore endeavoured to redress this balance through a more pragmatic approach towards the question of application. Although I cannot deny the derivation of my analytic methods from the discipline of European-based musicology, my approach does seek to examine the wider questions of aesthetic meaning by discovering how tastes in music are linked by musical structures to social and cultural manifestations. One of the critical dimensions of addressing the tensions that coexist in the text and the context lies in understanding the role of musical processes themselves. Yet in any such undertaking, it would seem prudent to continually exercise caution in the manner of employing traditional methodologies and models for textual analysis.

Another point to emphasise here is that textual analysis is not about interpreting lyrical connotations (Middleton 2000). It can be employed as part of a music analytic practice that takes on board the function of reading as a mission for elucidating what musical events signify. My goal here is to suggest the signification of compositional design in song form by reading the various functions of musical process. In many different ways, as I see it, deriving meaning from forms, styles and processes can offer the musicologist a spring-board for concentrating on the equally difficult problematics of contextualisation.

Throughout this book then, I attempt to escort the reader into various discussions of how musical elements interact with one another and correspond to style within the text. All along, I stress that the pop text is more than just the song. In a sense, it is an entity of motion determined by the variables of sonic structure that link it together. I would suggest then that reading the pop text be based upon a degree of subjectivity and perception of criticism from a variety of standpoints. In other words, the idea of the permutation of texts and their intersections with one another should draw out the full trajectory of musical narratology (Richardson 1999). I will return to this point in more detail later on in this chapter.

One way forward in debating the pop score is to elucidate musical codes and structures *aesthetically* within their 'culturescapes'[10] – this clearly requires an expandable method that focuses on the thematic loops and irreducible elements of music. Here I am referring to a kind of intertextuality where the process of identification implies always more than the denotative word. This approach offers a type of ideal for considering the nature of the *fragmented* text. Indeed, the problematics attached to methodologies of textual analysis are located in the challenge of distinguishing between the elements that comprise the musical text.

Allan Moore (1993, 2001) has considered this by arguing for the *primary* text in his interpretation of rock music from the past thirty-five years. In his development of a musicology of rock, Moore employs a concept of style to identify the internal consistencies that follow rules and practices in rock. His analyses of popular music through relatively traditional-based methods set out to problematise the extraction of affect and meaning. Well aware of the pitfalls of absolutism, Moore responds to the problem of textual analysis by situating his readings within a stylistic context where he theorises the question of self-expression. Like others, Moore's thesis supports the notion that musical structures must be recognised internally and externally in their shaping of aesthetic meaning.

Likewise, my readings of pop texts attempt to search for the relationships between one text and another. In principle, my approach is to analyse the interaction of the components that constitute the musical gestures of human agency. Hopefully, the more music-analytical aspects of my work will not deter others working outside musicology with an equal interest in the broader field of popular music research. In my development of a musical critique, the reader will note that I have been influenced significantly by the work of non-musicologists whose thoughts have impinged on the field of popular music research.[11] Their ideas have greatly inspired me to develop flexible tools and techniques for understanding music in the contexts that produce it.

Which brings me to the underlying tenet in this book: for music to signify anything, for it to assume its own set of meanings, it needs to be rooted in an organised system which exposes the traits of the author's and reader's identity through the text's purposive function. Central to this idea is the assumption that organised sounds are predicated upon their own currency within defined social contexts. Ultimately, it seems that this assertion boils down to the question of the individual's own tastes, attitudes and ideological predispositions (Frith 1996). Indeed, any tendencies towards musical understanding are dependent on personal modes of temporality, which are drawn together through the use of language. Certainly it is through filling in the semantic gaps that the variables of musical structure achieve their sense of meaning. How we proceed with questions is surely linked to what assertions we make about what music connotes and denotes. In carrying out this task, it is one's personal findings that explain the mediation of our own identities through music. If we accept Kristeva's and others' semiological positions, the reception of music can be perceived as a departure from the communicative function of language into dialectics between differential elements. In contrast to language, music is about those sonic moments in time where syntactic orders are surpassed by music's materiality. Aesthetic responses are thus linked to subjective interpretations that arise from the exposure of musical codes through the many discourses that construct them. To this I would add the obvious point made by other popular musicologists: that the uniqueness of pop cannot be measured by the same features we extract in the extensional musical constructions of, say, Palestrina or Penderewski. Rather, its codes of construction lie elsewhere. Like much non-European music, the primacy of Western pop is characterised by elements of musical expression that emphasise sensuality and physicality through channels of *intensional* development.[12]

Musical codes and compositional design

Multi-levels of organisation harness the intrinsic functions of musical codes and their processes in musical composition. My general concept of the code employed here is derived from music semiotics, where everything that we experience emanates from the structure of the signifying chains (Tagg 1987, 1992; Nattiez 1990, 1993; Cook 1990; Middleton 1990). In this section, then, I want to address the question of what kind of approach to the code might provide a flexible approach to reading the text, especially when this involves musical deviations through connotation. Although there may be some consensus on the structures of denoted meaning, there is always an element of ambiguity in the coded text. For in understanding musical structure, the emphasis also falls on the qualities of human imagination that language cannot possibly fully expose. This is why experiencing music makes it possible to 'foreground the character of people's involvement with their biographies, their societies and their environment' (Shepherd and Wicke 1997: 183).

Musical codes, by their very nature, are identifiable as auditory events in time and space. The implications of this for the music analyst lie in the task of code identification, which involves a range of levels of *acquired* listening competence.[13] Certainly, codes are articulated through their context, and to be sure, this always guarantees some form of affective encounter. Moving more freely in terms of their signification than codes in language, musical codes can only assume meaning through the cultural context of their location. This is especially relevant to music analysis as it prompts consideration of responses outside the realms of language.

What I am advocating here is an approach that is concerned with examining musical codes as they attach *arbitrarily* to the discourses that construct them. Middleton argues that 'musical content is defined through its structure' (1990: 220) which spells out its syntactic form and its materiality. Yet the primary signification of coding also operates through the consistency of the codes conditions within defined musical parameters. And, it is here that the very identification of musical codes raises a number of important issues.

Generally, semiologists have maintained a degree of immanence in the text when questioning value and meaning. I am referring to the work posited by scholars such as Jean-Jacques Nattiez (1990), whose theoretical leanings draw on those of semiologist Jean Molino. Of course, the focus on locating codes and reading immanence into the text can be viewed as solely reductionist in its mission. But, as David Brackett has outlined in his studies, codes are never static and are always dependent on acts of subjective interpretation (1995: 9–14). In this sense, the reductionist processing of musical codes is only the first stage in discoursing on how codes function. This would imply that when identifying fixity in coded meaning, music analysts should account for the procedures that negotiate their own musical experience.

In all the case studies presented in this book, I have sought to outline a range of syntagmatic primary musical codes that I broadly categorise as *stylistic* and *technical*. Grounded in a socio-cultural location, *stylistic* codes are relatively discernible through performance, genre and musical trend. In this way, they also relate to categories of idiolects, sub-codes, dialects and norms. On the other hand, *technical* codes are more specific and identifiable through established music-theoretical parameters that denote musical units and structures, such as, for example, pitch, melody, rhythm, chord progressions and texture. In addition, these technical codes can be extended to accommodate components of production: the mix, studio effects, the configurations of recording, and the polyphony of multi-tracking. Most importantly, it is through their arrangements within the recorded audio space, or in Moore's words (1993), the 'sound-box' (a useful term I employ throughout this book), that stylistic and technical codes are blended into the compositional design. Occupying a critical sphere of assimilation, the sound-box forms the prime site for music-analytic excavation, a space where codes interconnect to give rise to musical effects and gestures.

Possibly the greatest challenge of pursuing structural processes in the sound-box lies in the task of exposing the characteristics of music as auditory events in space and time. Certainly each phrase, each sound, each idiom that constitutes the code is different from the next, a phenomenon which certainly invites imaginative formulations of interpretation.

Again, to repeat a previous point, musical codes are extractable on the basis of the interpreter's listening competence – this being the first stage in the critical enquiry into *inherent* meaning. I am referring here to that sense of meaning which results from our responses to fragments and portions of musical material, where 'one "bit" of musical material leads us to expect another "bit", or [where] one bit reminds us of another bit, or one bit contrasts with another bit' (Green 1997: 6). Inherent meaning, in this sense, stems from the interrelationships that are imagined or perceived by the listener. Building on this a little further, let us consider how music is *communicated*, and in what manner our experiences of it adhere to specific social contexts.

Musical codes clearly refer to an unlimited range of meanings that are prescribed to by the reader's personal context. Lucy Green's two distinct categories of meaning (inherent and delineated), while functioning differently, are nevertheless contingent upon the other at specific junctions. Experiences of delineated meaning, like those of inherent meaning, rely solely on our subjective experiential states. Yet, there is an important distinction at stake here, as Green explains: 'The point of distinguishing between the two types of meaning is that, although they cannot exist without each other, each operates very differently in the way it impinges on musical experience and the way that it is "put into discourse" ' (Green 1997: 7).

Green's model assigns socialised meanings to musical codes through the process of delineation, which refers to a range of musical experiences that can offer a route through to a more holistic reading of the text. It then follows that only within a defined social and cultural climate can the process of delineation take place. But such a process leaves much to be explored as the term 'musical code' is always in great need of clarification.[14]

What I am keen to emphasise here is that interrogating the status of the musical code cannot bypass the elements of secondary signification within the externalised moments of musical articulation. For example, spectatorship in pop music (as in videos and live performances) delineates dialectical relations by positioning listeners according to their collective and unique identities. Studies into pop therefore need to locate the points of musical structuring that fix sonic and visual meaning. For it is at these junctures that delineation takes place. In turn, working out the conditions of one's own musical reception forms a useful basis for analysing the influences, reactions and attitudes of the numerous voices that shape our preferences for specific pop texts. Implicit in my method is the idea that the pertinent features of the pop text need to be identified in order to work out how the context connotes.

Although pop songs, on a basic level, might conform to relatively straightforward formal structures, it is worth emphasising that their inner workings are generally complex and multiform in style. For example, within the duration of three-minute-plus song forms, we are faced with an open-ended framework of intramusical organisation that defines compositional design and musical organisation. Below I have listed some basic types of compositional features into which the patterning of stylistic and technical codes slot:

1. Formal properties: the sections within the song's overall structure, often binary (verse-chorus-verse), that support the general progression of technical codes;
2. Harmonic idioms: the goal-directed or static progressions depending on genre and style harnessing tonal or modal systems;
3. Recording and production techniques: the controlling function of the production as manifested in the audio mix, which is responsible for shaping the compositional design;
4. Textures and timbres: the heterogeneous profusions of colours and

patterns that arise from vocal and instrumental gestures within the arrangement;

5. Rhythmic syntax: the recurring groupings and combinations of metric patterns that communicate the 'beat', groove, and 'feel' of the text.

In their interrelationship to one another, musical codes obviously function on many different levels. Clearly, the uniqueness of any single song exists primarily through the special combinations of its codes within the framework of the compositional features. That sound operates in an audio space where codes provide unity to expression, verifies the notion that exchanges of meaning can lead to arbitrary signification. In other words, how the ubiquity of meaning results directly from the organisation of structures or codes is the prime analytic focus in attempting to settle the pop score. In developing my approach then, I work with various representations of music with the intention to offer insights into the ways in which musical codes are manipulated to create expression through invocations of resistance, compliance and pleasure.

From this, the wider implications of identifying and then reading codes lies in illuminating the experiences that engender relationships between music and people. So, upon employing various analytic methods to reveal the details of music, we need to acknowledge the domains of connotation – primary and secondary – that influence our results. To be sure, the sounds themselves need to be foregrounded for the simple reason that pop music consists of a rich spectrum of codes that certainly equals that of any other musical genre. Given this, my proposal is to draw on what I consider to be appropriate methods for extracting musical codes in the pop text. In this way my readings aim to proceed from the structural function of codes to the manifestation of their signification alongside questions relating to identity.

Identity politics

It is true that music is sold on the basis of the pop star's identity as much as the apparatus of marketing and production linked to the recording industry. Two points need to be emphasised for the present argument: first, identities are performatively constituted by the artist's expression, and second, there are important links between music reception and identity. When we map the musical codes onto that of the performance, what is interesting is how the construction of the artist becomes a process for us to understand our own relationships to musical production and identity. In my research into identity formation in pop music, it has become more and more evident that pop culture forms a site where identity roles are constantly evolving to fit social needs.

Seen from this perspective, identity is based around notions of difference. The claim here is that the very task of conceptualising identity is one of identifying the oppositions of sameness and difference. As a concept, at least since Derrida, identity has come to imply difference as much as sameness. Identity is thus ascertained by differentiation: by distinguishing one person from another. In other words, only by identifying what someone is, is it possible to say what they are not. A key point of identity politics is also the insistence on a structure of sameness between more than one individual. For example, a person of ethnic minority will assert herself as part of a group, at the same time that the group will identify itself as different from a dominant group. Asserting one's difference is therefore about stating an identity with a group that perceives itself differentially. Historically, as illustrated in the work of Lacan, Lévinas and Hegel, such divisions have been theorised as the same and the Other, with the same being assumed as normative. In opposition to this, the discourses of identity politics have become directed against the power structures that are implicit in the *same–other* hierarchies of dominant groups.

Identifying the Other refers to a unitary grouping of any minority groups who are characterised only in so much as they are others. This would explain, for example, why the political agency of queerness is defined in relation to the dominant male group. For instance, pop stars might be considered queer because they transgress the norms of heterosexual male representation (from now onwards referred to as heteronormativity). We might say that the symbolic aim of pop idols such as Madonna, Morrissey, Prince, Annie Lennox and the Pet Shop Boys is to dramatise gender tensions and not resolve them. However, the key point I want to make here is that it is not by chance that gender ambivalence or destabilisation in pop representations communicates the politics of queer culture. This ambiguity has important implications for the pop performance as a condition of bodily seduction and theatrical presentation.

Given that patriarchal male identity is acquired through the idea that biology is destiny, patriarchal culture can never exist in isolation. In order to assert itself, the dominant group must set itself apart from that it is not, in order to seek that which it wishes to be. Let us take a specific music example: think of the way in which hard rock has pursued the ideal of white hetero masculinity to the extent that it has largely excluded female participation, gay representation and black stylistic influences. Although I am well aware of the generalisation of this assertion, it seems impossible today to disassociate rock's history from its awkward relationship to gender, although gradually the qualities that define rock representation have shifted. The point is that gender hierarchy presupposes an operative notion of compulsory heterosexuality. Certainly, pop identities revolve around movements of constraint and freedom that go a long way in illuminating the categories of gender, sex and the body as specific formations of power.

For the purpose of this argument so far, identity might be considered as flexible and free-floating and not divided into clearcut groups: women and men. On the political implication of this notion, Derrida insists that difference 'always involves the violence of a hierarchy, a forced inequality' (1981: 41). What Derrida shows in his work is that dominant identity is a dialectical concept partly constructed from its opposite. More specifically, as a structural entity, identity is never attained.

Positing difference through identity politics therefore has important social and cultural implications for understanding pop expression. This is because categories of identity no longer appear to be stable notions. In Derrida's now famous neologism of difference with an 'a' – *différance* – a sameness is perceived as never identical. Clearly, the consequences of this for feminism, for example, have been to address and identify the precise nature of political groups. Most significant here is a deconstructive positioning of 'difference', something that has allowed minority groups to claim that they are first the same and second that that they are different. The strategic spin on this is that positionings of difference form new cooperations between individuals and groups, thus enabling solidarity between various social groups. In this sense, a most effective way of comprehending identity is by disconnecting it from an 'essence' and perceiving it as a dramatic effect rather than an authentic core.[15] This seems a viable argument for any evaluation of pop music, and is as much a musicological as a sociological concern. A central assumption that supports this assertion is that musical expression has a performative dimension from the outset, and that pop artists reflect on their own communicative facility in relation to genre and style. The question here is, how do pop artists attach their identities to sites of gender, race, class, sexuality and locality? It seems that we need to respond to such issues of identity because they pose important consideration points on the nature of musical expression in general. Identity, in a sense, is not a noun, but neither is it some vague, superfluous entity. That people are constituted by a regulation of attributes that are performatively expressed is indeed a challenge for rethinking cultural postulations of identity. Accordingly, these issues are addressed in different ways throughout the following chapters; but for the moment there are good reasons for pursuing a little further the role of music in shaping notions of identity in pop.

Modelling identity

Music can profile identities through us mapping the symbolic with the imaginative. Shaped by people, music is an imaginative process capable of directing 'a purely symbolic structuring in awareness' (Shepherd and Wicke 1997: 199). Principally manifested through the ordered actions communicating via sound sources, we know that people are brought together by music and language to 'reproduce themselves materially' (ibid). This notion has some mileage when considering the everyday questions of identity, not least those concerned with the essentialisms that have plagued music historiography (McClary 1987,

1991, 1994b, 2000; Citron 1993; Solie 1993; Walser 1993a; Dame 1994; Green 1997).

Considering the behaviour patterns and attitudes that emanate from our lived experience of musical genres forms a useful starting point for working out ideologies in pop music (see Kerman 1980; Wicke 1990; Goodwin 1993a, 1993b; Frith 1996; Middleton 2000). In *feeling* music, there always seems to be a sense that emotional affect helps determine how we function – physically and cerebrally – in our responses to organised patterns of sound. How we experience sound, how we respond to it, how we engage in it through various forms of participation (listening, performing and dancing) is inextricably tied to the question of one's own identity. As an amalgam of sonic references, pop texts, as I see them, are a consequence of the complex set of connections between the body and countless modes of thought patterns. Frith has insisted that the construction of identity within musical expression can be perceived as a form of ritual in that 'it describes one's place in a dramatised pattern of relationships' (Frith 1996: 275). Frith's work retains an explicit focus on arguing the prime role of music in shaping subjectivities. Yet, the tenet of his argument is positioned within a sociological context where the connectedness between structures of music and their conditions for constructing identity are not always prioritised enough. At least from a musicological perspective, Frith's studies battle to sustain the material basis of the music code in its formation of relationships.[16] To some extent this same problem surfaces in Even Ruud's study, *Musikk og Identitet* (1997a), although I have found his engagement with models for categorising musical identity most relevant to this study. It is to some of these I will now turn.

Definable through four spaces, the personal, the social, the time and place, and the transpersonal – Ruud illustrates the various positions musical identity assumes. In the *personal space*, music discharges a wealth of emotions and feelings acquired from early on in our lives. By anchoring us in situations that account for constructing our individuality, music occupies a central position in our culture as a metaphor of our diverse feelings and sensations. In contrast, within the *social space*, definitions of the self are connected to larger social and cultural spaces in which 'music helps us to construct connective lines to other musical and cultural worlds' (Ruud 1997a: 106).[17] In this category, the role of the fan becomes an important issue for consideration. By identifying with the artist or group, one's responses signify a deepening of the individual's aesthetic experience of music. To this extent, musical taste is either an indicator of conformity or autonomy. And, thus, all facets of identity – gender, race, sexuality, class, community – assume a powerful significance.

In Ruud's third category, *time and place* refers to that which is interconnectable through musical experience. Here music functions as an indicator of the individual's life history: 'we look to music which creates the transition between the progression of time and phases of life' (ibid: 146).

Implicated in identity is the idea that experience is embedded within our sense of belonging somewhere. Indeed, the notion of having 'roots' becomes central to the construction of national and local identity. This idea also impinges on the fourth category, *the transpersonal space*, which constitutes that area located outside the personal space. Here, the main question deals with how we experience ourselves transpersonally as part of a larger and more holistic entity. Drawing on the work of various psychologists, Ruud conceptualises the different forms of experience – cognitive, emotional, existential, transcendental – that contribute to the personal development of identity.

One of the central difficulties facing the musicologist in linking these categories to musical experience has to do with the task of adjoining secondary signification to the primary text. It would seem that functions of musical process constantly need to be addressed as a principle for understanding how identity operates as a demarcator of musical articulation. This poses a problem when it comes to coupling identity with musical codes and structures.

In the transpersonal space, a zone I am most keen to explore, music is implicated in a process of signification that provides a channel through which we can examine how interpretation is exercised. If we accept that music always signifies a system of differences that is trans-linguistic, as Barthes and Kristeva argue, *unlike* language it cannot refer to anything specific. More provocatively put, such a position holds that music might have very little to say about identity at the end of the day. There is an argument here that a semiology of identity in music can easily be disclaimed because of music's non-linguistic nature. However, like Shepherd and Wicke (1997), I am inclined to see this position as troublesome, for it reproduces a hegemony of language that only serves to politicise linguistic discourses at the expense of others.[18] The issue, it seems to me, is not only one of interpreting the links between music and identity within a specified space, but also of working out the coded features of music in relationship to the socially constituted forms of identity in question. I would argue then that a critical pivot point to this structural homology is located in the theorisation of the individual in relation to the complementary musical processes.

Working out how music mediates sounds certainly forms a vital part of understanding ourselves within the context of distinctive musical expressions. As I will illustrate in the following chapters, examining musical codes within a critical context is necessary for examining the politics of identity from many perspectives. In this regard, I am interested in how the idea of the fragmented identity extends arguments of the Self into the arena of culturally constituted phenomena. In line with many recent studies on postmodernism, a central focus of this study is to concentrate on the questions of representation.

Perhaps the most characteristic feature of pop music lies in its smudging of conventions in order to give way to new spaces. Douglas Kellner's theorisation of postmodern identity (1995) addresses this concept alongside the question of pop music. Frequently Kellner insists that the importance of distinguishing between postmodernism and modernism is to arrive at some position on the fluidity of representation. Implicit in Kellner's readings of Madonna is the notion of performativity through playing around with images. An important constituent of the pop star's identity is indeed fashion, an ingredient that determines how the artist is received and accepted. The crucial point here is that postmodern forms of representation often flaunt traditions extracted from earlier genres by recycling them into (in)coherent narratives of pastiche and, arguably, 'blank parody' (Jameson 1983: 114). Blank parody, as Jameson cynically argues, is that moment when parody loses any sense of humour. By invoking this state (at least this is how the argument goes), it is pastiche that signifies the 'wearing of a stylistic mask' without any notion of laughter. To be sure, pop artists often unashamedly reinstate musical forms from the past through practices of pastiche and different forms of irony. But these forms of expression cannot be simply dismissed as humourless or void of depth. Often in pop, notions of authenticity are not only undermined through musical codes being destabilised, but also through the suspension of norms linked to the portrayal of gender and sexuality.

To date, many ideas concerned with gender and sexuality have been problematised by the interdisciplinary approaches provided by feminist music scholars (Koskoff 1987; Bradby 1990, 1992; McClary 1991, 2000; Solie 1993; Edwards 1994; Green 1997; Whiteley 2000). A central focus of my work draws on these studies and deals with accounts of spectatorship that are drawn from psychoanalytic theory. Laura Mulvey's controversial model of the 'gaze', for example, situates questions relating to gendered identity alongside that of sexual looking. Indeed, Mulvey's ideas (1975) on spectatorship in film texts have paved the way forward for explaining the phenomenon of the 'male gaze' as a gendered construction, at least in its relationship to the fetishised representation of the woman. As I see it, the merit of Mulvey's studies lies in a greater concern for the cross-cultural responses between receivers and viewers. We know that mediations in popular culture can produce very different responses depending on one's own relation to class, ethnicity, race, nationality and gender. In this respect, responses to pop videos are quite different ranging from the more abstract experiences of listening to music via the recording. Notably, Mulvey's extensively theorised idea that the *straight* male is unable to bear the strain of sexual objectification stems from her early work in the 1970s. Since then, of course, the extent to which men have been objectified in popular culture of the 1980s and 1990s – film, advertising, music, pornography, television – has escalated significantly, as have the studies dealing with this issue. In the light of this, essentialising the male gaze clearly renders Mulvey's earlier model quite obsolete (see Burston and Richardson 1995). Nevertheless, her writings expose the significance of the imaginary fictions that frame categories of the body within the transpersonal space. In this context, it becomes possible to *view* how the dialectics between body and mind are arranged through the possibilities of auditory communication. One of the principal points here is that bodily sonorities articulate identities within social contexts. Moreover, it is the continuous processes of identity formation that define our own positions and conceptions on subjectivity. When enacted through musical performance, it is as if the fiction of Selfhood extends notions of identity, not least when *différance* wilfully subverts normative gender positions.

Such arguments are expounded by Judith Butler (1990; 1995), who has pointed out that representations of ambiguity operate as acts of political negotiation. Butler calls for a greater involvement in questioning 'what political possibilities are the consequence of a radical critique of the categories of identity' (1990: ix). Grounded in Nietzschean ideas of self-creation, Butler's development of a queer theory considers the postmodern body as a product of discourse, not least in terms of power relations. Theoretically, Butler's formulation (which extends many of the concepts found in Foucault's work) denies any natural basis (or essentialisation) of the body, thus supporting the concept of gender identification as a fluid entity. The notion that identity is free-floating as a construct of performance is perhaps the most compelling idea to emerge from queer theory. Butler notes that because cultural configurations of gender have come to appear normal in our cultures, it is as if subversive action is needed to instigate mobilisation – in other words, gender trouble.

Given that the queer constructions often found in pop texts must stem from an awareness on the part of the spectator/listener, our identification of their fluidity offers up unlimited possibilities for evaluating them within a transpersonal space. Indeed, the representations commonly found in pop videos are about blurred and destabilised subject positions. Of course the type of decent-redness that results from this frames the causal mechanisms of a cultural ideology. Indeed, the case for arguing why cross-cultural fusions present in today's music should form an important part of any evaluation of Western music. The ground work for this in musicology has been done by Susan McClary who argues that we need to 'pay attention to the kinds of ferment located in boundaries, to fusions of unpredictable sorts' (2000: 168) in order to get out of the rut of always searching for authentic modes of expression. To this I would add the following: because the relationships between pop musicians and the technologies that construct them are continuously under development, critical readings of these mobile relationships in themselves are vital to pop analysis. In addition, we can assume that the impact of media and music technology has vastly contributed to the breakdown of divisions between art forms, artists and audiences. And this has significantly led to the celebration of fluid imagery and polyvalent identities in pop.

At this point I want to sum up some of the observations I have been making. In dialectical relationship to the external world, musical performances mobilise subjectivities by positioning our locations. Determining the ways in which the highly polysemic texts of pop music signify identity on many levels presents an imaginative challenge to the development of discursive models for analysis. This helps explain how, when positioning subjectivities ambiguously, music's innate function becomes an impressive mediator that serves to satisfy specific desires and needs. I mean that music's power lies in its ability to bring into play all those characteristics of identity that determine transpersonal spaces. So, within whatever soundscape we might find ourselves, music magically filters in and out those abstract feelings of wholeness through the technology of its articulation. Yet, most importantly, this seldom occurs without a great deal of pleasure and sense of playfulness.

Interpreting ironic intent

Assimilating how pleasure is derived from pop is inextricably linked to the many questions concerning identity. A feature well worth exploring in this regard is the issue of playfulness, a quality that is intrinsic within pop expression. In pop performances, play is often characterised to varying degrees by irony. Through ironic performance, the conscious subversion of norms involves us recognising, and more importantly, *enjoying* aural and visual images with delight and imagination. In all my studies of the artists presented in this book, I have observed how the closed, personal, and at times cynical, positionings of their playfulness are cleverly attached to the spectacles and sounds of performance. Certainly, this is a quality that either divides or unites audiences. At any rate, it is the very arbitrariness of performance that overflows into sonic grooves, patterns and inflections, providing a basis for enjoyment.

By the end of the 1990s, irony had spread everywhere. In particular, through popular culture it penetrated almost all corners of society as its proclamatory styles expunged the authoritarian word by retarding thought through joy, laughter and mockery. Endemic in most pop styles found today are the nuances of festivity, of banality, of indignation, of solidarity, of sentimental idealism, which position the peculiarities of the artists.

As I have discovered in my studies, reading the polemics of pop artists not only opens up possibilities for enquiring into how their identities are assembled, but also questions how we interpret their mannerisms of humorous affect. Yet, extracting irony in music cannot be reduced to simplistic disclosures of the repeatable, for everything expressed in music collapses into the inner worlds of the fans themselves. The significance of this point is based upon the idea that irony is only determinable by the interrelations of listeners/ fans in the context of the artist's performance. Importantly then, ironic undertones are never quite our own.

What might seem at first glance a scientific groundlessness attached to the question of ironic interpretation is bound to demand explication. How the viewer perceives aurally and visually the performing out of satire, parody, self-deprecating and teasing entities of identity is a most crucial issue here. Indeed, linked to our reception of humour through musical expression is always the notion of empathy, a quality I set out to theorise in Chapter 3 in my reading of Morrissey – a creature of ironic attitude who accrues his diversity and complexity through a compelling strategy of evasiveness and empathic appeal.

Because of its very nature, irony has few guarantees – a point I feel compelled to labour. In other words, irony always occurs with reservations. In my attempts to problematise its varied intents, I have found it useful to draw on a number of categories proposed by Linda Hutcheon (1994). These include:

1. *Reinforcement* – The intentional use of irony in everyday situations in a straightforward manner. This would be found in the communication of an attitude through emphasis.
2. *Ludic* – Associated with humour, this function of irony assumes an element of playfulness as well as teasing. Here, such a function can also be evaluated as trivialising and silly.
3. *Self-protective* – This function employs irony as a form of self-defence that can often occur in the form of self-deprecation. Such a function can also be read as ingratiating, for example, when a mistake is turned into a joke: 'I was just being ironic'.
4. *Oppositional* – This highlights the trans-ideological nature of irony. What might be considered subversive and transgressive to some might be offensive and insulting to others.
5. *Assailing* – This function relates to the sharp, destructive charge of irony. In a positive sense though this function can be corrective in its satiric role. Often it is satire which turns to irony 'as a means of ridiculing – and implicitly correcting – the vices and follies of humankind'. Here ironic modes, such as parody, piss-take and travesty might operate aggressively in their innocent wit.
6. *Aggregative* – The differentiation and potential exclusion of playing to in-groups within a community. While excluding, irony also includes often to the point of being elitist. The in-group function of irony is no better illustrated than in the seductive ironies employed by pop stars and the aggregative effect they have on their fans (1994: 52–3).

Hutcheon's above typology highlights the complex interplay of different ironic functions. Operating as *trans-ideological*, these forms of irony invoke both endorsement and condemnation by relating to the political ways in which their employment dismantles or fortifies positions. Put differently, while irony might work for some as a powerful political tool, it holds for others a destructive function. It is indeed this quality that signifies its trans-ideological nature.

I am referring here to its ability to frame debates whether or not we choose to interpret them as intentional. Clearly, the political impetus of irony lies in its ability to destabilise through a rhetorical strategy of serious play. In my various considerations of pop artists, I have found their identities to be based upon complex levels of ambiguity prompted by their politicised settings. This would explain why the thrill so often derived from ironic retort is tied up with an awareness that its lack of any guarantee (in terms of being grasped by all!) actually signals its subversive intent.

The obvious premise I am arguing for is that irony *regulates* play on many layers. As Hutcheon's categories demonstrate, nuances of irony, be they intentional, observable, or even incidental, are the prevailing characteristics found in many pop performances. Particularly relevant here is the participatory role of irony in terms of the cultural sharing of expectations. Yet, the fascinating point is that we know that a targeted audience will not necessarily respond to irony via an intended ironic utterance. Here reside the problematics of interpretation. Because cultures have widely different notions of humour, ironic readings by some inevitably occur in contexts that will not be guaranteed by others. In this way irony panders to exclusivity by playing to in-groups and elite communities. This would suggest that the seductive role of irony in creating in-groups, evident by the artist enticing fans while at the same time driving others away, should not be underestimated. This is exemplified by my discussion of the Pet Shop Boys' construction of an ironic detachment that intensifies their subversion of a variety of norms (see Chapter 5). Clearly the subject of such debate is complicated and is problematised from a number of perspectives during the course of the following chapters.

In taking into consideration the general scope of the pleasurable pop experience, we might be tempted to say that fans know when the pop artist/idol's strategies are diffuse. Of course such a realisation easily creates potential conflict when interpreting the discursive location of ironic expression. Clearly, this problem is analogous to any questions dealing with self-reflexivity in performance. When perceived as a discursive strategy, the ironic utterance can never be fixed. Often it is narrowed down to cultural location, where it combats the single-consciousness of *Einfühlung* and *Sentimentalität*. To me, it seems that the responsive nature of irony is all about implication – anything that we miss remains absent from dialogue. In this sense, understanding the process of ironic exclusivity becomes a loaded demarcator of self-reflexivity within the domain of reading performance.

So far my argument rests on the premise that irony permeates pop texts as a ritual by abstracting formal definition. Frequently I have discovered that the appeal of Prince is most discernible through a cunning performing-out of ironic difference that is mapped against brilliant virtuosity. Clearly, Prince's embrace of pastiche through playful acts of imitation underlies a sense of humour based upon affirmative pastiche. As one of the most androgynous figures to emerge from 1980s pop, he not only engages with fantasies but also fetishises the alternative through the intimacy of autoeroticism. Erotic pleasuring assumes a self-protective ironic function as displays of self-deprecation are framed shamelessly in Prince's videos. As such, his image signifies a knowing play on androgyneity that flirts with and confronts a large scale of norms. In Chapter 6 my account of his videos, 'Kiss' and 'Cream', sets out to problematise this.

From all this, we might say that the potential recourse to ironic interpretation forms the basis of most pop's appeal, pleasure and uniqueness. Because music, in Kristeva's words, is a 'system of differences,' it possesses a 'translingual status' (1989: 309) that renders it an unfixed signifier.[19] It is within this sense that music creates special relationships between the sonic signifier and the ironic gesture.

Thus, through an identification of the coded organisation of musical events in parallel to displays of ironic statement, we have an instance where primary signification is fully manifested in all the properties of secondary signification. To sum up, the questions that arise from this deal with how the conflation of our feelings for pop artists are realised as meaningful. Indeed, symptomatic readings of *différance* can position specific politicisations of ironic mediation in dubious ways. No doubt, debating the realm of ironic signification in pop texts can be a risky business. Again this is because irony is about stating transideological positions. In safeguarding the values of the fan, irony helps define the channels of communication that shape empathy, therefore advantaging the individual's position of temporal inclusion, or vice versa. And it is in such moments of hidden recess that the fan encounters those flashes of realisation where ephemeral fun coagulates with a strong sense of identity.

Most significantly, the act of recognising irony occurs in the dialogic exchange between the artist and the interpreter, and the latter's attentiveness towards constructs of identity. In this sense, irony can implicate deliberate insertions of struggle by feeding off forms of parody, satire, stylisation, Otherness, and so on. As I have discovered in my studies, its function is to elucidate by defining the profundity of fun. On such terms, we cannot ignore its prevalence in pop texts through the obvious or the ungraspable. This is because ironic codes have no axis; they are arbitrary and always adhere to the intertexts that connote both playfulness and *jouissance*.

Further discursions into the pop text

So far the questions of identity I have raised lie in the sphere of musical expression. This in itself is a discursive idea. How one's musical identity is constructed can be theoretically positioned around discursive approaches to representation. A number of recent studies in popular music have drawn on the work of the social semiotics of the Russian, Mikhail Bakhtin, whose work posits social and historical meaning in opposition to structural reductionism (Walser 1993a; Brackett 1995; Middleton 2000; Toynbee 2000). Bakhtin's value to music-theoretical scholarship can be seen as especially significant in that he brings certain paradigms to the surface, which are tied up in the discursive moments of intertextual exchange through dialogue. It is to this aspect that I will now turn.

Bakhtin's work offers an important way forward for considering various types of comprehension. For instance, he claims that to *comprehend* the author of a work one also needs to extrapolate the other Subject. In fact no dialogic relationship, Bakhtin argues, exists with only one object, as the process of *comprehension* requires two subjects in order to function *dialogically*. In this way, 'there are no paths from the pure author to the author as person' (1986: 110) because the author masks his/her images and thus him/herself. The critique that Bakhtin expounds confronts the structural analysis of the narrative. From this standpoint, semiological systems are soon rendered imperfect – for the dialogical relationships that structure narratives are only possible because dialogism is a part of language itself. In other words, such relationships cannot be solely reducible to concrete semantic relationships for they always possess their own specificity. So, when Bakhtin refers to *the discourse*, he perceives writing as the place where one reads the other. This notion is useful in coming to terms with how dialogism identifies the act of both reading and writing as subjectivity, or better, as a function of intertextuality.[20]

What most interests me here is the positioning of the discourse surrounding the sound-box in its dialogic relationship to other texts. When reading pop texts, dialogism opens up new approaches to the structural space of the musical text. If we extend the problematics of definition I have provided earlier on in this chapter, we might consider the pop text as a construction of narrative; narration being the process constituted as the dialogical field by the analyst (in this case the musicologist) for whom the narration refers. At least two types of narrative arise from this: on the one hand, a scientific reading of musical description and the construction of the narrative by the analyst, and on the other hand, the readings of others' writings, as well as the (re)constructions of such readings themselves.

The working premise I am proposing then is that the pop text becomes mobilised only through its contact with other texts: this relates both to the listening and the reading process. Only at the point of contact between texts does the first dialogic stage of understanding take place. And indeed behind this intertextual contact are the identities that live to tell, fill in, or receive the multiplicity of the narrative as it unfolds. Clearly, the trajectory of the pop song is impossible without the concatenation of voices that bring together different and irreducible meanings through forms of utterances. In a Bakhtinian light, we might consider the pop text as oriented towards the responses of others – responses that are actively based on diverse forms of comprehension. How musical codes within the pop text acquire their expression is thus based on how they are received individually and abstractly. Their total combined expression can be regarded as what constitutes the effect of their stylistic aura. From this it would seem that the task of identifying musical codes is determined by the listener's proximity to the text along a scale from the intimate to the unfamiliar. Notwithstanding all the diversity within pop expression, pop texts, in actuality, receive their listeners in much the same way as any other texts, namely through the process of interpretation.

As I have already suggested, music can be understood as organised through a wealth of stylistic and technical codes. Within the pop score, these constitute the intramusical components of the textual grid of sonic communication. Most of all, stylistic and technical codes implant the artist within a dialogic relationship where the identity of the receiver is enveloped in subjective desires, social attentiveness and preferences of taste. Herein lies my prime thesis for framing the pop text.

Like other forms of musical expression, pop songs function as open-ended revelations of the performing artist. This would suggest that any theorisation of textual meaning hardly seems feasible without some form of aesthetic evaluation, a task located in the spaces between the subject (musicologist) and object (musical example). This means that in the quest for comprehending (and often idealising) the musical text, everything becomes positioned not only in the miniature worlds of each person but also in the limitless worlds of others. So, what then do discursions into the pop text accomplish?

Deciphering pop music, and undertaking readings of its codes through the subjectivity of personal interpretation, clearly constitutes a formidable task. This is because, as with the exegeses of visual arts, pop texts are scopogenic, in that they 'open up personal readings based on that which is presented to us; herein lies their meaningfulness' (Hawkins 1996: 34). Given this, it would seem that the purpose for interpreting pop lies in our ability to capture the very discourses that make music tangible.

For the music scholar keen on interpreting musical codes and structures, there is a demand for discursive assimilation. This is because pop music consists of representations that cannot exclude the ear from the eye. Once visual representations reverberate with audio images, it is as though the equation *music=identity* is totalised. The dialectics between music and identity are thus realised through the pauses, the junctures, the symbols, the sights, the rhythms felt through CDs, videos, MP3 soundfiles, all of which epitomise recorded music as a vibrant dialogic process. In fact the most profound networks of comprehension are found in the banal, ironic, crude, erotic, obscene, romantic, threatening, or self-indulgent sonorous threads that directly impact the body. For the pop text to exist, the listener has to merge into the music's internal and external space through responsive and imaginative action.

Thus, the secondary signification of music is always infinite, and can only be realised through the understanding of one person's meaning over another. And as pop texts are always contextualised through commercial packaging,[21] the power of the music industry, with all its economic targets of cash flow, has a strong bearing on the interpretation of musical meaning. Without doubt, the concept of production becomes crucial to any understanding of the conditions and practices that surround the pop text (Negus 1992; Burnett 1996). And, as Middleton has suggested, when interpretations of songs are made to seem 'monologic', it is quite likely that the mechanisms of production and dissemination have had some role to play. To all intents and purposes, the dialogic chain between the text's internal and outer spaces needs to be assimilated before pop music analysis can escape its 'formalist dungeon' (Middleton 2000: 15).

To summarise so far: discursions into the pop text need to take place in correlation with other texts, and involve dialogue in new contexts. From this, the dialogics in the boundaries between text and context are a central issue. It would seem then that the task ahead consists of transforming musical cognition into a semantic context for thought and reflection. Thus, the question remains: how might dialogism assist our cognition of listening experiences? And how does the text *emulate* the music through the controlling metaphors that assume music exists as a single organism? It would seem that the way to address such questions is to enter the picture from a critical musicological angle that acknowledges the relevance of cultural expression within a musical context. Indeed discursions into this realm are necessary to seek the dialogic boundaries that intersect and produce meanings in the pop text.

Towards a critical musicology of the popular

When situated historically, the impact of popular music during the past hundred years has been momentous. As Derek Scott reminds us, when '[m]easured in terms of social significance, the twelve-bar blues has been of greater importance to twentieth-century music than the twelve-note row'. In his socio-musicological studies, Scott highlights the problems of artistic hegemony in musicology through a poststructuralist concept of 'cultural relativism', whereby he insists that 'all values are relative and there are no independent standards of truth' (1990: 407). Obviously, the weight of the modernist aesthetic tradition is left exposed and vulnerable when it comes to re-examining assumptions of aesthetic autonomy in art. Two salient questions surface from this: first, what procedures are necessary to instigate a more accommodating framework for musicology, and, second, how far can a broader perspective of musicology be taken before it becomes lost in its sense of purpose?

It is to these issues that the following points were drawn up by Derek Scott and myself for a Critical Musicology Forum at Sheffield University in 1993. In our view, we insisted that a critical musicology needed to engage itself with:

1. Social, political and cultural processes that inform the arguments surrounding musical practice within a new historical context, by avoiding teleological assumptions attached to meta-narratives;
2. Aspects of critical theory necessary for the analysis of the values and meanings that are linked to the musical text;
3. Issues of class, gender and race in music by addressing the dimensions of production, reception and positioning of the Subject;
4. Problematics of canonicity, universality, aesthetic hierarchy and textual immanence, with reference to the binary divide between the classical and the popular;
5. Studies of different cultures in terms of their own specific and relevant social values with a focus on the diversity of musical forms;
6. Questions relating music to political, anthropological, philosophical, psychoanalytical and sexual discourses in an attempt to recognise meaning as intertextual;
7. Explorations of the multiplicity of music's contemporary functions and meanings, with particular emphasis on the evolution of new technologies within late twentieth century post-capitalist cultures [Scott and Hawkins 1994: 3].

Preparing the ground for defining a critical musicological critique, the above points probe the paradigms of traditional music scholarship (also see Cook and Everist 1999). Given that social, political and cultural processes underpin musical experiences, our first point emphasises the need to explore musical texts within an everyday changing social climate. An approach is therefore required that casts a critical light on the conventions, ideologies and practices of social groups and subcultures. Adopting a pluralistic approach to the field seeks to open up the possibilities for considering the prevailing attitudes and concerns of our cultures. Indeed, the problematics of musical historiography, in particular the genealogical networks that are drawn up, are a reminder of the teleological conclusions inscribed within the meta-narratives of the musical canon.

Situated within much the same frame of reference, the second point positions the analysis of the musical text within a more critical context that takes into consideration contextual, philosophical and political discourses. Here, hermeneutics and homological models are useful for accommodating the values and meanings of musical texts. At the same time, issues of class, gender and race become central to any interpretation of music and identity, as our third point suggests. They are inextricably connected to the modes of production and reception of music within a socially grounded context. This would suggest that any positioning of the Subject needs to lock into the debates that envelop traditional notions of genius, universality and aesthetic autonomy. Notably, post-structuralist and feminist critiques dealing with the positioning of the Subject have gradually assumed a certain historical signification, which, in turn, have problematised the gap between reader and text.

Common arguments about popular music are often based on a series of binarisms supported by ideological premises: the classical versus the popular, the intellectual elite versus the worker. Through deceptively liberal and hegemonic ideologies of late modernism, the criteria relative to qualitative value judgements have protected high art from the invasion of pop and schlock art (Hawkins 1994). Our fourth point flags up this issue by raising questions concerning notions of universal truths, aesthetic superiority and textual immanence through a range of discourses. In addition, as our fifth point claims, there is a need to engage in the study of different cultures within and outside our own society as an important route into understanding how music can only be evaluated according to its social currency. This notion is broadly predicated upon a repudiation of the idea that cultural and artistic values are in some way attached to objective truths. On this matter, the ideologies of 'romantic primitivism' (Middleton 1990: 169), which have characterised the study of much non-Western, popular, and Third World cultures, now seem reprehensible.[22] While an ethnomusicological approach might contribute to the emergence of a popular musicology, its application to music outside one's own culture has not been without its problems. As Brett asserts: 'the love of transcription and glorification of fieldwork often make ethnomusicology as positivistic as historical musicology – and the frequent recourse to jargon is a sign of the desire for mystification and abstraction' (Brett 1994: 15).

The above warning is worth taking note of, for, as Brett puts it, the crack of the 'postcolonial whip in the master's hand' is often discernible in the systematic theories that have dominated musicology since the German *Aufklärung* – a movement historically nurtured by logic and rational scientific thought and based upon the exclusivity of knowledge.

Returning to the issue of intertextuality, our sixth point emphasises the significance of the ongoing debates in areas such as political science, philosophy, anthropology, psychoanalysis and feminist studies, just to mention a few interrelated fields. Accounting for intertextuality within pop texts is contingent on assimilating the various layers of meaning in musical expression. In this context, intertextual readings potentially highlight the transposition of a multiplicity of texts that lead to a sense of polysemy through the interconnection of different sign systems (Kristeva 1980: 38–41). Above all, processes of intertextuality circumvent the domination of one interpretation over another, or, to put it differently, the totalisation of any specific singularity.

In considering the interpretation of pop music, the dialogistic nature of intertextual readings, as I have pointed out in the previous section, is helpful for extending the comprehension of the play of difference between the musical text and its other surrounding texts, such as the personality, the social context, the imagined addressees. In this context, I am referring to the open-ended possibilities and matrix of analytical operations that contribute to the text. On a cautionary note though, it needs to be stressed that the concept of intertextuality is often misunderstood as being only a matter of influence by one author on another.[23] Within a critical positioning of the term's trajectory, we also need to consider the transposition of one system of signs into another, which articulate new denotative and enunciated positions. In a Bakhtinian sense, the text can never amount to the work as a whole.[24] For the work is always embodied in the cultural context in which it is evaluated, and the functions that incorporate identities within musical texts are determinable along with the independent variables that emanate from the development of a typology of numerous discourses. Moreover, intertextuality, in musical terms, relates to the sounding of one text in and through the other. This basis for this notion concurs with our seventh and final point that emphasises the social significance of music through its technological mode of production within a multimedia landscape.

In pop's short history, there can be little doubt that recording technology has had the greatest impact on both the production and consumption of its music. Reproduction and regeneration through the ever-changing and evolving processes of technology, such as bit-centred forms of production, is central to understanding how pop music functions. Pop artists' identities might be considered as hybrid constructs of technology and the human performer. Essentially, technologies function as the interface between the artist and their audience to the point that the musician and technology in pop can easily collapse into one single entity (see Gay 1998). In this sense, as Théberge (1997) has argued, the use of the term 'sound' in pop music analysis cannot be detached from the sound recording or the music. Through its technological production, the sound transports with it a range of signifiers, which emphasise the multiplicity of its musical function.

Now all the points outlined in this approach to a critical-based musicology can be connected to one central premise, namely, that the interpretation of any single text is based on an understanding of the juxtaposition of a range of discourses. Above all, we need to continually remind ourselves that pop music is also about entertainment; it is about fun, fantasy, play and self-irony. Any musical interpretation cannot avoid the consideration of these politics of *jouissance* that shape the text.

Musical interpretation, however, as I have discovered, is not always indicative of the preferred readings of audience groups. While the need to engage in surveying the opinions of others should be implicit within the musicologist's search for patterns of reception, it is more the continual construction of a sense of social reality on a personal level that comes into play in my various readings of music texts. Perhaps the greatest challenge in learning to read the pop score lies in us devising interpretative tools that can be mapped to a wide range of musical influences and conflicting values. An aim of critical musicology is surely to release certain forms of music from the attitudes and beliefs that dominate conventional modes of musicological enquiry. One way forward is to redefine the historical map in order to liberate music scholarship from the constraints of its rigid ideologies. Arguing this point, Middleton has asserted that '(t)he need then becomes the identification, within the musical field as a whole, of different historical levels – at each of which a different pattern or focus of change, continuity and contradiction may be found' (Middleton 1990: 122).

From this, the task ahead seems twofold: first, to develop a diachronic mode of analysis for constructing a discourse that constantly challenges and shapes such differences by addressing historical contexts, and, second, to make discrete choices concerning what codes are most appropriate for music analysis. To this end, I would suggest a gradual broadening out of analytic musical competence that involves us searching beyond the confines of traditional musicological practice by entering into intertextual dialogues on many levels.[25] With this in mind, let us return to some of the conceptual criteria referred to earlier in a more general concern to focus on the texts of the pop score.

Mobilising the pop score

Pleasures in recorded sound are located in a multiplicity of sensations that are immediate in their effect. We know that compared to Western art music, gratification in pop is instant rather than deferred. The appeal of the sound in pop is derived directly from the music's immediate *effect* on the body. For example, in dance-based genres, how the pulse, the groove, the joy of repetition drives the music is what induces immediate physical and aesthetic response. Yet, to be sure, the pop experience is also affiliated to sensations based on learned listening experiences that adhere to bodily movement.

As I have suggested, making sense of different genres within an interdisciplinary study can be pursued through a non-linear approach into historical issues. Addressing this throughout her studies, McClary (2000) has called for a *decentred* approach to music history that defies linear development. Instead of seeking out authentic traditions and practices in contemporary Western music, she argues that we need to discard them for rereadings of our cultural landscape. McClary emphasises that the throwback to nineteenth-century aesthetic autonomy 'can no longer be privileged as somehow true' (2000: 169) in the meta-narratives that preserve the classic-music tradition. The point worth underlining is that a critical approach is imperative for the music scholar keen to understand how music delineates meaning through a range of subject-positions. Implicit in such an approach, however, should also be an awareness of the politically subversive and manipulative potential of musical expression, which, in the case of much pop music, promotes those vital aspects of cultural, social, and political tension.

We might then begin by investigating pop texts through a more diagnostic approach; an approach that focuses on the everyday struggles of politics and identity roles within a media-saturated culture. Certainly a popular musicology is required to assess the musical text alongside the rapid emergence of new technologies to comprehend the networks of everyday communication. Quite simply, the relationships between technologies and their use are constructed through the constant cultural reconfigurations of musical genres. My studies are therefore concerned with such developments, and seek to demonstrate how musicology can serve to shed light on the inextricable links between technology and culturally delineated practices.

Above all, I consider musical experience as a form of social and cultural sharing. This, indeed, holds true for both the artist and the onlooker. In this respect, music functions as a powerful metaphor for collective identity through the countless opportunities it offers up for interpretation. And, this would explain why identity becomes a matter of social and cultural relevance based upon a sense of shared performance. To reiterate a point made earlier, what seems most significant is that music functions as a vital force for understanding others and ourselves.

What I am proposing then is an approach to music interpretation that is intent on exploring how sets of different musical rules shape our aesthetic responses. This, in turn, can form the basis for exploring identities in the transpersonal space. Clearly, discovering what the specific sound of an artist signifies is important in identifying the stylistic codes of expression. In other words, fathoming out the *sonic trademark* of a musician should be about understanding the developments and trends in musical production and consumption while finding new ways to approach the creative act of interpreting music.

Originating from a wide range of different subject-positions, the five chapters that follow pick up on many of the theoretical issues presented in this introduction. Each chapter presents a case study of an artist, raising questions relating to aspects of their music and identity. In Chapter 2, the reader is introduced to several songs and videos of Madonna Ciccone as I situate her musical codes alongside her multiple constructions of identity. From the point of view of performance, the focus rests upon her musical creativity, an important aspect of her texts seldom addressed. Emphasis on femininity at play emerges as an important aspect of Madonna's rhetoric, and this is situated within the problematics of a modernist vs. postmodernist debate. Drawing on various readings by other scholars, mine seeks to demonstrate how this extraordinary artist gains her empowerment through a special kind of performance. In particular, I set out to discuss how an ironic sensibility positions her as a Bakhtinian subject-of-difference through a series of identities that augment the complexity of her performances through the layering upon layering of voices. There can be little doubt that the output of Madonna stretches through the 1980s and 1990s pop scene into the twenty-first century, and as an artist, she is now recognised for her agility in changing image and style – a strategy that flirts with ambiguity in order to reinvent identity. In an Irigarayian sense, the pleasures derived from Madonna's music emulate the joy she derives from her sexuality, a sexuality that is displayed as non-linear and plural in its charge.

In Chapter 3, a very different type of identity is scrutinised through the music of the Manchester-born singer Steven Morrissey. Far from the glamorous, showbiz manner of American pop stars, such as Madonna, Morrissey is a reminder of another type of pop icon emanating from the music industry in the 1980s, namely that of the 'indie' star. His songs negate, in one sense, the idealism of New Pop, forcing him to be reflective by immersing himself in personal relationships with himself. Morrissey's sensitivity to the simplicity of song form, at least in comparison to the other artists I concentrate on, is well worth consideration. It is no coincidence, however, to discover that he shares many of the characteristics found in Prince's and the Pet Shop Boys' texts. For example, the manipulation of image, the blurring of stereotypical sexual divides, the camped-up mode of delivery, the play on irony, are just some of the features that surface in my readings of his songs. Knowingly, Morrissey romanticises the anti-hero in pop by expressing the political despair and disenchantment of a predominantly white, northern English, working-class generation growing up in Britain during the 1980s. Through his texts the path is made clear for employing a methodology that explores irony and empathy through musical codes, lyrical content and performance strategy.

If Morrissey articulates the problems of the male in crisis, Annie Lennox certainly brings to the fore an antagonistic empowerment of female identity in British mainstream pop of the 1980s (and 1990s). In Chapter 4, I consider aspects of her identity through a detailed reading of the song and video, 'Money Can't Buy It', from her debut album, *Diva*, released in 1992. Here I trace the construction of her identity as it is assembled through a range of musical, lyrical and visual components. How does a pop song's narrative work in conjunction with the musical codes? What are the links between primary and secondary signification that contribute to musical narratology? Such questions are problematised when I examine the nature of Lennox's performativity. Indeed, this poses a tricky undertaking as her politics of power seem to be grounded in what, on one level, might be read as a satire on gender. In particular, it is the array of musical and visual codes that put into motion the full gendered force of Lennox's rhetoric. Through shifting positions of masquerade – musically and visually – Lennox not only challenges but also playfully taunts the heteronormative male gaze. At the same time, her video performance of the song, 'Money Can't Buy It', provides a provocative text for tracking down the teasing, heterosexual constructs of representation that typify pop artists of her generation. With this study, my goal is to reveal numerous musical codes in an attempt to position their affective power in a space that gives rise to tensions centred on gender.

Whatever the dialectics between music and the body might represent, the issue of banality in pop texts should not be ignored. This constitutes one of the most dominant forces in the aesthetics of 1980s UK pop. Accordingly, acts of ironic commentary in the Pet Shop Boys' music are critiqued in Chapter 5. Musically, ambiguity and the politics of male identity are problematised within a historical setting through music analysis. As I seek to point out, this duo's music percolates with all sorts of flavours that are hinged to arguments concerned with authenticity and authorship in popular music. My presentation of music and video examples therefore seeks to illustrate how (in)authenticity becomes the focus of debate through readings of the artifice of 1980s and 1990s pop performances. In particular, Neil Tennant's vocal display signifies an important role in the creation of the construction of the nonchalant pop star. Often the pessimism of his lyrical content is washed up by the optimism of the musical score. For the Pet Shop Boys, performing and parodying their Englishness is negotiated through a very different structural design than that of Morrissey's. Indeed, it is through these artists' quirky satirical position (not least through appropriations of tacky disco!) that we are provided with a basis for interrogating camp identity and masculinity in 1980s and 1990s pop. Furthermore, their songs open up the space for considering the dialogics of queering within a critique that draws on intriguing extensions of English identity towards the end of the twentieth century.

Generally, in my consideration of all these artists, I have concentrated on how the dialectics between identity and musical codes can surface as a central part of musicological concern. My reading of Prince's texts in Chapter 6 illustrates this intention through a consideration of his performance strategies. The manipulation of his identity in a multitude of ways underlies his special kind of narcissism as a sleekly controlled exercise in the rapid exchange of signs and symbols. How his music is shaped through an engagement with style is microscopically explored in a semiotic analysis of the large-scale stylistic and technical musical codes in the album *Diamonds and Pearls*. Within this chapter, I also touch on some of the more recent debates concerning the impact of race and identity on pop music. The African-American discourse in popular music seems relevant for examining Prince's curious racial and sexual blend alongside the question of musical crossover. As I attempt to illustrate, political rhetoric in musical expression has the power to pull together a wide range of issues that form the basis for unravelling meaning. Prince's identity politics thus take us on as many excursions as do his stylistic codes. Tangential inquiries into his parody relativise themselves through a consideration of the full impact of his virtuosic enunciations of pleasure. In fact, it is the act of blending so many signs and symbols together that result in the very appeal of his queered performance. This, as I have found, simultaneously attracts his fans to his music while causing others to dislike him with a vehement passion. In effect, Prince epitomises the first wave of the MTV generation, in particular, the first group of African-American crossover performers to turn the video into a vehicle for entering the fiercely competitive marketplace. My references to Prince in this final chapter are thus situated dialogically within a highly visual context, where the dimension of visual performance always empowers the musical codes, and vice versa.

Finally, in my interpretation of all these artists, the central question of compositional design and musical coding is kept in focus as much as the social and cultural phenomenon that shapes their identities. An underlying intention here is not to be exhaustive in the form of biographical examination, but rather to explore a number of viable approaches to interpreting music as an autonomous source of affect and meaning. While my methods include examining patterns and processes of musical codes, others concentrate more on modes of enactment by investigating the question of performance reflexivity. Above all, this study attempts to reflect my standing as a scholar/fan, and is thereby grounded in a deep concern to discover how musical expression can be read *culturally* through its communicative power. My preoccupation then lies in the task of interpreting a range of codes that disclose a world of disparate identities within a context that I believe I am able to relate to personally. And all this returns me to the title of the book, which holds the clue to my intention.

No amount of transcription or conventional musical analysis can ever render the pop score fixed. As I was writing this book, I imagined a score without manuscript paper, without staves, without bar-lines, without time signatures, an open audio space to occupy in whatever way one deems most appropriate. Indeed it is salient that all the musicians, fans, students, teachers and producers I have entered into discussion with have acknowledged the crucial function of popular music in shaping their identities culturally and socially. Ultimately then, the pop score is an abstract and experiential one. It is based not only on the dynamics of the pop recording but also on the individual listening patterns, emotions, aesthetics and cognitive responses we have to sound. In this sense, the score symbolises the recorded soundtrack of our memories, experiences, and musical reflections – everything that makes music fun and meaningful.

To settle the pop score then brings into line my endeavour to address the study of commercial pop music alongside the many developments taking place in other interrelated disciplines. Daunting, yet necessary, the mission is to uncover some of the qualities that are implicit within the provocation of pop music texts. And so, it is to the intricacies of such texts and how they function that the hub of this musical enquiry is directed.

Notes

1   In particular, I am referring to the studies undertaken by Tagg 1982, 1989; Hamm 1982; Björnberg 1985, 1994; Middleton 1990, 1993, 2000; Shepherd 1991; Whiteley 1992, 2000; Moore 1993; Walser 1993a, 1993b; Brackett 1995; Cook 1994, 1998; Covach and Boone 1998; Everett 2000.

2   This idea has been expanded on and presented by new musicologists from the
     United States, such as Lawrence Kramer, Gary Tomlinson, Rose Subotnick, Susan
     McClary and Ruth Solie.
3   For further reading, see Cook 1990, 1998; Kramer 1993; Middleton 1990, 1993;
     McClary 1991, 2000; Green 1988, 1997; Cook and Everist 1999.
4   As J. Beadle (1993) has pointed out, the synthesiser – the main component of
     1970s 'disco' – became an acceptable substitute for the 'live' performer in pop.
5   Nicholas Cook has discussed how with post-modernism the approach to composi-
     tion has changed. Rather than concentrating on 'notes' in the traditional sense, the
     idea of composing with styles and genres has emerged as one of the most impor-
     tant recent techniques in multimedia music composition. In his analysis of televi-
     sion commercials, Cook examines such issues of compositional structure and
     process in relation to specific social and cultural values (1998: 16–20).
6   Also see Frith (1981) for an account of *how* the study of rock music, as a phenom-
     enon of emerging youth cultures, first took place in the field of sociology.
7   For a more extensive account of this period, with a full discussion of the problems
     encountered in the musicology of Hamm, Mellers and Wilder, see Middleton
     (1990).
8   An insightful explanation of this is provided by Shepherd and Wicke (1997) who
     argue for the social constitution of cultural forms through musicology.
9   In particular, I am referring to the fields of Cultural Studies, sociology, feminism,
     ethnomusicology, film theory and psychoanalysis. Clearly, the interdisciplinary
     implications for musicology can be perceived as both advantageous and disadvan-
     tageous.
10   See Frith and Savage for a critique of their use of this term: 'The 'culturescape' –
     that pattern of aesthetic symbols and rituals through which people determine their
     individual identity and social place . . .' (1997: 15).
11   In particular, I am indebted to scholars outside the musicological field who have
     inspired my thoughts on secondary signification, such as Bakhtin, Lacan, Barthes,
     Foucault, Kaplan, Bourdieu, Grossberg, Butler, Goodwin, Kellner, Frith, Hutcheon,
     Baudrillard and many others.
12   See Andrew Chester's dichotomy (1970) of intensional and extensional qualities
     that distinguish between the aesthetics of art music and popular music, especially
     with reference to musical composition. For critical reactions to Chester's position,
     see Brackett (1995), Moore (1993) and Middleton (1993).
13   Nattiez (1990) insists that a degree of structuralism is necessary for there to be
     communication and connotation. His models are of course based upon assumptions
     of musical competence, a point Gino Stefani (1987a) stresses in his model relating
     to the following codes: General Codes, Social Practices, Musical Techniques,
     Styles and Opus. Situated within this model are two distinct approaches to musical
     competence: the 'high' and 'popular' which emphasise the matter of context. See
     Frith (1996), Brackett (1995) and Scott (2000) for different critiques of Stefani's
     theory, and Moore (1993) for a detailed and useful discussion of the role of
     'listening competence' in determining codes and styles.
14   See Rolf-Inge Godøy for a thesis based around how different meanings become
     attached to any single sonic substance or musical code. In dealing with the *ubiquity
     of meaning*, the problems that confront us are, as Godøy insists, 'not "neutral"
     problems, but precisely problems of meanings' (1997: 22–3).
15   On the problems of essentialising race and ethnicity in African-American popular
     music, see Tagg (1989).
16   Moore problematises this same point in his reference to Frith's position. Especially

in his detailed pursuit of aesthetic questions, Frith is unable to qualify how his statements on the effect of music are 'musically constituted'. This raises a general problematic in sociology whereby sounds are not deemed to warrant that much explanation or exploration (Moore 1993: 16).

17 Note that in his reference to the work of music anthropologist Martin Stokes, Ruud (1997a) concurs that it is through performance that we shape a context in which a series of phenomena can occur; here the emphasis falls on the quality of performance which creates the social space.

18 Also see Middleton (1990) for his similar observations on Barthes's writings.

19 On the idea of 'unfixed'signifier, I prefer this to that of the 'empty' signifier as applied by Kristeva. Also note Kristeva's position generally tends to idealise music although her argumentation displays more caution on this matter than Barthes does. Also see Richardson (1999) for a useful perspective on Kristeva.

20 Jason Toynbee has applied a Bakhtinian approach to interpreting popular music by concentrating on heteroglossia in the novel as a way forward to understanding authorship. Like Bakhtin's utterance, the musical voice is socially and historically positioned, occupying textural properties that are linked by the author to a vocal site. Toynbee emphasises the point that the sound of the voice located within its specific context is a form of citation (See Toynbee 2000: 42–45).

21 For a detailed account of the systems of consumption and production of popular music see Burnett (1996). In this important study, Burnett sets out to examine the complexities of consumption by exploring who the consumers are and what they demand. The purpose of his investigation is to reveal how the popular music industry functions through the use of a cultural model.

22 Note that Derek Scott has cited how the meaning of *piobaireachd*, a cultural and musical form from the Scottish Highland Gaelic communities, 'depends on [its] sociocultural context rather than on universally valid musical devices' (1990: 407). Also see Blacking (1976, 1995) whose writings extend far further than ethnomusicology and anthropology to include medicine, religion, African social politics, and cultural theory.

23 It was Kristeva who originally introduced the French word, *intertextualité*. Also, see Robert Stam (1989) for a detailed discussion of Bakhtinian theories of dialogism and intertextuality.

24 It should be stressed that Bakhtin's work is highly contemptuous of the Western canon and its 'great works'. His social theory of the utterance reveals a degree of scepticism towards the idea of 'mastery', thus forming part of his combat against patriarchy. The rationalism that characterises the Western Enlightenment, with all its monologic binarisms, is theorised within the framework of his carnival aesthetics.

25 As I have already implied, the traditional methodologies available in musicology are often misplaced in the analysis of pop music. Furthermore, as Charles Keil states: 'For music in which good process and spontaneity are the avowed goals, it seems unfair if not ludicrous to frame an evaluation *exclusively* in terms of coherent syntax and architectonic principles' (1994: 74).

Chapter 2

'I'll Never Be an Angel': Stories of Deception in Madonna's Music

I'll never be a saint, it's true
I'm too busy surviving
Whether it's heaven or hell
I'm gonna be living to tell[1]
          –'Survival'

Introduction

For many pop musicians, the struggle to stardom in the early 1980s occurred within an industry that was undergoing enormous change, especially with the advent of the pop video and launch of MTV in 1981. It is to this phenomenon of televisual development that Madonna owes her fame. By the mid-1980s, a rapid increase in star celebrities in the wake of the New Pop mainstream emerged that depended on high visibility through the music video (see Kaplan 1987; Straw 1993). Within just fourteen weeks of its release, the album *Like a Virgin* had sold over 3.5 million copies. Before Madonna had even started touring, this album became a triple platinum, and by 1985 was the first album by a female artist to be certified by the Recording Industry Association of America (RIAA) for sales of five million units.

Capitalising on the power of this visual medium for commercial promotion, the majority of pop artists in the 1980s started to gain control of their image alongside their music in new and exciting ways. Most significantly, the female musician's traditional relegation to vocalist could now be turned around into a powerful vantage point in videos where the soundtrack could 'operate like a narrator's omnipotent voice-over to guide the visual action' (Lewis 1993: 131). In short, video iconography provided a new dimension to performance – a form of exposure never seen before. Close-up shots of facial expressions, bodily response, costume details could be more adventurous and manipulative on video, with pop stars taking advantage of this intimate mode of expression to control all aspects of their performance. In this way pop videos became the prime outlets for encoding new identities and trends in popular culture.[2] Moreover, they constructed a simulated space where the fetish of spectatorship could be eagerly realised.

There can be little doubt that music television asserted definite shifts in the ways in which music could be disseminated and received in the 1980s (see Goodwin 1993a). Characterised by a very distinctive style, Madonna's authorship surfaced during a period when male-oriented rock and pop styles had also started to change. Rapidly she influenced a generation of fans growing up in the 1980s who began imitating her style in their quest for recognition and empowerment.[3] Against this historical backdrop, Madonna's identity and eventual rise to corporate power can be read as a testament to the development of media culture in the late twentieth century.

On the general question of pop criticism, my main contention in this chapter is that the bulk of Madonna scholarship has steered away from any serious consideration of her music.[4] A familiar assertion during most of the 1980s and early 1990s was that her music lacked any 'real grain and swing', and was more often than not 'totally flat on its own' (Reynolds and Press 1995: 322). Similarly Frith, in the early 1990s, suggested that her *weakness* as a singer was borne out by her 'thin' voice and vocal chords, arguing that it was rather through producers, such as Pettibone, that her 'technical failures' could be *faked* through production (Frith 1993: 88). The significance of these reactions is aligned to the kind of value judgements that have defined authenticity in rock music. I would suspect that underlying the all-too-familiar denigration of Madonna's performances is the suspicion that certain types of musicianship are void of any original or authentic expression. Such assumptions neatly fit the agenda of a modernist critique in which the role of the 'mass media' (with all its commercial pursuits) is perceived as socially subversive rather than constructive. But the point I wish to labour most is that in concentrating on practices of production and consumption patterns (I am referring to those raised by the debates commonly encountered in Cultural Studies), qualities of musicianship should not be ignored for the sake of economic deterministic arguments.

Without wishing to advocate canonicity around Madonna (this has already been done by others), I do feel compelled to challenge the assumptions embedded in arguments for authenticating one genre over the other. My methods therefore seek to demonstrate in what ways Madonna's music is informed by aesthetic function. And, as I believe it is her music that constitutes a primary mode of her expression, I am keen to explore why so little consideration of this aspect of her output has been undertaken.[5] My central aim then is to argue how Madonna's music might be assessed without it necessarily being confined to the straitjacket of music analytic formalism. Indeed, what has prompted this study most is a personal reaction to the *absence* of sufficient debate around the signification of this artist's music.[6]

In his response to Madonna's music, Jeremy J. Beadle wavers considerably in his evaluation. While quite prepared to acknowledge her achievements as extraordinary, Beadle dismisses her music by describing it 'formulaic to the point of cynicism' (Beadle 1993: 69). Yet, uneasy about his own assertion, Beadle is swift to modify his position later on in his critique by conceding that 'formula or no, several of [Madonna's] singles are, in their way, small classics: "Borderline", "Vogue", "Papa Don't Preach", "Like a Prayer", "Express Yourself" are *all good remarkable songs* encompassing a variety of styles, and, inevitably, visual images' (1993: 70, emphasis added). Somewhat reluctantly, Beadle ends up deflating his own value judgements, admitting that '... to be fair, both [Madonna and Jackson] are painstaking and particular about the musical quality of their output within the terms they set themselves...'. This is the closest account of the music we get, as Beadle fails to acknowledge Madonna's musical reflexivity in any critical enough manner. Not dissimilar assertions are also found in John Fiske's more intellectual approach to Madonna's output when he makes the following claim:

> ...I concentrate on Madonna's appearance, her personality, and the words and images of her songs, for these are the main carriers of her most accessible meanings. This is not to say that her music is unimportant, for it is the music that underpins everything else and provides the emotional intensity or affect without which none of the rest would *matter* to her fans. [Fiske 1989: 95]

Yet, directly following this statement, Fiske admits that *his* 'real' dilemma is in the task of tackling the musical text. He claims this in generalised terms by stating that 'the pleasures of music are remarkably resistant to analysis, and are equally difficult to express in the words and images that are so important in the circulation of culture' (1989: 95). And here we arrive at the crux of the problem of interpreting music. As Fiske and others steer clear of any sustainable inquiry into Madonna's musical expression, we never learn what constitutes the musical support of the 'words and images of her songs'. Instead, what we are presented with is an argument that seems to dismiss musical interpretation in one fell swoop. For the most part, denying any criticism of musical expression surely brings to the fore the ethics of one's responsibility. Thus, while engaging in terms of its heuristic rigour, Fiske's analysis of Madonna falls short of any convincing discussion of her music. This poses a central flaw in many reviews of her music.

Generally, of the studies that have focused upon commercial music of the 1980s and 1990s, the majority have skirted around the question of *aesthetic function*. The reasons for this have been extensively debated by others. Richard Middleton maintains that 'we can regard the general subservience of the aesthetic function in popular music ... as an example of the "politicization of the aesthetic"' (Middleton 1990: 257). From this we might beg the question: how does pop music function *aesthetically* as a discourse when its role is so often politicised on the basis of the music's own communicative value? Indeed, the concerns surrounding this question should be implicit in any approach to music analysis.

Another key issue here involves the manner in which musical codes *appear* to the interpreter. Undoubtedly the *jouissance* and erotic value of Madonna's texts are located primarily in the spectrum of her 'produced sound'. As I have argued in earlier studies, the importance of a musical evaluation of sound is all too often ignored at the expense of lengthy excursions into questions of star persona identification. Styles such as Hi-NRG, 1970s disco, Afrocentric hip-hop, house, acid-jazz, rock and techno disclose the sociocultural location of Madonna's sound. Notably, these idioms are rooted in all aspects of her performance. Moreover, they are located in the quality of her talking voice, her singing voice and her produced voice, all of which articulate her identity in different ways. Most of all, I would argue that it is in how the voice is recorded through the inventiveness of production that instantly thrills her fans.[7]

In general terms, we could say that Madonna's performativity is discernible in the physical gestures of musical motion that articulate progression from one phrase to the next. How her sound is offset with technological processing forms a starting point for understanding not only how pleasure is disseminated within her texts but how she as producer/performer sustains control. The effect of this is discussed a little later in my analysis of a number of her songs. But, before I proceed with exploring such questions, I will provide a short background to the album from which I have selected songs for analysis.

Released in 1994 by Warner Brothers, *Bedtime Stories* consists of eleven tracks with words and music written by Madonna and Dallas Austin. An impressive team of well-known producers, musicians and writers contributed to the project.[8] Situated within what Douglas Kellner (1995) has referred to as Madonna's third phase, this album signifies a period in which she set out to emphasise her role as a 'serious artist'. In contrast to the bold sexual overtones of the albums like *True Blue* (1986), *Like A Prayer* (1989), *Erotica* (1992), the soft-porn picture book, *Sex* (1992), and the MTV-banned video, *Justify My Love* (1990), Madonna, albeit probably ironically, has claimed that *Bedtime Stories* is a lot more about romance than sex. In what follows, the effect of her musical codes is read through the recordings of the songs, 'Don't Stop', 'Bedtime Stories', 'I'd Rather Be Your Lover', 'Human Nature' and 'Survival'. Again, my goal here is not a comprehensive musical analysis of formal structures, but rather a reading of the intertextual junctures that engage me as a music scholar/fan.

Reading musical codes in Madonna's performance

Overlaid by strings, a pulsating bass line transports the track, 'Don't Stop', a song which stylistically revels in the sheer bliss of disco. Remaining in the same catchy rhythmic mode throughout, the bass underpins the instrumental and vocal lines with a magnetic pull that makes dance irresistible. The transposition of the bass's register an octave lower (Example 2.1) and its compression within the mix contrasts vividly with the shrillness of Madonna's vocal sounds, as the rush of strings and the guitar riffs fill up the audio image with a range of dazzling colours. Rhythmically, the syncopated, grinding motion of the bass line constitutes a central musical code that could not be more erotic in its innuendo. Quite earnestly, Madonna urges us to *let the bassline pump you, bring your body over.*

Example 2.1   Bass line in 'Don't Stop'

Codes, such as the booming funk bass, the caressing disco strings, the clean guitar strokes, and irresistible kit tracks, remind us of struggle and celebration as Madonna strains on musical traditions that are linked to conflicts over freedom of expression. All through her career, her trademark as a female artist has been grounded in dance music. Often dismissed as trivial or vain, it is notable that the music she indeed turns to falls 'decisively on the side of the feminine body' (McClary 1991: 153), a position held in polemic opposition to many male-biased genres. It is as if the rhetoric of 'Don't Stop' verifies the connection between body and mind as Madonna commands us to: *Don't stop doin' what you're doin' baby, Don't stop – keep movin' – keep groovin'.* Carried along by the undulating groove, these words, in their repetition, repudiate closure. And, as Walter Hughes argues in his analysis of disco we have an instance here where 'language is subjugated to the beat, and drained of its pretensions to meaning' (Hughes 1994: 149). When we surrender to the beat, verbal meaning becomes an accessory rather than a main focus. Madonna endorses this when she claims in 'Don't Stop' how the music *brings your body over.* Such poignant moments typify the *Bedtime Stories* songs as Madonna reflects on her own 'subjugation of words' within a performance setting.

But, above all, the pleasure of Madonna's performance is commonly located in the groove, particularly in the beat. The significance I attribute to this feature is exemplified in the title-track, 'Bedtime Stories', where Madonna sings in a low, husky register, *Today is the last day that I'm using words, They've gone out, Lost their meaning ....* In this song a muddy bassline propels the groove forward as reverbed organ chords punctuate the cyclical groove with anticipated, off-beat stabs. Non-stop repetition creates a Ravelian-like sense of build-up as rhythms simmer for a while before tangling up into more dense and compressed twists within the mix. Into the sound-box,

Madonna's vocal utterances are digitally imported into the swirling torrents of the groove's multi-layers, as her words dissipate into rhythmic bliss.

In addition to the groove in the song, 'Bedtime Stories', the arrangement of the vocal tracks are worth mentioning. The vocal strands coagulate to stress a deep rhetoric of desire, as the cyclical repetition of the word *travelling* is expanded metaphorically. Suspended over only one chord throughout (Gm9 in G Aeolian mode), the song's harmonic structure outlines the repetitive nature of the groove, while, positioned in the foreground of the mix, the bass, synthesiser parts and percussion tracks pan about with dazzling virtuosity. Quivering with desire and nervous expectation, Madonna's voice is phased into the mix with two deep-throat moans which introduce the first verse. Positioned to the front of the audio image, the jumpy bass and synth riffs swiftly take charge of the rhythmic action. Here, a full throttle of vocal colour is released and mapped against instrumental sequences that negotiate musical euphoria on all fronts.

Simultaneously, the aural sensation of the trancey textures and swirls construct a multi-layered audio image that focuses on the vitality of rhythmic energy. In such instances, all the pleasure is in the erotic effect of the wide variety of sounds mapped against the sexiness of the voice. With the arrival of the final verse, the textural space of the recording gradually reaches its plateau of transcendence. Now charged with overwhelming passion, Madonna's trembling voice is eased to the front of the mix as the low register bass, synths and kit drop out. Candidly, she unleashes the full force of her desires through the poignancy of the following melodic phrase: *And inside, we're all still wet, longing and yearning. How can I explain how I feel?* Ironically (again in the context of Madonna's insistence that *Bedtime Stories* is more about 'romance' than sex), these words taunt, amuse, arouse and tease. Only a brief moment of respite resides before the cyclical action of the groove starts up once more, this time with more intense, organ power-stabs, further energising the musical current. The erotic pull of these codes is heightened by the application of

Example 2.2   Melodic phrase in 'Bedtime Stories'

effects in the mix, as Madonna's voice is heavily reverbed to create an overpowering sense of sonic intimacy that is orgasmic in its effect.

Throughout the song 'Bedtime Stories' waves of energy are controlled through Madonna's voice as she surfs the groove. Moving towards a conclusion, the instruments gradually drop out of the mix as the groove grinds to a halt leaving the voice naked and vulnerable. Madonna trembles, with a vocal close-up: *I'll never explain again*. At this moment in the song an overwhelming sense of sentimentality envelops the full potential of her solipsistic nature as her whole being becomes dramatised through an eroticisation that signifies the full assertion of her identity.

Madonna's control as performer prevails at all times. This is not only discernible through the audio images in the sound-box, but also through an autoerotic manipulation of the camera in her videos and films. Always the slipperiness of her identity contributes to the construction of a pluralism that is magnetic. In her performances a strategy of changeability is assured within a shifting heterogeneous setting. This forms the basis of Madonna's aesthetic. As if through mockery, her 'scrambled' identity achieves its continuity through a high degree of self-reflexivity, with her turning inwardly and searching for *who she is*. In the song 'Bedtime Stories', there can be little doubt that we are meant to learn about who this artist would like to be with. This is executed through a narrative where the agents of desire have no fixed standpoint, and where the listeners can easily allow themselves to be seduced!

In musical terms, Madonna locates her identity through a spatialisation of her own idiom – I am referring here to structural qualities of static tonicity, unresolved harmonic tension, distinctive voice leading, steady beat repetitions and porous arrangements, which are just some of the features that contribute to her sonic trademark. Through her sound, one soon senses the complexity of Madonna's personal history, something that affords her a calculated dimension of musical ambiguity. Often through parody, the sexual is blurred by the erotic as Madonna's *performing voices* queer a host of gender rules. And, ultimately, the enjoyment we derive from her music is located in the subject's pursuit of fantasy through the voices of her own texts. I will return to a more detailed discussion of the role of the voice later on.

Moving on to another song, 'I'd Rather Be Your Lover', I want to consider a different stream of desire that flows forth as Madonna lusts after the unattainable through processes of negotiation: *I could be your sister, I could be your mother, We could be friends, I'd even be your brother....* This time her desire to be someone's lover, on her terms, invokes a cunning game of 'cat and mouse' that provokes and confutes. In the guise of intimacy and (in)sincerity, the lyrical sentiments provide yet another instance whereby deception is teased out as the main thread of ironic intent. This state of affairs is encapsulated by the juxtapositioning of a range of musical codes with the lyrical sentiments. For example, the quirky two-chord riff, which opens the song (Example 2.3), implies some equivocacy through its I-IV shape, while still remaining non-committal in its tonal direction. In this instance, harmonic ambiguity helps capture the full implications of Madonna's intended rhetoric.

Example 2.3 Chord and bass riffs in 'I'd Rather Be Your Lover'

By teasing out the narrative to its full, this chord sequence (Example 2.3), with its regular metrical structure, increases the musical tension through a play on tonal uncertainty. At the same time, the groove becomes a symbol of escapism and fantasy. Towards the middle of the song an eight-bar rap break is taken by the black female singer and bassist, Me'Shell NdegéOcello: *Tell me what you want, Tell me what you need ... .* In direct contrast to Madonna's vocal colour, Ocello's timbre feels weighed down by its low chest register, with the anticipated accents and idiomatic African-American rap speech rhymes richly enhancing the levels of musical colour. It is not long before Madonna interrupts Ocello, her voice foregrounded and juxtaposed in contrapuntal delight over the short interjections of Ocello's rap part. The affective charge of this gesture is increased by the juxtapositioning and foregrounding of Madonna's vocal parts. Here, the unequal status of the two characters, at least in real-life terms, is enforced musically: Madonna as authorial-diva, Ocello as young, up-and-coming, backing support. Culminating in what might be read as biting rhetoric, Madonna sings: *Aren't you surprised?* Refusing any harmonic resolution (F#m7 shifts up a tone to G#m), the suggestion of a slow fade-out through the softening of dynamics (a cliché in terms of resolution in pop songs) is disrupted by the unlikely interjection of the vocal fragment, *Are you?* At this point, traditional cadential closure is subverted yet again by an unexpected redirection of musical expectation; a common ateleological technique deployed by Madonna.[9]

Perhaps the overall musical effect of 'I'd Rather Be Your Lover' could be best described as one of sentimental introspection and fantasy. Performed at a moderately slow, grinding tempo, the song sustains a duplicity of meaning throughout. Although the dissonant interjections of a G#m chord at cadence points pose little threat to the stability of the F#m7-B9 progression (Example 2.3), they assume their position as substitute chords for B9, while all the instrumental strands blend to construct a texturally thickened line cushioned against the enticing musical gestures of the vocal lines.

Musical tension is further enhanced by the cross-rhythmic pull between bass lines and chords in 'I'd Rather Be Your Lover'. Punctuated by snares kicking into the second beats of each bar, Madonna's voice is swept along in short spurts above the polyphonic textures. Transporting both Madonna and Ocello's vocal tracks, the groove expertly blends these vocals with all the other musical codes to affirm the song's narrative. Once again the meticulous details of the groove signal one of the most effective features in the song's production. Skilfully controlled through its cyclical pull of motion and textural build-up, this groove strives towards blissful transcendence. Madonna's fantasy to *rather be your lover than your mother, brother, sister or friend*, is convincingly established by the technical and stylistic codes of the musical gestures. In this respect, vocal intimacy in the delivery of these lines functions to prise open a space where anything can happen. At this point, I would suggest that the codes of phrasing, timbral inflection and voice leading in Madonna's melodic lines set up a degree of conflict while, contingent on such musical ambiguity, her lyrical acclamations tease out any pretensions of conventional expectation.[10]

There can be little doubt that all along Madonna consciously privileges her authorial intention by coercing the fan to participate in her establishment of meaning. Yet, as much Madonna scholarship has hitherto revealed, her texts can also be read as her simply cashing in on a constructed femaleness as fetishistic commodity. Of course not everybody is willing to accept her ironic spirit and sharp sense of self-reflexivity, especially when her strategy is one bent on attaining commercial success and fame!

In stating this, I am suggesting that Madonna's subversion of her own personae through a unique degree of musical performance forms a central point of consideration when investigating her music and identity. In the form of many guises her rhetoric is never reducible into the simple binarisms of: postmodern/modern, conservative/revolutionary, politically right/left, straight/gay. Rather, it would seem that her star personality is situated within a range of markers that signify a plurality well worth taking note of. Above all, her manipulation of irony raises a central issue concerning shared assumptions and aesthetics in pop.[11] If we accept that irony is only dependent on *shared norms* of communication, the position of the spectator can never be essentialised. As Linda Hutcheon points out, in the workings of irony the 'rhetoric of approval and disapproval takes many forms' ... (Hutcheon 1994: 46). Likewise, any evaluation of musical codes as ironic markers is also problematic when theorising the motives of intent. Because the reflexive markers delineated by musical codes are only understandable through their acquired social and cultural contexts, they, in turn, invoke or denounce ironic intent. Yet, I would

Figure 2.1   Madonna on the album cover *Bedtime Stories*

insist that the limitations of this practice of interpretation should not be shirked in the interest of theoretical merit. Choosing to read a text as ironic, in fact, asserts an intention well worthy of illumination. With this in mind, let us pursue this issue in conjunction with the interrelationships of voice and gender.

Hearing, seeing, feeling gender

Vocal delineations of identity are linked to processes of enjoying music, especially when the voice is experienced as playful and appealing (McClary 1991; Dame 1994; Middleton 1990, 1993; Walser 1993a; Cook 1998).[12] In all our responses to music, there is a tendency to associate the voice directly with the 'closed positionings' of the body when it comes to identifying notions of gender. Yet, rather than existing as 'natural' or fixed, gender constructs are historical categories which are socially articulated. The Dutch musicologist, Joke Dame, has argued this extensively in her work. She emphasises that when we hear music we inevitably 'hear a body' (Dame 1994: 143).[13] In her enlightening article, 'Unveiled Voices', Dame argues that vocal categories are never permanent but instead open to choice. Her examination of the castrato's singing style sets out to problematise the numerous descriptions of gender found within traditional musicological analysis. In particular, the case she makes is one for considering the 'denaturalising' of sexual and vocal features: [b]oth the denaturalization of sexual difference and the denaturalization of voice difference make it in their own ways possible to sever the link between sex, voice pitch, and timbre' (Dame 1994: 140).

By interrogating motives behind established theories on the liberation of sexual classification, Dame scrutinises the basis of Barthes' concept of plurality. She exposes how his interest in the castrati as neuter, in fact, denies the issue of sexual difference in males in any in-depth manner. Her argument here is that male curiosity in the androgyne, at least for Barthes, might be considered as a 'one-sided appropriation of the female by men' (1994: 142): Whereas in the case of women displaying power through androgyny, classification is different from the female portrayed as threatening within a heteronormative context.

In Madonna's case, narratives of physical desire, erotic insinuation and the play on sexual variation are implicit in most of her texts. Often the intimacy set up between her and the listener is regulated through the erotic underlay of her talking voices, with a range of variables, such as whispered words and seductive moans (on the second beats of 'Inside of Me') closely foregrounded in the mix. In such instances, the aesthetic of the voice lures us into a world harnessed by the body. This takes place through the stretching and straining of vocal chords, in the overall control of breathing, and other vocal techniques that arguably denaturalise gendered difference.

Generally, the seductive rhetoric of her narratives mediates an indomitable desire, which, when empowered, continues the battle against patriarchy through the vocalisations of the ruthless female diva bent on becoming a success.[14] No better is this exemplified than in the song 'Human Nature', in which Madonna aggressively confronts chauvinism head on, as she sings, *And I'm not sorry, I'm not your bitch, don't hang your shit on me*, while reassuring herself and the Other in whispered tones to *express yourself don't repress yourself*.

Again, any conformity to functional harmony is obscured by the ambiguous, static harmonic structures which flirt with the unlikely pitch centre of D natural within the opening and recurring instrumental riff superimposed over progressions within B major (or, enharmonically, Cb major). Weaving its way around the chord progressions and vocal parts, this synth riff appears deliberately timid and fragile in stark contrast to the rough, jungle-like bass pedal, which binds the various layers of material securely to the overall formal framework of the song. The effect of this is heightened by the almost indiscernible dynamics of the whispered vocal hook, *Express yourself...*, a common aphorism that runs through two decades of her songs, which offers the opportunity for identity-confirmation on the part of the listener.

Texturally, the vocal lines in 'Human Nature' are dense in their polyphonic arrangement within the mix. The full punches that accent the phallic beats through the dry foregrounded compressed snare reinforce the sentiments of her voice in the chorus by the introduction of a door-slam sample. Quite viciously, this slaps the off-beat as a warning, increasing the level of aggression in the music. Codes, such as these, are diverse in 'Human Nature,' with Madonna's voice(s) blending into the instrumental parts through its low register. In keeping with the harmonic and melodic flavours, the vocal tracks splinter off into two distinct tracks – one whispered and one sung. Such details intensify the introspective dimension of the narrative. And between the sung and whispered articulations of vocal expression, the ironic markers of (in)sincerity are cunningly situated. By openly soliciting pretence through a sense of affected nuance in the jarring, nasal-type vocal sound, we are presented with a whole range of sonic innuendos that can be likened to the physical gestures of nudging, winking and smirking (also see Middleton 1993; Shepherd 1991).

Perhaps what delights most in the songs from the album, *Bedtime Stories,* is the manner in which Madonna (de)constructs her identity through vocal production, and how she 'denaturalises her voice' as a text of difference through identifying with other subjects and objects of desire. In a Bakhtinian way, her texts exist as free disclosures of her many voices. This means that when we perceive and relate to her through the channels of the recording (sound and visual), we never actually experience her in the same manner that we do when we receive the images of her on their own (see Cook 1998).

In particular, it is the integral positions, multi-voices, and fractured personalities embodied in Madonna's sound that produce the greatest musical intensity. As Bakhtin has argued, the combination of voices alters our understanding 'through the layering of meaning upon meaning, voice upon voice, strengthening through merging (but not identification), ... [It is] the combination of many voices (a corridor of voices) that augments understanding, departure beyond the limits of the understood, and so forth' (Bakhtin 1986: 121).

I would add that in pop, it is this 'corridor of voices' that draws us as listener/fan into the body of the artist. Clearly, the physicality of Madonna's sounds alone cannot be reduced to words, vocal parts, or melodic lines. This is because they include a wealth of physical sensations, as well as multiple meanings, that exist well outside the limits of description. But arguably, it is the *felt* qualities of her vocal grain that best denote joy, ecstasy, sadness, melancholy, and sexiness in the *utterances* themselves.

What is at stake then in the responsiveness of the vocal utterance? Consistently, Madonna's politics are harnessed by her personal identification through musical codes. Like Prince, Morrissey, and Lennox, Madonna's codes dislodge normative categories of identity in specific ways, not least through her tendency to queer her act. Let us now turn to this question in more detail through a consideration of the link between musical coding and spectatorship.

Spectatorship and seduction

To date, a wealth of studies have been forthcoming that concentrate on Madonna's videos.[15] Arguably, any form of music analysis cannot be fully executed without understanding the interrelationships between sound, visual spectacle and the question of identity politics (see Cook 1998). To take a couple of well-known examples, let us consider how her identity is positioned visually. In the video, 'Justify My Love' (1992), filmed by Jean-Baptiste Mondino, Madonna's positionings frame imaginary cameos of her explorative identity. Clearly, the fluidity of references appropriated in this monochrome video, from 1930s Berlin cabaret, leather erotica, to the sex fantasies of transvestism and lesbianism, visually pander to queer culture, which, in turn raises issues of a constructivist nature. In this video, the choice of iconography brings into play all the strains of sexual objectification.[16] On this aspect, Sheila Whiteley has described how Madonna *appears* to positively endorse a wide range of sexualities regardless of whether such an act might be 'labelled as exploitative' (Whiteley 1997a: 271).[17] Yet, the full political motive behind attempting to de-essentialise gender categories in this video is debatable. How this positions Madonna in dialectical relationship to those she appropriates problematises any consideration of her spectacle.

Systematically, Madonna has positioned subjectivities of difference through the force of her political agency (see Irigaray 1985). Grasping the power of the 'feminine' through satirical mimicry, she liberates herself from the ties of any singular track through the trans-ideological functioning of irony. Rich in its spectacle of high-fashion snapshots and poses, the now famous *Vogue* video, from 1990, alludes to a narrative centred upon Hollywood historiography. As Madonna commands her troupe to *Strike a pose! Vogue, Vogue!*, she positions herself in a line of fashion and film celebrities: Greta Garbo, Marilyn Monroe, Bette Davis and Rita Hayworth. Most notably, Madonna grabs the opportunity for serious self-promotion through the incongruity of her masquerade. Through fun and pleasure, Madonna is allowed to confront her critics with ingratiating defence: on the one hand, by parodying the superficial fashion and showbiz world (through the rubric of oppositional irony), and, on the other hand, by *ludic*(rously) promoting Hollywood culture. Opening up a text where internal oppositional positions prompt new things to occur, Madonna's camped-up

Figure 2.2   Madonna striking a pose in 'Justify My Love'

arrogance in the *Vogue* video creates liminal spaces around the components of hyperbole, understatement and cliché: all the familiar markers of ironic intent.

Notably, in both the videos I have referred to, the influence of Mae West is discernible in the manner with which Madonna celebrates the realm of female desire by toying with sexual ambiguity.[18] Like West, she constructs her identity around a specific camp sensibility which satirises narcissism (see Robertson 1996). Yet, as much as this might seem frivolous, her deployment of camp constructs a potent statement of defiance which functions as a vehicle both for resistance and empowerment. Moreover, her references are often situated in a range of personalities, not least Marlene Dietrich's, whose 'androgyny has filtered into pop through Madonna's direct imitation' (O'Brien 1995: 245).

Such strategies of appropriation slot into MTV's wider display of camp through the artifice of its self-promotion. Indeed, the absence of any monolithic gendered agenda in MTV's decentredness accounts for its appeal amongst a diversity of spectators, not least of all a sizeable portion of gay culture, as Steve Drukman explains: 'This relatively new form is an open field for any and all spectatorial positioning, and its symbiotic intersections with the gay community (from the many gay/video bars to Madonna's *Vogue* video) are already apparent' (Drukman 1995: 84).

Drukman's reference to audience positions importantly highlights the impact of MTV on viewing trends to emerge in the 1980s, which we know Madonna has set to exploit as a medium for eliciting a wide variety of gazes. In a way, the kind of political positioning I am referring to here highlights a postmodernist strategy, where normative portrayals of gender and sexuality can be read as fake, as the artist masquerades all those fantasies of heteronormativity, or, indeed, vice versa.[19] Whether read as drag queen, diva, girl-next-door, porn star, or leather-clad dominatrix, her impersonations remain a powerful strategy for shaping her identity. Quite consciously, she *plays out* the cultural codes of femininity in her refusal of any single identity, and like Siouxsie Sioux, Annie Lennox, Bjørk and Grace Jones, Madonna reinvents herself continually, while still seeming sexually available to those who want her. It is in such display-related delineations that she 'implicitly calls into question both her musicianship and the inherent quality of her music itself' (Green 1997: 42). As Green insists, it is ultimately the physical spectacle of the artist that becomes an important part of how we comprehend musical meaning. In this way, the gendered connotations of vocal and instrumental expression constitute the discursive context for understanding the roles of artists in musical performance.

The implications of ironic intent has already been connected to critiques surrounding postmodern identity which are useful to this debate (de Lauretis 1986, 1987; Kaplan 1987; Goodwin 1993b).[20] In one way, Madonna fulfils the criteria of the postmodernist identity by deceiving through the agency of masquerade. Yet, I am not in agreement with Reynolds and Press's assertion that 'behind the shimmering surface of make-up and masquerade, there is no authentic identity' (Reynolds and Press 1995: 321). By reinventing herself through masquerade, Madonna's 'mask' is intentionally transparent for fans to gain access to the 'real' her. On this issue, E. Ann Kaplan also probes the question of her authorship:

> And one might well examine just why the 'real' Madonna fascinates. Why do fans and audiences want to know her? Why, even, does the public that resents and scorns Madonna want to know about her? Why is selling the real Madonna – in magazine and TV interviews and now in the documentary film and the much-touted unauthorized biography that followed (C. Anderson 1991) – such a commercial success? Why do groupies need to relate to stars through imagining their offstage lives? What can we learn about Western culture's investment in the construct of the 'individual' and of a split between inner and outer selves (the real Madonna is inner, the one she shows merely a mask or outer) through fans' needs? [Kaplan 1993: 150]

Kaplan's investigation into the 'real' or authentic Madonna opens up a range of debates relating to the theorisation of stardom. While she maintains that there is no 'core' to Madonna's authenticity, she overlooks the possibility that it might be precisely this 'absence' that positions the 'real' Madonna's in a *social space* where we, the listeners, choose to place her.[21] Put differently, the act of changing one's identity through posturing can shift the 'core' to a range of new positions. Acknowledging the conditions of this construction, Nick Cook, in his musical analysis of the video 'Material Girl', claims the following:

> [T]he effect of such contradictions ... is to project a further, privileged position from which Madonna I may be seen to be duped, or hypocritical, or simply fictive. To this extent, the real person constructed by 'Material Girl' is not Madonna II nor Madonna I; it is an unseen, authorial Madonna whom logic compels us to call 'Madonna O'. [Cook 1998: 171]

Cook's reading of the authorial Madonna (Madonna O) in 'Material Girl' leads him to conclude that meaning is no more circumscribed in her videos than in her songs, owing to her reception being so diverse. From this, it seems that how Madonna's music and identity is *felt* through her texts – how it is inferred by an array of positions – is about the construction of subjectivity. Certainly the force behind the fictive consciously operates as a powerful form of resistance to the ideologies subscribed to by rock authorship (Toynbee 2000: 25–33).

As part of the 1980s New Pop mainstream, Madonna grasped early on that one of the stakes in pop music is the constant modification of image and music. Intentionally, she learnt how to *perform* out her identity by contesting the 'coherent subject' through references of diversity rather than conformity.[22]

I will explore this in more detail in the next section. Meanwhile, the potential of her 'authenticity' has been to offer the possibilities of transformation as an index to her artistic success. Her authorial position today remains bound up in the construction of herself through visual and sonic production. Indeed, through all her texts, she demonstrates that the promise of stardom in pop is about the dialectical conjunction between modes of identity and their marketability.

Production and (post)modernist 'Survival'

Madonna's career began in the early 1980s when the New York club scene 'was in the midst of its glorious ride along the cusp of the mechanical and the soulful, when old r & b conventions of vocal dirt and desire were being deployed by a new generation of engineers'. This was a period in pop history, as Frith explains, that marked the beginning of a new sense of 'temporal order', where the care taken to layer the dance grooves 'turned even the most sweaty work-out into an intellectual exercise' (Frith 1993: 87). Moreover, Madonna's climb to fame started out when all over New York studios were producing 12-inch hip hop records as a result of the increasing popularity of new dance trends. Displaying innovative processes of mixing and editing for their time, the dance tracks of this period showed off the advances of technology in production that were about to revolutionise the industry. For Madonna it was these new technologies that would mediate her performance, and indeed her eventual role as producer, by providing her with access into the industry.

Contextualising this period in social-historical terms raises the question of the role of the female pop artist leading up to Madonna's rise to fame. Acknowledged as another one of her main influences, it was Debbie Harry who played an important part in paving the way forward for her.[23] With her striking Bardot-like, peroxide blonde, glam-trashy image coupled with sharp ironic expression, Debbie Harry formed the central focus for the group Blondie. Considered a punk group (at least in the US sense), this group produced intelligent and sophisticated pop songs which became commercially successful during the mid-1970s (see Greig 1989). Frith provides the following account of this in respect to Madonna: 'she became a pop diva in the wash of Debbie Harry, who had pioneered the craft of marketing the tough as the tender and turning thrift-store sex appeal into performer art' (1993: 87).[24]

Discernible in many examples of performer-based art during the last twenty years of the twentieth century, there has been a blurring of roles between musician and producer. Investing in her own studio and record company, Madonna was quick to learn her way around the recording studio – the most male of all domains. By the late 1980s Madonna had achieved considerable fame, albeit controversial, as a shrewd business entrepreneur. And, in 1991, her position in the music industry was further elevated as she negotiated a deal with Time-Warner for a $5 million advance on each of her next seven albums. In addition, she received an advance of $60 million for her own newly established Maverick company, which sealed her success as business woman, positioning her in line with the corporate power of Michael Jackson (O'Brien 1995). Finally, by the end of the millennium, with the release of her album, *Ray of Light*, even her staunchest critics would concede to her skills as an artist-producer-entrepreneur.[25]

Seen in the light of media priestess of the late twentieth century, Madonna symbolises the Dionysian and Apollonian split. Her displays of promiscuity and, for some, her 'madness', represent the full-blown objectification of Apollonian obsessiveness through the voyeuristic demonstration of idolatry. More than any other female pop icon of her generation, she epitomises the empress of deception by playing slave to lust through the erosion of sexual barriers. Her catalogue of videos might be considered as the most decadent portrayal of ritualistic masquerade in the history of mainstream pop, which, not surprisingly, when first shown, positioned her as the ultimate target of misogyny.

The erotic pulling power of the gaze had first been tested out in the video, 'Open Your Heart', in which Madonna, dressed in a black bustier, parodied the pornographic culture of male voyeurism.[26] The effect of this video was to have far-reaching implications for the music industry, as O'Brien describes: 'With a complete understanding of the camera she turned it into a fetishistic gaze. The exuberance of her control, together with the fact that she was the highest-earning woman in pop, meant that Madonna became the yardstick for executive decisions on marketing' (O'Brien 1995: 228).[27]

Indeed, the spectacle of her identity 'on set' would be further magnified by her corporate position in the pop industry 'off set'.[28] In campaigning for her rights towards freedom of expression, and unashamedly acknowledging her construction as a commodity, Madonna succeeded in authenticating her standing as an artist,[29] which returns us to the critique of authenticity. One central argument has been that when the chips are down Madonna's identity refutes any distinct categorisation. In fact, through the deployment of a range of strategies 'the putatively postmodern Madonna' has been seen to enact 'a pop modernist aesthetic' (Kellner 1995: 286). In this respect, there are important aesthetic implications at stake, as Kellner argues:

> A complex and challenging phenomenon like Madonna puts in question and tests one's aesthetic categories and commitments. Yet Madonna does deploy a wide range of aesthetic strategies and so if one's definition of 'postmodernism' is a set of cultural practices that combines traditional, modernist, and new postmodernist forms and themes, then Madonna can be interpreted as 'postmodern.' However, one should note the extent to which she draws upon

classical modernist strategies, images, and forms in her most impressive music
videos and concert performances of the past few years. [Kellner 1995: 286]

It is notable that while she might be prepared to accept her fluctuations in
popularity, Madonna's authorship is verified by her own evaluation of her
status as an artist. In fact, by having a clear-cut point of view, with all its
extended codes and defensive reflections, she has gradually demarcated
her modernist stance. This is situated in striking contrast to the aspects
of her fragmented identity. Aware of the risks involved, she seems clearly
concerned with articulating a certain coherency. To this end, the very resistance Madonna discharges in terms of her ostentatious oppositionality is
constructed by a labour that thrives on not only commodifying but also
parodying itself.

    This issue is taken up in depth by Judith Butler in *Gender Trouble*, where
the notion of gender parody is challenged, especially in the face of cultural
configurations. Significantly, in the case of drag, cross-dressing and sexual-
ising butch/femme identities, the relation between the 'original' and the 'imitation' is a lot more involved than that which first meets the eye. One cannot
assume that there is an 'original', as parody only operates as a notion of an
'original'. Butler understands imitative practice in parodic style more as an
imitation of the 'myth of originality' (1999: 176) – something that constructs
the illusion of a primary gendered self. Further, that gender attributes are
performative suggests that there is no preexisting identity by which an act or
attribute might be measured' (p. 180). In this sense, gender is a bearer of
attributes that is neither apparent nor real, neither original nor derived.

    Implicit in Butler's reasoning of identity politics is the notion that an identity
does not need to be assumed in order for political action to be instigated.
Rather, the task of locating the discursively variable constructions of the
Subject within a context where the Subject is understood, is to redescribe the
paradigms that assume the naturalisation of sex, gender and the body.

    Now aligned to the Dionysian principle of theatricality, Madonna could be
considered a vandal forever manipulating and deceiving through imitation in
order to survive. This is visible through the hysteria, promiscuity and euphoria
of her parodic address. Interestingly, while she aspires to 'strong' females,
such as the singer P.J. Harvey[30] – women who speak their mind – she has
nothing short of contempt for female pop stars who do not speak out. She has
claimed that: 'to remain popular you can't go against the grain. Janis Joplin, at
this time, in the world would not be a popular artist. Chrissie Hynde does not
sell as many records as somebody like Mariah Carey. And that's because
Mariah Carey and Whitney Houston don't have a fucking point of view' (in
Ellen 1995).

    Now the venerable criticism waged against others not only denotes an air of
theatricality, but also discloses a thirst for power. Based upon ambitious

intention, Madonna's scripts are rooted in her playing out her dramas for her fans. At the same time, the nature of her neurosis is identifiable by her reactions to a world consisting of rival performers, both female and male. If we hold that the plot of such a dramatisation of identity conflates her economic cravings, it is in this context that her calculated intentions grant her empowerment through musical expression.

During the 1990s Madonna continued to explore and exploit areas of sexual expression, such as sadomasochism, pornography and same-sex erotica. Her press interviews to date have been littered with the same sense of self-reflexivity and sexual awareness we find in songs, such as 'Survival', where she faces her critics head on with the biting lyrics ... *does your criticism have you caught up in what you cannot see?* Spiced with accusation and pain, Madonna informs us, in no uncertain terms, and quite sarcastically, that she has little time to behave properly because she is *too busy surviving*, thus assuring us that she *will never be an angel or saint*. Contrasting with each other, the verse and chorus sections in 'Survival' contain an array of musical codes through which Madonna defiantly insists that she is *living to tell* regardless of whether it is *heaven or hell*. As with most of the tracks in *Bedtime Stories*, empowerment is actualised in the form of the production of the groove (see example 2.5) which transports her emotive messages through a range of codes, such as the bass figure, the harmonic gestures and chords, and the melodic shapes and vocal phrases. Let us look at these technical codes more closely before turning to the question of musical production:

- Bass figure – Placed on the first two beats, the heavy, compressed bass line in 'Survival' anticipates the third beat by 'hitting' the preceding quaver beat. Filling the audio space with its booming low frequencies on the first two beats of each bar, the bass regulates the levels of tension/release and call/response within the groove. Reminiscent of a Massive Attack track, at least in terms of its production, the timbral effect of the bass is muddy yet exquisitely erotic. Its shape throughout is highlighted by the intricacy of the kit track. Juxtaposed over a steady hi-hat quaver beats, the snare shots smack the second and fourth beats with ferocity. The effect of this contributes to the overall energy of the rhythmic impulse, which is further enhanced by the other instrumental parts (guitar, synths, percussion) entering and exiting the mix at various points.
- Harmonic gestures and chords – In the verse, the harmonic tension spans two bars with Gmaj7 resolving to F#m7 in the second bar. Only in the bridge passage does this tension break when Gmaj7 falls down a minor third to Em9 in preparation for the chorus. The overall harmonic shape – one chord per bar – is reinforced by the root notes taken in the bass part. However, despite any stability or comfort created by the harmonic gestures, a general sense of ambiguity is promulgated by the lack of a clear

tonic centre.[31] The likelihood of any tonicity is further confounded by the incessant repetition of the pitch B, taken by the backing guitar, which doubles up with the bass rhythm more than two octaves higher. These harmonic codes thus contribute to the levels of tension and energy within the groove.

- Melodic shapes and vocal phrases – Layered over the bass lines and chord sequences, the vocal phrases provide yet another dimension to the intensity of the groove. Internal melodic shapes, such as intervallic motives, rhythmic ideas, tune segments, always correspond, albeit in a variety of ways, to the regularity of the two bar rhythmic and harmonic cells. Gesturally, the vocal phrases tend to be shaped by two bar melodic sequences, whose cadences rise and fall alternately; this tempers the mood of the song by again projecting stability and control (especially on the part of the vocalist). Through the smooth, undulating quality of the melodic phrases, it is as if Madonna 'surfs' the groove. As the lyrics suggest circular motion, so the vocal phrases move *up and down and all around* in sync with intervallic upward and downward motion, highlighting the sexual connotations of Madonna's intentions.

- Rhythm – Possibly most striking about the vocal part is its rhythmic pull against the regularity and rigidity of the quantised bass and kit tracks. It is indeed this aspect of rhythmic irregularity that widens the scope for us to wallow in the expanse of sonic gestures. In this way, the vocal phrases contribute significantly to the levels of energy within the groove (Example 2.5). The pleasure then is derived from the overall arrangement of the groove, in particular, the compelling juxtapositioning of the tracks.

A lit-tle up and down and all - a-round, it's   all a-bout sur-viv-al.

Example 2.4   Melodic codes in 'Survival'

Following on from this, I am keen to point out some of the ironic markers located in the 'sounds' themselves. The choice of instrumentation in 'Survival' encapsulates a range of synthesised sounds, such as the fashionable cheesy-flavoured 1970s analogue samples. Laced with digitally controlled scratch samples, the disco retro feel is conjured up through the song's 'synthetic' quality. Here the artifice in choice of sound secures the song's ironic emphasis, not least through the phallic snare shots on the second and fourth beats. In her references to Madonna's musical expression, McClary explains how 'the options available to a woman musician in rock music are especially constrictive,

Example 2.5   Groove in 'Survival'

for this musical discourse is typically characterized by its *phallic upbeat'* (McClary 1991: 154, emphases added). On a cautionary note, she adds that while it might be possible for female artists to play down such 'upbeats', there are dangers in the music becoming stereotypically feminine. The terms of McClary's debate here certainly beg careful consideration. From another perspective, we could say that Madonna has never recoiled from appropriating so-called phallic beats as a pronouncement of her own femininity. In other words, the phallic beats of cock-rock seem reinscribed quite intentionally through all her songs. In actual point, there can be little doubt that she has revelled in the accenting of the *phallic* upbeat at the same time that her rooted-ness in African-American musical styles has been highly profiled. Reading this as a creative strategy assumes a repudiation of authenticity in the context of a white, male-based rock musical discourse.[32]

In the cyclic coda section of 'Survival', a multiplicity of musical codes unite through three central lyrical hooks: *up and down and all around*; *I'll never be an angel*, and *survival*. And, before gradually fading out, the groove (Example 2.5) transports us into the song's moment of transcendence, a space where we are permitted to revel in the climactic delight of joyous repetition. Here, as with most of her songs, 'Survival' refuses any traditional tonal definition and resolution through its modal staticity, as, once again, repetition functions as a metaphor for her persistence, her ambition, her determination to survive. From humiliation to provocation, the wide range of sentiments evoked by this recording are based around a set of musical rules which delineate meaning in performance. The result is a kind of musical repartee that functions as a rejoinder by suggesting a detached sense of feelingness. But most of all, the codes in this song are representative of part of the production quality of the sound, and it is to this point I will now turn.

In 'Survival', as in all the other tracks I have considered so far, the role of producer is critical when considering Madonna's approach to music-making. Obviously in collaboration with the other producers she employs, the choice of process in finding the best sound and effects is implicated in the total effect of the production. For example, the layering of sounds in 'Survival' is achieved through technical enhancement made available in digital editing, sampling and post-dubbing. It is important to emphasise that Madonna's sound is controlled by everything in production terms, from the choice of microphones to the type of editing software used. Implicit in her songs, as with her videos, is a particular penchant for innovative production. In historical terms, Madonna's sound can be traced through many of the dance-style productions from the early 1980s onwards. Her preferences for dance trends, evident in all her productions, emphasise the significant changes that have linked technological innovation with sound in the pop world. Théberge has argued that nowhere has the 'link between "sound" and musical genre been so intensely formed as in rap and various forms of dance music since the 1980s' (1997: 196). And, in this case, the capabilities of digitalised instruments – drum machines, synthesisers, samplers – have had a great bearing on the articulation of the artist's technical and stylistic codes, all of which define a specific period.

Drum programming alone, in its development during the past two decades, constitutes a multitude of variables that requires great expertise and understanding of the intricacies involved in getting the desired effect in a groove. One only has to compare the use of drum machines on Madonna's first album to her latest (at the time of writing this book, *Music*), to appreciate the full impact of this on the emergence of her style. Perhaps the point worth stressing here, though, is that it is not only the technical manipulation of material that defines the recordings, but also the imaginative choice of instrumentation (digital and live). Often the sounds themselves prompt the musician to play and produce in a certain manner and style, while their treatment in the studio, through say phasing, gating, multiply delay and reverb, can function as a stimulant for determining the compositional design and production. Thus, it is the techniques of production that can most inspire musicians to draw on new compositional possibilities in music technology.

Techniques employed in production are closely linked to the demands of the music industry, and the demand for different and exciting sounds with which the market promotes new artists. And, here we have a clue to Madonna's standing as a musician. Her ability as a producer/performer to embrace new trends and sounds as part of her musical commodity, has placed her in a context where the fusion between demands of commerciality and production techniques are complete. From 1983, when her career took off with *The First*

Album, which featured tracks such as 'Holiday', 'Borderline', and 'Lucky Star', to her album *Music* (released in 2000), there has been a digital revolution in sound recording. And again, Madonna's achievements as producer need to be measured against this. Digital technology in sound reproduction has become one of the main means for changes in musical practice. As a result, the artist's recourse to production brings to the fore the immanence of the musical skills of the artist and how they translate into commercial success. This perspective is important because it identifies how in the music industry artistic credibility is measured by the imperatives of risk-taking and change.

Final concluding thoughts

What these considerations of Madonna's music most demonstrate is the intricate relationships between musical expression and the pop personality. As Madonna has developed her sound, so have new techniques in production steadily evolved. Pop music functions as a springboard for interpreting a variety of cultural expressions within a framework that confronts fixed dualisms and rigid categories of identity. Significantly, it is as musician and producer that Madonna is one of the few female artists to have broken into the male domain of the recording studio. Undoubtedly, Madonna is fully aware that women have been excluded from the musical workplace on most levels, and has set out to change this (McClary 1991; Gaar 1993; Green 1997; Bayton 1999; Whiteley 2000).

At issue here is the consequence of this through the construction of performative texts that are predicated upon a special type of difference. Here I am also referring to the sound of different cultural voices. Difference in musical voices could be best described on the basis of its effect and aesthetic intention. From this perspective, we need to remember that our responses to Madonna – be they pleasurable, repugnant, or indifferent – are also constructed upon our sense of *cultural imagination*. This would imply that we need to get to grips with the complexity of our own ideological preferences and dislikes in order to adequately evaluate the effect of musical expression. However broad the generality of such a function might be, there are two critical concerns at stake: first, the task of assimilating the artist's sound as an integral part of their social circumstances, and, second, the need to shift from stultified pure musical description into the sphere of analysing it alongside other texts.

Identity constructed through self-parody is a feature typifying much pop. It is worth considering that such constructions in Madonna's texts are performative in that they display a range of performed acts which emphasise a kind of virtuosity in representation. In one sense, the self-recognition of the representation of herself as a white, heterosexual woman can assume a melancholic dimension.[33] Significantly, Butler has argued how an adherence to fixed forms of sexuality and gender can often lead to states of psychopathological melancholy. This concept is well worth extending to Madonna's type of performativity. Through performance, gender can become constructed as 'a ritualized repetition of conventions' which is forced into a category of 'compulsory heterosexuality' (Butler 1995: 31). Thus, the workings of gender through the performance of drag, masquerade, and camp in pop texts can be read as oppositional and subversive. Often such constructions of femininity in videos raise the issue of mimicry in performance, a point of further debate I enter into in Chapter 4. When the woman plays out a femininity 'different' from her own, such a role 'allegorises a loss it cannot grieve' especially when the act of mimicry exposes a heterosexual melancholy (Butler 1995: 31). In *Bedtime Stories*, Madonna's narratives of love and sex are often tinged with a boldness and sarcasm that confess to the artificiality of scripts that contain floods of sentimentality.

Butler has described how there are costs attached to the expression of *coherent identities*, especially when these are performed out at the expense of rejecting the 'specters that threaten the arbitrarily closed domain of subject-positions' (1995: 31). Only through reversing this and repositioning an incoherency of identity does any connection become possible. In this sense, the decentred subject, Madonna, becomes vulnerable, yet liberated, and thus open to desire. It is therefore the suggestion of incoherency through mimicry in her texts that potentially creates new modes of authenticity, and, in turn, compounds essentialist notions of naturalness around any one real identity.

In opting for identities that evoke a variety of subject-positions, Madonna inevitably clashes with conventional concepts by the trading-in of the notion of a single, true identity with that of a multiplicity of conflicting constructs.[34] But, even this ploy is not bereft of the terms and conditions of the modernist Subject. Madonna's many identities are positioned as knowing transfer points – points that function to negotiate authenticity through blatant displays of inauthenticity. In a sense, Madonna's authorial position exchanges one totality for another to the point that it becomes redundant to argue whether her real personality is separated from the varied representations that we experience.[35]

In performance terms, the political charge of her personal rhetoric is grounded in a history of Western culture. There is always an air of difference that functions as a transparent form of resistance to the status of a single, coherent, universal subject. Yet, such displays of difference are vulnerable to distortion through various complex constructions (see Solie 1993). Given this, how we locate the sites where 'cultural forces permit or encourage resistance to the construction of difference' becomes a tricky undertaking (Solie 1993: 9). Yet, no matter how much Madonna's representations are played out, she continues to provide a compelling site for examining a musical sensibility not dissimilar to that of the avant-garde artist. Indeed, the distinctions between the modernist and postmodernist identity are easily blurred as Madonna's authority continues to goad her staunchest critics.[36]

But most of all I am inclined to argue that Madonna's texts arbitrate tension through the fusion of her musical labours with political resistance. While the distinct groove-based codes of her songs can of course be read in many ways, I would prefer to interpret them as part of the aesthetic formations found in pop culture. Clearly, there are those who hold that Madonna simply *mainstreams* her identity too far. But because she might not resist in the way one might expect, this does not mean she does not resist at all. For me her greatest resonance lies in a musical celebration of the liberation and empowerment of herself through the eroticised body. To some extent this demonstrates how the commercial marketplace – the site of pop's consumption – turns into the location for rebirth, revolution and new forms of human behaviour. Viewed in this context, Madonna's texts raise many critiques on the modalities of commercial success and desire. The implication of this is that beneath the musical surfaces there lurks an ambition and passion that is quite insatiable.

Contrary to the bulk of scholarship centred around this artist, again I would insist that her musical texts should not be dismissed in view of their 'simplistic formulae'. At a general level, Madonna's sound points towards a specific historical moment in pop music, where representational strategies became exceptionally polyvalent. Thus, it is hardly surprising that she has continued into the new century to explore realms of musical expression that continue to redefine the genres found in popular music. Indeed, Madonna's extraordinary celebrity status must be linked to her ability to grasp the rapidly changing technologies and styles of a multimedia industry and apply them creatively to her texts.

Finally, if we fast forward from the mechanical disco thrusts of her first album, *Madonna/The First Album* (1983) to her most recent albums, *Ray of Light* (1998) and *Music* (2000), Madonna is impulsive in adapting to the times. While the nostalgic, psychedelic sounds and ambient dance grooves incorporated into *Ray of Light* display yet another change in identity, the use of raw guitar acoustic performance set alongside elegant electronic flourishes in *Music* idealise the new heights that Madonna has reached at the dawn of the twenty-first century. Yet, the hyperreality of this icon continues to be enigmatic as, captured in the click of the record button, she openly confesses, *I traded fame for love* (in *Ray of Light*) and that *nobody's perfect* (in *Music*). Even in the song 'Music' everything is redefined once again as she plays out mimesis in an attempt to recover the banality and universality of pop itself by proclaiming, *Music makes the people come together, music makes the bourgeoisie and the rebel.*

So through a fascinating display of musical performance and ambivalence, Madonna has continued to capture the imagination of millions where the infatuation with idols is no better illustrated than through a craving for pop. Tirelessly, she has persisted in manipulating and soliciting media response through the flamboyancy of her musical rhetoric. While hard and persistent, her quest for freedom of expression is manifested in her exchange of one identity for another. And lest we forget, her creative agency is underpinned by an ardent ambition, a sadomasochistic allure, and a lewd sense of exhibitionism that continues to seek out fame at all costs.

Acknowledgements

Much of the content of this chapter first appeared in an article with the same title in the internet journal, *Critical Musicology Journal*, University of Leeds, 1997.

Notes

1   The quotation is from the song 'Survival' from *Bedtime Stories*, Words and music by Madonna Ciccone and Dallas Austin (WB Music Corp., 1994).
2   The start of female address on MTV has been traced back to 1983 with the release of Cyndi Lauper's video, 'Girls just want to have fun'. Between 1983 and 1984 female stars, such as Tina Turner, Pat Benatar, Cyndi Lauper, and Madonna, opened up the field for challenging assumptions on gender and sex-roles by drawing audiences into the narratives on girl culture and female social relationships. A full detailed discussion of videos featuring female musicians from the period 1983 to 1986 can be found in Lewis (1990).
3   Despite the countless critical critiques of MTV, it is worth stressing that sexism, misogyny, homophobia and gender inequality have been often vehemently opposed in many of the videos of the 1980s by both male and female musicians.
4   See Cook (1998) for one of the few musicological analyses of Madonna's videos. His method is to demonstrate through music-theoretical concepts the important relationships that exist between visual shots, words and music. For another important perspective, see Bradby (1992) who emphasises the complete lack of attention paid to Madonna's music by cultural theorists. Importantly, she reveals how the correlation between music and lyrics can serve as an aid to comprehending Madonna's videos.
5   Note that the bulk of Madonna scholarship has taken place in culture, media and film studies, with very little musicological attention paid to Madonna being instigated by feminist music scholars.
6   It is worth emphasising that only in the late 1990s have her skills as a producer finally been acknowledged by more of her critics. Although in some cases critics have insisted that Madonna's success is mainly attributable to the work of others, and her ability to cherry-pick the best and most trendy producers on the market. See, for example, Paul Moody's review of *Ray of Light* (1998), in which he extols Madonna's success and musical ability.
7   For an interesting perspective see Stefani (1987b) who has argued that this might be because the singing voice is less demanding on the listener than other constructions, and therefore an easier 'message' for the brain to decode. Also Moore (1993) has insisted that greater conceptualisation of the role of the voice is necessary before we can fully account for its communicative quality and aesthetic affect.

8   This includes an array of producers and musicians such as Dallas Austin, Dave
     Hall, Herbie Hancock, Anne Preven, Scott Cutler, Babyface, Kevin McKenzie,
     Shawn McKenzie, Michael Deering, Nellee Hooper, Ndége Ocello, Bjørk
     Gudmunsdottir, Marius Devries, Colin Wolfe, Rudolph Isley, Ronald Isley and
     O'Kelly Isley. Notably, the title track 'Bedtime Stories', written by Nellee Hooper
     with Bjørk, inspired the album's title.

9   On the issue of closure, McClary makes the following pertinent observation:
     '[Madonna] offers musical structures that promise narrative closure, and at the
     same time she resists or subverts them. A traditional energy flow is managed –
     which is why to many ears the whole complex seems always already absorbed –
     but that flow is subtly redirected' (McClary 1991: 154–5).

10   In making this assertion I am keen to emphasise that I am locating my argument
     firmly within the comparative domain of Western art and popular music.

11   McClary (1991) identifies irony as one of Madonna's most obvious strategies and
     describes how through parody she disrupts 'a much-treasured male illusion' (1991:
     155). However, this assertion could be seen as fairly problematic as it assumes
     (rather than theorises) irony as gender-specific.

12   Cf. Roland Barthes (1977, 1988), whose work has influenced much musicological
     thought. Exploring the links between the voice and gendered sexuality, he proble-
     matises the binary divides that frequently lead to essentialist assumptions. Classifi-
     cation according to biological determination forms an important part of Barthes'
     investigation into the transgression of sexual difference. One of his projects is to
     dismantle stereotypical notions of female and male sexuality by concentrating on
     the neutral centre of the androgyne.

13   Frith (1996) approaches the analysis of the voice under four headings: as a musical
     instrument, as a body, as a person and as a character. Like Joke Dame, Frith
     maintains that by listening to the voice we are listening to the physical sound of
     the body. Also see Middleton's critique (1990) of Barthes, in Chapter 7 of *Studying
     Popular Music*.

14   It seems that like Strauss's *Salome*, Berg's *Lulu*, Wagner's Kundry in *Parsifal*, as
     well as Balzac's castrato, Zambinella, from the tale *Sarrasine*, Madonna is one in a
     line of strong females who have challenged bourgeois male ideology through
     blatant displays of power and parody.

15   For two such recent studies, see Cook 1998; Whiteley 2000.

16   However, it should be pointed out that numerous gay and lesbian critics have taken
     issue with Madonna's appropriation of gay culture. Arguably it is precisely her
     heterosexuality that makes her appropriation of gay culture unacceptable (see Gill
     1995).

17   In response to Whiteley's study (1997b), I would contend that as well as providing
     female fans with a sense of empowerment over their sexuality, the 'Justify My
     Love' video also has an immediacy with male viewers. From the numerous
     responses to this video I have measured in my classes, male responses vary far
     more than Whiteley's findings suggests. Generally, many male viewers tend to pick
     up on the ironic intent of this video, enjoying the spectacle of Madonna's perfor-
     mance. To suggest, as Whiteley does, that the video might function to 'alleviat[e]
     masculine psychological insecurities or simply stimulat[e] masculine pleasure' is
     essentialist through the neglect of a range of important common responses that are
     felt across cross gender divides. Of course, it must be emphasised that in both
     Whiteley's and my research into response, our subjects are limited to music and
     media students working in the field of popular music studies. As Whiteley's class
     of music students overwhelmingly felt, Madonna engages equally with both male

and female viewers. On a cautious note, we should remember that readings of music students cannot be considered as representative of mainstream rock and pop audiences in any thorough empirical-based study. See Steve Sweeney Turner (1998) for a similar critique of Whiteley's position.

18   Importantly, we cannot dismiss the fact that she attracts gay and heterosexual fans alike through her gender-bending antics, something which is by no means a new strategy in pop culture.

19   See especially her videos, 'Material Girl', 'Like A Virgin', 'Express Yourself', and 'Papa Don't Preach'.

20   In her studies, Teresa de Lauretis (1986) draws the distinction between the deployment of masquerade and 'mask' as a strategy of empowerment. While masquerade can be enjoyed by the bearer, especially in terms of the quality of its mimicry, the mask is negatively imposed to the point of inhibiting the 'real' personality.

21   As Grossberg (1992) asserts, it is the strategy of pop artists to perform their authenticity through a display of fragmentation and contradiction which thus results in an inauthenticity.

22   For a useful critique on sexual subversion in pop culture, see Geyrhalter (1996).

23   See Moody 1998.

24   In addition to the prominent position Debbie Harry held in the pre-Madonna era, mention should be made to key black girl artists and groups from this period, such as the Brides of Funkenstein and Parlet (protegés of George Clinton), the punk-funk group the Mary Jane Girls, and Vanity 6 (produced by Prince), who expressed themselves in an explicitly sexual manner.

25   In his retrospective review, 'Berühmtheit als Kunstform', Thomas Groß (2000) has ·
pointed out that one of the greatest misunderstandings when it comes to her music has been to underestimate Madonna's inventiveness. His argument for her creative authorship rests in the assertion that her talent has been cast in her shrewd perception of the changing music industry. This is something Madonna has frequently acknowledged in live interviews.

26   See McClary (1991) for an account of the interplay between the visual and musical dimensions of representation in 'Open Your Heart'. McClary concludes that the feminine erotic can function as nonsexual pleasure in a patriarchal setting.

27   Madonna has always acknowledged her threat to women as much as to men. For example, in one interview Madonna claimed that 'powerful women are a threat in any society which is why I am such a target. Even other women are threatened by me. It's disturbing but at the same time it's inspiring because it makes me want to destroy all that, end it' (in Moody 1998).

28   Within this context, it is not surprising that Madonna's role as musician is regarded by many with a certain scepticism, often blocking any chance of serious musical analysis.

29   Perhaps her strategy to *appear* oblivious to popularity, insisting that her standing as a musician has increasingly gained more respect from the public, might be interpreted as a shift towards a more modernist position.

30   In contrast to Madonna, P. J. Harvey problematises the qualities of her sexuality often with reference to her physical awkwardness and dislike for self-eroticisation.

31   For a lucid discussion of 'tonal space', see Middleton (1993), who demonstrates in his analysis of Madonna the importance of exploring tonal space in conjunction with the tension that is produced by the effect of gesture and movement.

32   Forming a central point of her thesis, McClary (1991) discusses this extensively through her analyses of gender.

33   Building on Freud's work on the formulations of the ego, Butler (1995) has

suggested that gender identification might be the result of a certain melancholic identification.

34 This idea has been theorised in much detail by Grossberg (1993) who insists that it is indeed inauthenticity that produces new orders of authenticity in the context of pop expression. Such an interpretation of authenticity can be read as ostensibly ironic in itself. Also note that others, such as Brian Longhurst, see this somewhat differently, from a more postmodernist position. He has argued that in the case of Madonna 'there is no real identity, no authentic way of being' (Longhurst 1995: 126) as she exchanges so-called reality with a constant flow of deceptive identities.

35 This begs the question of how we read her live performances in contrast to her videos. In the live stage performance of *Vogue* (from MTV's video music awards 1990) Madonna masquerades in one of her most provocative live performances as Mozartian operatic diva.

36 Given my concern for a better understanding of Madonna's music, I do not intend to become too engrossed in the debates around her postmodernity and modernity. I am more keen to bring my own experience as a musicologist to bear upon the task of acknowledging the feelings, emotional and intellectual, encountered in pop songs.

Chapter 3

Anti-rebel, Lonesome Boy: Morrissey in Crisis?

'I often pass a mirror, and when I glance into it slightly
I don't recognize myself at all. You look into a mirror and
wonder, "Where have I seen that person before?" Then you
remember – it was at a neighbour's funeral, and it was the corpse.'[1]

Introduction

Once the creative passion had died down between the songwriting duo, Johnny
Marr and Steven Morrissey, it was only a short period before one of England's
most influential post-punk, indie pop groups broke up. Much to their fans'
dismay, the Smiths were disbanded in 1987. With over seventy songs recorded
in just four years, they had brought into mainstream English pop a sensibility
that contrasted strongly with the glamour of synthesiser and sequencer-based
1980s pop. Consisting of Johnny Marr[2] (lead guitar), Mike Joyce (drums),
Andy Rourke (bass) and Steven Morrissey as vocalist, the Smiths put on the
market a brand of music unique to the independent sector. Their impact on
English pop would pave the way for groups such as Happy Mondays and
Stone Roses in the 1980s, and, one decade later, the Britpop band explosion
headed by Oasis, Blur, Suede and Pulp. Above all, the songs of the Smiths
expressed the romantic ideals and myths of English identity during the
Thatcher years.[3] It was from this background that Morrissey emerged as a solo
artist in 1988.

In this chapter my aim is to explore a number of issues relevant to
Morrissey's musical expression. I begin with considering questions of style
and identity and how the Smiths constructed a realness or artistic authenticity
for their fans. Of particular interest to me is how this affected Morrissey's
characterisation and how it raises a wealth of questions relating to masculinity,
sexuality and race within an English context. But the central question that runs
through this chapter is concerned with how musical expression creates
empathic responses. By looking closely at the nature of such responses, I
suggest a way forward in attempting to understand their significance with
respect to the wider concerns of musicological analysis.

Part of this study also examines some of the tensions that have defined
Morrissey's distinct style by my approaching aspects of his performance
through a consideration of a range of musical codes. In addition, the

distinctiveness of Morrissey as a lyricist needs to be evaluated alongside issues of authenticity, which, as I debate, are primary markers in the construction of his identity. Perhaps the most awkward aspect of Morrissey's musical identity is tackled towards the end of my discussion. Often a suspicion of pretence accompanies ironic expression and playfulness. When combined with musical performance, working out ironic intent can be a cause for unease. As I make clear in this chapter, there are always negative and positive aspects applicable to ironic interpretation, and when the political dimensions of an artist's work, such as Morrissey's, are so overt, the problem of attributing ironic readings is indeed complex.

There are, however, many ways to read the range of emotions in his songs as a desire to ironic recourse, and I do this through my own personal readings. The very trope of the ordinary, down to earth musician, displaced within the context of the MTV pop mainstream, is in itself a formidable arsenal for speaking out. Thus, grounded in this notion, I seek to demonstrate that the multiple voices in Morrissey's performance are inseparable from their cultural historical roots. As I will debate, his musical rhetoric becomes a channel for addressing the local space in relation to the central while opposing the dominant positions that instill power and belief ideologically.

With a thorn in his side

During the same year that Elvis Presley reached number one in the charts with 'A Fool Such as I', Steven Patrick Morrissey was born in Manchester on 22 May 1959, of Irish parents. His youth was spent listening to and absorbing vast amounts of pop music. Years later he was to claim: 'When young I instantly excluded the human race in favour of pop music' (in Bret 1994: 9). From an early age he had started writing so that by the time he met up with the other founding member of the Smiths, Johnny Marr, in 1982, he had cultivated a striking poetic style. Impressed by Morrissey's lyrical brilliance, Marr was able to quickly work out melodies and arrangements that best suited their songs. In fact, Marr's musical influence would prove to have a major effect on the Smiths' success and later on Morrissey's musical style when he pursued his solo career.

Self-deprecation has always formed part of Morrissey's texts. Thriving on this, his rhetoric is structured around an ambivalence to his own identity. On another level, themes of social rebellion in Morrissey's texts can be read as pointed defences of Arcadian values in England. An ability to convert social observation into witty aphorism is a skill he shares with numerous other English artists and groups, whose treatment of national sentimentality echoes England's decline. Mixed with feelings of loathing and hatred for the social and political conditions of his country, Morrissey's songs are rooted in a sense of loss of Arcady through the modernisation processes of cultural change. And through his songs, the culturescape of a postmodern generation growing up in England of the 1980s and 1990s is chronicled.

Historically, English pop music started off as a working-class reaction to traditions and values centred around class. Based on a sensibility consisting of contradiction and perversity, the portrayal of Englishness through popular song has always flourished through the illusions of Arcadian dream. In the wake of Oscar Wilde (an acknowledged source of inspiration for Morrissey), a new cult sensibility emerged at the end of the nineteenth century that defended the Arcadian values of English culture. With the onset of the First World War in 1914, British youth had despaired at the social and cultural decline of England. As Michael Bracewell points out: 'England as Arcady – the rural democracy of the green and pleasant land, translated into the suffocating fabric of English society – had been a pretty disguise for much that youth of the twentieth century would refuse to tolerate' (Bracewell 1998: 15).

If we trace this back to the end of the First World War, ideals of English identity were also challenged during this period as the values of the Victorians conflicted with the aspirations of modern youth. Indeed, for writers such as Graham Greene and Evelyn Waugh, the mushrooming of suburbia had become both a source of repulsion and fascination in a context where rebellion was driven by what Bracewell describes as a 'statelessness' arising out of the 'collision between two opposed states of mind: the Arcadian and the suburban' (1997: 25). Certainly, this notion of statelessness was embedded in the despair of suburbia which would become central to the fostering of English talent in the 'dismal bedroom in the suburbs' during the latter half of the twentieth century.

As the century progressed, a greater ambivalence towards British identity was further articulated by a serious reaction to European fascism and the moral hypocrisies of England during the onset of the Second World War. In the 1930s, W.H. Auden continued the tradition of sharp social critique by his predecessors and contemporaries (Howard, Betjeman, Wilde, Waugh et al). Frequently imbued in irony and satire, Auden's writing and thoughts on Englishness would be what the Pet Shop Boys and Morrissey would pick up on some fifty years later. Indeed, the affected mannerisms and witty satire of writers such as Auden and Coward led to a re-evaluation of Arcady.

Manifested in an ambivalent response to England, through the mourning of Arcady, Morrissey's texts, like Auden's, would encapsulate those deeply mixed sentiments of a changing political climate, something that continues to create great unease among certain pop artists today. It is interesting that Auden's visions of England in the 1930s would be retained in some of the most famous pop songs of the second half of the century as the class system, firmly positioned by the monarchy, continued to be an issue of contention within a majority working-class society. Indeed, part of the Smiths' (and later

Morrissey's) appeal lay in their construction of a sense of Englishness which centred around arousing notions of sentimentality through empathic response. From the outset, their musical style developed steadily in a direction that was predicated upon nostalgia.[4] While each member of the group possessed his own distinct style, their songs were carefully constructed around Morrissey's personality in order to, as Stringer suggests, 'capitalise on the public's growing fascination with his star image' (Stringer 1992: 16). Most importantly, the nature of his image, in particular his gendered construction, played a major role from the outset:

> Morrissey's contradictory traits (an ordinary, working-class 'anti-star' who nevertheless loves to hog the spotlight, a nice man who says the nastiest things about other people, a shy man who is also an outrageous narcissist) were already being mulled over by reporters (he must have been the most interviewed star of the 1980s); and so the diverse, yet instantly identifiable, 'sound' of the Smiths could testify, at once, to their skill as both music and image makers. [Stringer: 16–17]

In the wake of the New Pop mainstream that was sweeping the world during the beginning of the 1980s, the Smiths represented for many something alternative and 'authentic'; a cunning fusion of old and new values. Johnny Marr's traditional guitar style, with its references in the rock styles of artists, such as Roger McGuinn and Keith Richard, fused with the unlikely flamboyancy of Morrissey, who was influenced by specific artists of the 1960s and 1970s whom he modelled his performance around.[5] In addition to his musical tastes, a general interest in feminism and the plight of women in society had a profound effect on his songs:

> Morrissey's intense fascination with the blurred distinction between masculine and feminine roles was heightened by such reading. Looking back at his successive championing of Bolan, Bowie and The New York Dolls there is evidence enough of a youth celebrating celebrity androgyny. Not surprisingly, the stress on 'demasculinization' encouraged Steven to question his own sexuality. [Rogan 1992: 90–91]

This account goes some way in explaining why issues of gendered identity are so central to Morrissey's songs. In one respect, his apparent confusion about his own sexuality has led him to a curiously non-committal position in which he has repeatedly stressed his asexuality and disinterest in sexual activity.[6] On the one hand, such declarations might be read as distinctly English, reflecting a moralistic and satirical take on the Victorian approach to sex (see Simon 1996). On the other hand, they could be evaluated alongside many of the pop stars of the 1980s whose display of sexuality concertedly conflicted with heteronormative models of masculinity. Yet, paradoxically, claiming asexuality in oneself, as he would later discover, soon reproduces many of the fundamental axioms of sexual essentialism one sets out to avoid. That Morrissey realised full well that sex is taken far too seriously within our Western culture, has been manifested in his decision to distance himself from any declaration of his own sexuality. This seems hardly surprising when situated within a late twentieth-century context, where varying degrees of persecution by the media have formed part and parcel of the celebrity world on a daily basis. In being a pop artist, Morrissey knew there were costly penalties for breaking out of the narrow confines of what is socially normative and acceptable. So, while the 1980s might have seemed like a period for new possibilities, they were also witness to times of severe suffering based around prejudice towards gender and sexual difference.

Contextualising this helps reveal how Morrissey's identity has been constructed through the very conventions that oppressed it, not least through his staunch opposition to conservative traditions and values. In this way, his songs and performances offer thoughtful commentaries on notions of social stereotyping, with his trump card being a calculated construction of playfulness that has on more than a few occasions led the tabloids up the garden path. Of course this has always had consequences for fans delighting in the resisting subject of wit and misery, whose categorisation of identity crises frequently set out to challenge.

Which returns me to the issue of English identity. The names groups select for themselves are intimately tied into their notions of how they perceive themselves and wish to be perceived. Notably, it was Morrissey who decided on the name for the Smiths. In stark contrast to the spate of bands that emerged in the early 1980s, with zappy names – Spandau Ballet, Duran Duran, Wham!, Culture Club, Kajagoogoo, Wet Wet Wet, Bananarama, Tears for Fears, Curiosity Killed The Cat – the Smiths captured the essence of Englishness through the mundaneness of their name.[7] Constructed against the pop mainstream of the day, the notion of them depicting a sense of realness was paramount, as Morrissey explains:

> The Smiths are absolutely real faces instead of the frills, the gloss and the pantomime popular music has become immersed in. There is no human element in anything more, and I think The Smiths reintroduce that quite firmly. There's no facade. We're simply there to be seen as real people. [Morrissey in Bret 1994: 25]

Quite instinctively, their sonic trademark was developed around a musical sensibility that had its roots in English groups, such as the Who, the Kinks and the Stones. Notably there was little direct reference to African-American artists and music styles,[8] as the Smiths' authenticity – a kind of back-to-basics approach – drew on a combination of musical traditions that shrewdly blended rock with pop styles. What principally distinguished their sound was a resistance to many of the cliched musical features, especially in terms of production style, that typified international mainstream pop and rock of the day.[9] The significance of this would be emphasised by Morrissey years later when he claimed, 'The Smiths make music which sounded very affordable to people.' And of course it was this aspect that appealed enormously to their fans, primarily because it contrasted boldly with the pop and rock of the day, that in Morrissey's words was 'overbearingly glittery, overbearingly rich and very conservative' (in Uhelszki 2001).

With reference to song structure alone, a defiant rejection of the formulaic predictability and structures found in pop songs was discernible in their texts. This was borne out by the absence of middle sections, easily discernible choruses and instrumental solo passages. Stylistically, there were also implications inherent in their choice of chords and voice leading, where there would be a 'momentary disorientation' or anxiety relating to where 'harmonic and thematic resolution' might indeed take place (Stringer 1992: 24). In actual fact, the Smiths' avoidance of such harmonic teleology could be linked to the wider ambiguity surrounding their musical reception. Stylistically, all this was tied up in a calculated characterisation of ordinariness which resisted the gloss of technological slickness found in pop productions of the day. And yet, their image as 'normal lads' was still bound up in the contradictions that distinguish the pop industry and cults of authorship (Toynbee 2000).

In terms of his own personal style, Morrissey has drawn on referents that stretch from 1960s popular music to rock and punk of the 1970s. Many of his songs are structured around distinctive guitar lines (lead and rhythm) with bass and kit as their comp backing. The density of instrumental textures in his songs can be measured by a distinct quality in timbre which is stratified through the mix in studio and live performances. Frequently, Morrissey's voice is foregrounded in its relationship to the bass and kit, while the backing guitar parts often appear in the mid-ground. The use of effects, such as reverb, frequently serve to pad out the textures of his songs, while separation of parts within the mix through technical manipulation varies quite considerably. A comparison of songs from Morrissey's early solo period in 1988 to his most recent album releases soon reveals a tendency towards employing studio technology in new ways. In addition, the inclusion of other instruments (synthesisers, samplers, drum machines, etc.) also feature in many later songs.

In pursuing the question of musical performance throughout this chapter, I intend to focus on the details of vocal expression as a main code defining Morrissey's style. I suggest that it is through his unique manner of controlling rising and falling pitches in his melodic lines that our attention is drawn to the special quality of his delivery. Notably, there is frequent emphasis on major seventh leaps that significantly determine the modal flavour of melodic and harmonic content. Importantly, the types of chords and functions he draws on are realised at the guitar fretboard rather than the piano. This distinction is relevant to any discussion of the derivation of harmonic sequences and melodic patterns in rock and pop music (Moore 1993: 54–55).

In general terms, the harmonic rhythm in Morrissey's songs appears to be moderately paced with very few exceptions of rapid change, while the disposition of kit patterns, generally constructed around solid rock riffs, serve to control the pulse of chordal change. In fact, the very consistency of his rhythmic patterns and their alignment to harmonic change is that which typifies most the post-punk essence of his musical idiom. Certainly, Morrissey's debt to punk groups, like the Jam, is most significant with regard to his performance delivery and attitude. This of course stems from a range of rock and pop genres that the Smiths appropriated and helped redefine in the 1980s. But within the confines of this chapter, my interest is less in defining the history of Morrissey's musical style than in investigating the qualities of his performance that help shed light on some of the most compelling questions of his identity – it is to this issue that I now turn.

Constructs of male identity in Morrissey

The main assumption running through this book is that pop texts are interwoven with identity politics. Clearly, music is experienced as something special that opens up the possibilities for recognising and imagining forms of identity in ourselves and others. The position that Even Ruud (1997a) takes by insisting that music functions as a storage compartment for biographical and cultural memory can be implemented as a guiding principle in the understanding of the relationship between music and identity.[10] This also raises a wealth of questions concerning idealised representations of male identity in pop texts and how they promulgate gendered privilege in a social context. That is, normative notions of gendered identity are largely about defending those values. According to Laura Mulvey's formulations of classic narrative cinema (1975), representation forms the basis for political struggle in all cultural forms. Pop texts are no exception from this. In pop of the 1980s and 1990s, the objectification of the male body gave rise to questions of identity that have been tackled in many postmodern studies on MTV spectatorship (Fiske 1987; Kaplan 1987; Goodwin 1993a; Lewis 1993; Berland 1993). In this light I want to consider how masculinity operates as a mode of expression in Morrissey's songs.

We know that as the production of new images in popular culture started redefining traditional masculinity in the 1950s and 1960s, questions linked to sexual politics became all the more prominent. It is interesting though that even at the end of the 1980s, while dominant forms of masculinity were contested (and at times turned upside down) through the assertiveness of new forms of political expression, men, in the main, according to Rutherford, 'remained remarkably silent in the face of this unmasking and criticism':

Exposed to a growing questioning men have used their silence as the best form of retaining the status quo, in the hope that the ideological formations that once sustained the myth of masculine infallibility will resurrect themselves from the fragments and produce a new mythology to hide us in. [Rutherford 1988: 23]

The critical issue that emanates from this observation concerns the *rigidity* of male expression and its conflict with the libido in a cultural and social setting where the body is detached from its sexuality and emotions. Historically, the battle for control and empowerment has been about the domination of others, and, in this respect, assertions of male heteronormativity have existed in a constant state of tension. What gradually emerged in the 1980s was a politics based on the understanding of the trajectories that discursively constitute binary categorisations of sexuality.[11] Moreover, critiques of the essentialisation of the male subject were forthcoming in order to consider the more fluid models of gendered identification. A key to this endeavour lay in dispelling the intellectual contempt for emotion that dated from the Enlightenment to the present day.

With many pop and rock stars, sexual identity has often conflicted with repressed models of masculinity. Polemically positioned to traditional male role models such as Springsteen, Bon Jovi, Sting and Ricky Martin, Morrissey's construction is insistently far more ambiguous. No clearer is this evident than in the way he slips into an address of his own insecurities and what his masculinity means for him. In ridiculing dominant forms of masculinity by claims to asexuality, Morrissey actually appropriates qualities of Otherness in order to highlight the awkwardness of his difference. Yet actually, such a strategy could be interpreted as a deliberate attempt to foil our grasping the orientation of his sexual identity.[12]

In my studies I have observed how Morrissey's characterisation of the anti-hero through his songs, videos and interviews, often emphasises his attachment to women and gay men, albeit in a non-sexual manner. This forms part of a strategy that not only positions him polemically to the traditional male hero's plight from women, but also emphasises an ambiguity which is discernible in many of his songs. The implications of this are that his identity is constantly renegotiated through the process of performance, appropriation, and representation. In short, his representations can signal gender trouble especially when read as queer (Butler 1990). Again Butler's theorisation of identity subversion within a postmodern landscape provides a usesful marker for measuring and problematising the multiplicity of gender. And, if situated within a framework of queering about with gender, Morrissey's strategies could indeed be interpreted as deviant, slippery and downright misleading. In a sense, any reading of subversive intent in his constructed ambiguity is not necessarily politically benevolent.[13]

Within a cultural context, Morrissey's identity also needs to be mapped against the politics of England in the mid-1980s, a period marked by a continual movement towards the far Right. It was during this period that the New Right's operations in the South Atlantic became part of an intention to expose the so-called enemies within. This had far-reaching implications domestically, and would prove to have a profound effect on the shaping of male identity during the early 1980s, not least among pop artists and groups. Above all, the political party-line that led to the Falkland War was inextricably attached to clearly defined ideologies of identity, as Stringer explains:

> The Conservative Government's ideologies of race and nation were filtered down to the ideals of the monogamous, heterosexual family unit, so that homosexuality, and the rights of women to determine their own autonomous sexuality, were once more marginalised as evil and undesirable. It is not hard to see how the Smiths react against this. [Stringer 1992: 23–4]

Interestingly, on the basis of the above account, Stringer reads the Smiths as genderless through what he describes as a typical English lack or concealment of sexual desire. Such a positioning is helpful for us in understanding the qualities of Morrissey's identity, an identity that promotes celibacy, put-on awkwardness, ordinariness and ambiguity. In this way, his construed genderlessness could be perceived as a construction intended to set up a special tension through the play on difference. The possibilities opened up on this level thus present us with a useful starting point for considering the nature of musical expression alongside identity.

One way into this is to consider the frustrations of the angry, self-destructive, anarchic pop male. Historically, this identity-type is nothing new to pop music (Walser 1993a, Frith 1996; Nehring 1997). Explored vividly in moving songs such as 'The Boy with the Thorn in His Side' – the ninth single released by the Smiths in 1985 – Morrissey sets out to localise his innermost emotions: *The boy with the thorn in his side, behind the hatred there lies a murderous desire for love.* Executed with an upbeat, energetic, fast rhythmic pull, the euphoric nature of the music in this passage clashes with the desolate emotions of these lyrics. This sets up a duplicity that emerges as a prime marker in all Morrissey's songs. Frequently, in his songs, misery and despair are masked by euphoric musical gestures that blend countless references. It is as if Morrissey's ongoing crisis is in constant need of relief through the execution of jovial musical narratives – a strategy that pinpoints the counternarrative quality of his musical expression.

In another well-known song from 1984, 'Heaven Knows I'm Miserable Now' – the single that trailed the Smiths' album *Hatful of Hollow* – Morrissey affords himself much emotional recourse through lines such as: *In my life why do I smile at people who I'd much rather kick in the eye.* A ploy here is to satirise conventional musical gestures alongside self-reflexive anger. By playing on the niceties of simple, polite, musical gestures, he exposes the violence in his thoughts. As Stringer explains, 'the music will not allow what the lyrics seem to ask for, or the lyrics sublimate what the music seems to offer' (Stringer 1992: 23). This trait continues into songs recorded thirteen years later, for example, 'Trouble Loves Me,' from the 1997 album, *Maladjusted*, in which Morrissey inflames the passion of his cultural predicament and ambivalence towards his Englishness: *faced with the music as always I'll face it, in the half-light so English ... frowning.*

As if enshrined in misery and contempt, Morrissey's lyrical impulse forcefully wrestles with his social background. For Morrissey, like Wilde and others, the reality of English social conditions and cultural history brings to the fore the deepest sentiments of anger and despair. It is as if a morose sense of introspection characterised the crisis facing the pop star of the 1980s, something Bracewell has traced historically:

> Still bloody from the womb, so to speak, the new pop male in England took a look around himself in the early 1970s – the decade in which space travel, boyishly celebrated in the 1950s, would be seen in popular culture as a metaphor for existential crisis – and found progressive rock and novelty singles wherever he looked. [Bracewell 1998: 91]

For many of Morrissey's generation, it was punk rather than rock that mobilised the search for new identities and spirituality. But, as Bracewell argues, the sheer impact of punk on the male fan gave way to a loutish, homosocial bonding of laddishness. Artists like Elvis Costello, Joe Jackson and Ian Dury became the favourites listened to by males, while groups like Dexy's Midnight Runners and the Jam lost some of their mass popularity through being 'too introspective' (p. 107). In this light, the path was made clear for groups like the Smiths to enter the arena and redefine the contemplative English male pop star through Morrissey: '...once the dust had settled, the bedsit philosophizing had dried up, and the hospitals had finally been closed down, the method-acting, new pop male, for all of his testosterone and tears, muscles and moods, was left with his arms full of air. What was required – as ever – were *bisexual icons*' (Bracewell 1997: 108, emphasis added).

Epitomising exactly the kind of pop icon described above, Morrissey swiftly established an aura around himself that was charged with an ambiguity that could be loosely interpreted as bisexual. Aware that male authority is based upon the act of looking (read: Mulvey's male gaze), he set out to flaunt his masculinity like numerous other pop stars. His manipulation of blatant homoerotic imagery on album sleeves, flyers and videos, of course provoked at the same time it thrilled. In the context of the 1980s, Morrisey's texts offered a means through which it became possible for young heterosexual and gay fans alike to address the complexity of their own sexualities and desires. There can be little doubt that representations of masculinity during this period underwent transformations by prompting less rigid spectatorial positions (Mort 1988; 1996). In actual fact, Morrissey demonstrated how the male could avoid locking into the pressures of a fixed sexual identity. Through the pretentiousness of denying categorisation, he showed how one could jump on the bandwagon of queering identity by playing about with sexuality as a cultural construction. In short, such a crafty strategy set out to encourage polymorphous identification by circumventing the constraints of heteronormative representation.

Characterisation and 'star' depiction

In *Viva Hate* (1988), Morrissey's first solo album, his songs abound with social protest and acerbic political comment. A range of emotions are embraced by a single-minded determination, which were based upon a self-belief that Morrissey could succeed on his own without the support of his other half, Johnny Marr. Perhaps Morrisey's intention during the start of his solo career was caught up in an attitude that translates back to the romantic notion of the anti-hero silently suffering rejection. When one changes the course of one's path to make it alone as solo artist, redefinition through struggle opens up new sites of conflict and conquest. And this brings us to a central point for consideration: the connection between musical expression and the characterisation of the pop star.

The English tradition of popular song has always focused on the character song (Frith 1996). In acting out a part that functions as an exercise in style, at least in contrast to the more critical commentary one finds in German theatre songs, the English performer has often turned to self-ironic characterisation. At their most touching, Morrissey's songs, like his interviews, are self-reflective, ironic and contradictory in their enactment of a range of attitudes and sentiments. Moreover, the literary excellence found in many of his songs highlights the integral processes of characterisation at work. Of course understanding how this works is dependent on the fans' relationship to the star's persona, and how they respond to characterisation.

As powerful modes of address, Morrissey's texts not only question social and political issues but also strike at the core of the crisis concerning male identity. How the pop star looks, how he displays his body in performance, how he dresses, how he defines his own social space, and most importantly how he sings, affects the ways in which we experience the artist in relation to ourselves. With regard to image, it is noteworthy that while the Smiths' albums used images and photographs from other sources, all Morrissey's albums have included photographs of himself. On one of the promo shots from the *Viva Hate* period, Morrisey willingly plays on the notion of coming out. In a close-up photo by the well-known Anton Corbijn, we are presented with perhaps the most homoerotic of all Morrissey's poses to date. Shot from the torso upwards, Morrissey is naked with his right arm raised camply behind his

Figure 3.1   Morrissey during the *Viva Hate* period

head. The gaze here is awkwardly sidewards on in the glare of the studio lighting. Unmistakeably, the narcissistic construction of the image is a startling blend between Elvis Presley and James Dean – not uncoincidentally the two stars Morrissey has most admired. Indeed, from this we might ask to what extent his intentions are ironic, not least of all in the wake of the shy, anti-rebel position he had worked on during his entire career with the Smiths.

Bound up in the complexity of his identity, Morrissey's songs often allude to a melancholy that is introverted. Self-pathos and paranoia are the cornerstones of his texts. Reynolds and Press shed some light on this:

> Morrissey, 'castrated' by those invisible threads that attach him to his mother's apron, and thus incapable of any other attachments; Morrissey, with only misery for company, forever licking that 'unnameable narcissistic wound' in the word-less falsetto that climaxes his greatest songs. Morrissey has always insisted on the impossibility of the sexual relation, always argued that 'being only with yourself can be much more intense'. [Reynolds and Press 1995: 214]

However, we might also read Morrissey's declared vulnerability and sexual emasculation simply as a 'new twist on the old business of boys misbehavin'' (Reynolds and Press 1995: 332). As if seeking to resist the rigidity of his own masculinity, Morrissey constructs his cult authorship through a play on the Other. There can be little doubt that by constructing his own breed of masculi-nised power through such tactics, his intentions are designed as problematic on many counts. In her evaluation of the 1980s male, Suzanne Moore insists that 'these new hysterics with their male bodies and optional feminine subjectiv-ities cannot speak of a desiring subject who is actually a flesh and blood woman' (Moore 1988: 190). To what extent then would the new hysteric *knowingly* grasp his own inadequacies as he set out to highlight the disillusion-ment of his own personal dilemma? And if we accept that the artist sets out to tease through calculated characterisation, how do we go about assessing the role of music in this process?

Pop songs always transport with them the singer's ego, which often speaks out as the protagonist in the lyrics. Indeed, central character in popular songs generally possesses 'an attitude, in a situation, [as if] talking to someone' through the lyrics which function as stories (Frith 1996: 169). In other words, what is taken for granted is the manner in which singers utilise their own personalities to capture the song's story. Obviously this is a strategy that entails a high degree of seduction through the representation of characteri-sations as stylistic markers. For Middleton, the construction of subjectivity is linked to how 'character roles' are not only determined by social categories but also by 'personality types' with which audiences can relate (Middleton 1990: 251). Given this, we might consider Morrissey's authorship as always culture-specific. This is because his performances are about ideologically embracing cultural forms in order to affirm his construction as a star.

So, more than mere storytelling, Morrissey's songs signify theatricalised representations of the storyteller. It is as if he *enacts* his own character by exhibiting a self-consciousness through the intensity of his music and lyrical expression. The main element of Morrissey's songs is that they serve to characterise him in a self-conscious manner that portray a range of feelings that capture some of the moods of the 1980s and 1990s – a period characterised by nonchalance, greed, despair, cynicism and frustration. Frequently his texts are imbued with a sobriety of real-life down-to-earthness – an embittered Mancunian wryness – which position them beyond the hedonistic domain of much mainstream pop. This is borne out by mannerisms which delineate credibility through the 'ordinariness' of a Northern working-class setting.

For the purpose of this analysis so far, I am suggesting that the characterisation process in many pop texts involves a degree of role-playing which brings to the fore questions of motive, sincerity and intention. To explore the implications of this further, let us turn to the question of intention. Paisley Livingston makes an important distinction between assertions of sincerity and lying:

> We are often interested in knowing whether a statement is accurate or inaccurate; but we are also often interested in whether it is sincere or insincere. People who are sincere but misleading should get credit for sincerity – but not reliability – and it would be unfortunate if we had no concept with which to distinguish such cases from those where someone purposefully attempts to mislead someone else. [Livingston 1996: 151–2]

Clearly the negotiation of the artist's intentions is inextricably tied up with a critique of authenticity. Consider Morrissey's ability to manipulate and deliver his songs in a deliberately glib and insincere manner. Not only does he provoke issues concerning his credibility, but also he parodies his own status of star persona. Quite aware of the empowering effect of his motives, Morrissey stylises his choice of words in a way that appears reliable and intentionally seductive to his fans, albeit utterly superficial and repugnant to others. What is most revealing is his play on characterising the snobbish, proper and camp Wildean subject.[14]

Camp has always been the unruly response to the construction of appearance and reality and, accordingly, derives its humorous content from the play on a range of contradictions. In translating the serious into the frivolous, camp is engaged with the double-take. Building on Sontag's definition of camp (1964), Steven Drukman (1995) has argued for the more serious side of its intention. Imbued with camp, many pop texts expose the artificial constructedness of the star's identity as a necessary fiction. Yet we know that when interpreted as an apparatus for defiance, acts of campness can flounce multiple roles on the basis of fun yet seriousness. This quality is frequently encountered in the camped-up portrayal of the English gent, a distinguishing marker that is reinforced by theatrical intention.[15] Of course identifying camp in pop texts is about reading a specific cultural significance into the text. This might explain why pop songs are often felt to possess a subtext which permit them to be appropriated by their fans in ways that will not be picked up by others. Registered through a construction of ludic humour, camp has the potential to transform points of identification into something pleasurable, although, on this note, it might be worth considering that camp as a strategic gesture can easily be experienced as intimidating.

From this it becomes clear that working out such categories of characterisation and how they function on various levels is a complicated yet important task in the reading of pop texts. But, in the end, the act of identification is only made possible through shared experiences, the basis of which needs to be understood culturally and politically. However, attempting to work out the intentions of the artist alone is insufficient in determining intended meanings. Similarly, discovering the source of appeal in one's own response only goes part way in determining how the *communicative* process functions in musical expression. In short, the messages we receive from the songwriter can only be evaluated along the lines linked to the listener's social background and taste in musical style.

What is often assumed by fans is the pop star's authenticity.[16] We cannot overlook the significance of this in the light of the cult following Morrissey has enjoyed; something which is tied up with the romanticisation of the individualised artist. What particularly interests me here are the junctures of authenticity and musical materiality. I am referring to those points of contact that result in characterisation,[17] and, more specifically, the intentionality of contradictory representation that constitutes the notion of realism in pop expression. Let me clarify this position further.

The power of Morrissey's rhetoric emanates from a range of idiosyncrasies which shape his musical style. Continually there is evidence of apparent contradictions that fuel an ambiguity, which, in turn, embodies a very specific type of characterisation. If we return to the question of Englishness in male identity during the 1980s and 1990s, this pop star represents a cunning blend of the eccentric and the ordinary, the enigmatic and the familiar. Frequently, as I have argued, the male pop artist of the 1980s drew on a construction of identity that was diffused by an underlying sexual ambivalence.[18] With this came an air of constructed self-consciousness and awkwardness that was strategic in its adherence to the coded behaviour that enchanted an audience; an audience, at least in Morrissey's case, who thrived on the parody of a style that flirts with punk while siding with pop.

On the question of performance style, Morrissey's musical approach needs to be traced back to the Smiths, whose construction of identity was based upon a deliberate 'lack of emotional expression' (Stringer 1992: 22). While the generality of such a point is potentially provocative and not altogether sustainable, it does however touch on a certain tension of detachment that exposes the traits of Morrissey's identity.[19] Throughout his career, Morrissey's songs have been located within a social setting where the issue of emotional expression can be equated with a sense of calculated discomfort. This is characterised in both his lyrics and musical delivery.[20]

The title of *Viva Hate* alone, encapsulates Morrissey's anger and dismay, especially in light of the Smiths' split. Commenting on the choice of title he flippantly proclaimed: 'I find hate omnipresent and love very difficult to find. Hate makes the world go round' (in Bret 1994: 79). Throughout the album the sentiments executed are notably depressive, defiant and vulnerable, with Morrissey centred in the foreground of all the narratives. Easily outstripping the success of any of the Smiths' singles, the song 'Suedehead' from *Viva Hate*, soared to number 5 in the UK charts in 1988.[21]

Deriving its title from the Richard Allen novel of 1971, the song has little to do with the subject content of this novel – a vivid account of the adventures of a group of anti-gay skinheads. Rather, the song dwells on the awkwardness of someone who discovers their privacy is invaded by another person. Morrissey laments: *Why did you come? You had to sneak into my room just to read my diary.* Notably, the music in the opening passage creates suspense through the highly reverbed arpeggiated guitar crescendo on a held G9 chord (VII), followed by a dramatic two-quaver upbeat on C#, superimposed over a syncopated bass line with kit.[22] Light-hearted and almost trivial in mood, this introductory material builds up a groove in the A mixolydian mode. Coerced through a sudden shift to E major (V), the verse is characterised by Esus4 chords resolving to E major which evoke a sense of harmonic ambiguity. Any sense of diatonic assertion is temporarily overted through the mixolydian flavour of the chordal progressions in the verse. During the chorus phrase, *why do you come here ...*, a certain pathos is captured by the doleful, A mixolydian progression (A-Bm7-G-Bm7-A). Musically, the underlying tension of this song is shaped by a denial of diatonic cadential closure.

Embellishments of modality are often exaggerated in hooks and refrains, although no modal centre ever overrides the other. Principles of voice leading, such as those illustrated in Examples 3.1 and 3.2, capture the mood of Morrissey's performance, and betray his ironic edge. This is most discernible in the vocal inflections and timbral qualities of his voice, particularly in the relaxed, sung-spoken phrasing of delivery. Importantly, the offsetting of vocal pitches with the chords to which they belong emerges as one of the most prevalent features of Morrissey's performance style. Seldom are his melodies aligned vertically with the harmonies. The effect of this lies in a contrapuntal tension that draws us into the emphasis of specific words and sentiments. Thus, the nature of vocal linearity not only defines the musical idiom but also heightens the level of poignancy, especially in terms of resistance and expectation. For example, all the way through 'Suedehead,' Morrissey laments the intrusion of his privacy, and the desire on the part of the intruder to discover his secrets. Quite like the Pet Shop Boys, the seriousness of his lyrics are parodied through the superficiality of the tunes, against which depressed, tongue-in-cheek sentiments are positioned. When Morrissey asks *why do you hang around*, the word *why* (Example 3.1) is drawn out over three bars in an exaggerated manner, the effect of which is induced by a move from the chords E major to D major (I-VII) with suspended passing tones. Similarly, the phrase *I'm so sorry*, (F#-C#m/E-D) one of the worst possible English clichés (Example 3.2), is stretched out in a sarcastic tone that heightens his camp sensibility.

Example 3.1   'Why do you hang around' from 'Suedehead'

Example 3.2   'I'm so sorry' from 'Suedehead'

For me what is most striking about 'Suedehead' is the articulation of sentimentality through a tightly controlled level of musical intensity. Morrissey bemoans the invasion of his life with his characteristic tone of mournfulness. He discovers there is a price for success that pop stars have to pay. Here the display of personal frustration attached to fame is epitomised by the pop star's dilemma about 'selling out' on the one hand, and trying to retain his cult image of ordinariness on the other hand. Such contradictions are not only discernible in the lyrical content, but also in his style of singing, in the straining of large intervallic leaps, the breaking of pitches, and the glow of an almost tearful vocal timbre. At times, he hardly exerts himself to the extent that his performances appear effortless and nonchalant. Embellishing the spoken meter of his verse, he communicates the meaning of his words in no uncertain terms. Yet always there is a control in his manner of delivery, as we are made aware that every nuance is calculated. The result of all this is the characterisation of a morose and ill-treated subject who is prepared to lament the hurt and pain of having his privacy invaded, at the same time as admitting, as he does at the end of the song, that *it was a good lay*. The effect of this claim is to instantly dissolve everything we have ever been told about his celibate life-style or so-called asexuality. And to ensure that we 'get it', this phrase is repeated at random as a teasing coda. In such moments we are exposed to the potential of manipulation through technical codes of repetition.

Finally, in projecting himself as a victim of social circumstance, Morrissey parodies the very individual he sets out to characterise. Through the conflict between his lyrics and musical material, his characterisation in songs like 'Suedehead' jostles cheekily with notions of ambiguity. And, of course, he knows full well that the portrayal of himself as lonely, depressed and anti-heroic, can trigger off all sorts of compassion in his fans. Thus, it seems to be through such manipulative strategies that his dependency on empathic response truly relies.

Modelling empathy through vocal 'sound'

Feelings of remorse dramatise the majority of Morrissey's songs. Interwoven into the narrative of the song, 'Satan Rejected My Soul' – the last song on the album, *Maladjusted* (1997) – a range of mixed feelings are explored. Indeed, there are a number of issues here worth considering that have a great deal to do with working out the imaginative activity of entering into another's feelings. In particular, the tensions inherent in Morrissey's music make available to us the possibilities of our own emotional responses. I am therefore keen in this section to explore how characterisations in pop texts draw on *empathic* response through vocal expression.

In 'Satan Rejected My Soul', through a narrative of self-ridicule, Morrissey pleads us to accept his soul which Satan has rejected. His personal crisis in this song can be interpreted as a two-way pathological process whereby his and our responses are prone to playful self-deception. What I am suggesting is a kind of special compassion that reveals not only the scope of his own characterisation but also the relationship between him and his fans. Nothing could be more heart-wrenching than the torrent of tormented emotions he exhibits as he laments over the fate of his soul, *so take it – please come on, come on, call me in haul me in*. Through empathising with the artist's misery, the fan is able to quickly access the domain of musical fantasy, a domain where musical expression intensifies (if not alters) the tensions with which emotional involvement is experienced on an intimate level; a point I will return to when I discuss further the signification of Morrissey's vocal technique. It is as a result of our responses to artists via their music that songs ultimately gain their currency – a concept that offers us a useful route into exploring the artist's intentions.

Working out what a song signifies is certainly predicated upon the position from which we *imagine* things as fans. If we accept this, what then are the qualities that generate the imaginative flow that constitutes one's empathic response to a singer? According to film theorist Alex Neill, individuals possess sets of *beliefs* that concern fictional or make-believe characters through imaginative projects which are 'characteristic of empathising with another' (Neill 1996: 190). Encountering empathy, as Neill insists, is surely an imaginative process as well as a belief. For, by empathising with another, 'one imagines the situation she is in from her point of view' in a way that represents the other's feelings as if they were one's own. If we are to accept this, then, where does this lead us in terms of evaluating how music provokes empathic response?

In problematising this notion a little further, I want to look at some of the ways in which empathic responses might be aroused musically in 'Satan Rejected My Soul'. First, let us consider the connection between the lyrics and Morrissey's performance. His unique vocal style generates a spectrum of sonic nuances that are culturally identifiable. For example, his inflection of pitch alone allows him to emphasise words, phrases or vowels with a sense of detached, self-irony.[23] In addition, his phrasing and shading accentuates a locality that reveals his cultural context. To be more specific, this is evident in a style of singing that accommodates certain rounded vowel and syllabic emphases that pronounce, with clarity, the subtleties of his English elocution. Stringer notes how Morrisey's method is to employ 'very clipped, precise enunciation' while avoiding 'the kind of "blue" or "dirty" notes associated with Afro-American vocal traditions' (Stringer 1992: 19). To this I would add that the quality of vocal timbre through melodic embellishment contributes significantly to the overall effect of Morrissey's enunciation. Clearly a wide range of devices offset the vocal sound against the other instruments which shape the distinctiveness of his voice. Moreover, it is the distribution of pitch, register, intensity and contrapuntal organisation that provide us with access into the world of the singer.[24]

In 'Satan Rejected My Soul', the musical treatment of words tends to dramatise their 'spoken' effect. Because music creates different stresses on words, it prompts responses to lyrics in a different way from if they were read. And, in this way, the song can emerge as 'the preferred reading of the words' (Frith 1996: 181).

For example, by repeating the line *I must find somewhere else to go* twice, Morrissey intentionally stresses the words, *somewhere else*, on the strong beat during a descending major seventh scale (Example 3.3). Here his phrasing, his vocal timbre and emphasis of vowels help highlight the emotions that assert his personal dilemma. With heartfelt conviction, his low-range register dramatises the despair felt in the lyrics, and, moreover, the pain of recognising his recourse to a narrative of self-actualisation.

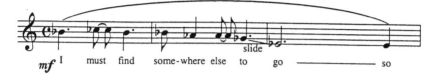

Example 3.3 'Satan Rejected My Soul: I must find somewhere else to go'

At least two points of interest arise here. First, the articulation of a distinctly English mannerism which serves to underpin the nature of his song's narrative. As we have seen, Morrissey's avoidance of any obvious African-American inferences (in accent or style) and mainstream pop idioms has much to do with him asserting *his* construction of Englishness through mannerism.[25] Second, with reference to Morrissey's precise diction, it is his conscious evasion of sounding very local that can be read as oppositional in ironic intent. Yet by employing a middle-class, educated accent, he does not deny his Northerness.[26] Contextualised within the broader terrain of pop music, Morrissey's sound is about the articulation of a voice that is distinctly English and Northern. This transports a special sensibility with it. And here I would suggest that the overall effect of his articulation becomes a *sonic metaphor* for the authorial voice.

But, in the end, all this links us back to the question of empathy and how it is evoked through the performance of pop songs. Certainly, what the fan encounters in Morrissey's songs is an invitation to partake in sentiments of self-pity and loathing. It is through the processes of mediation that his innermost emotions become the best guarantee for his truthfulness. In this regard, the argument I am proposing is based upon the premise that performance styles have much to do with charming over audiences. It is indeed the attitude which marks out all the conditions for musical reception, which, in turn, delineate meaning.[27] From this, it becomes obvious that through reflexive performance, words and phrases are intensified in a deeply personal way that entice the listener into the singer's world in a very different manner from that of just speaking the lines in a non-musical context. When Morrissey delivers his poetic phrases, he exerts a specific control over his musical reinforcement of words to a point of exaggeration. Especially, the inference of camp strikes up an intimate rapport between singer and listener. In fact, such a manner of delivery is so personal and localised that its subjectivity can easily be convertible into irony. This helps explain why Morrissey's lyrical skills (particularly in his handling of rhyme and meter) translate so effortlessly into melodrama – herein lies the basis of his appeal.[28]

Let us now consider in more detail some of the musical features inherent in Morrissey's vocal style. Music scholars have referred to the distinction between the 'untrained' and 'trained' voice, and how this connotes ideological meaning. Allan Moore, for example, has referred to the 'trained' voice as usually represented by the acquired technique of singing 'in-tune' which fixes pitches as accurately as possible, a prime characteristic of European bel canto singing. In terms of vocal tone, the trained voice is usually apt to 'employ an even, full-throated tone with rich vibrato' (Moore 1993: 42) which avoids the inflections of tone so often found in styles like rock and punk.[29] Undoubtedly, Morrissey's voice fits into an untrained category which legitimises his vocal style as authentic or natural – at least from a fan's perspective.

Other stylistic traits that bring home the untrained quality of his expression are discernible in techniques which include inflection of pitch, vocal resonance, the control of register and rhythmic phrasing. In particular, the technique of controlling pitch is one of the distinguishing features of any singer. For Morrissey this involves the sliding around of pitches in a manner which avoids precise pitching. Instead of pitching his notes 'accurately', he often strains for them by slurred, sharpened or flattened inflections. And, offset against the backing parts in many of his tracks, his articulation of pitch contrasts vividly. In fact, the aesthetic pleasure derived from his control of pitch is offset by the tension that exists between the instrumental lines and vocal parts.

Inadvertent or not, Morrissey's avoidance of pitching tempered notes in a 'trained' manner of delivery spells out the naturalness of his style. In his melodic phrasing, stresses on long notes often coincide with random pitch variations. Upon reaching a sustained pitch through inflection or embellishment, he will hit it before colouring it with heavy vibrato in an attempt to fix it. In such moments, his handling of pitch and register control holds the greatest clue to his sound.[30] To clarify this further: subtle variations in pitch inflection function to emphasise certain words in a way that accent the lyrical connotations. Morrissey's approach to pitch is characterised by the nature of his intervallic leaps, where voice leading is often allowed to slip around the targeted notes. It is such performance techniques that emphasise his style as 'natural' or untrained – a quality that everyday people can identify with – which reaches out to others.[31]

In any form of vocal performance the manner of controlling pitch, and thus register, plays an important role in conveying information concerning the personality of the performer.[32] What becomes clear in Morrissey's performances is that his register sits most comfortably within his mid-range.

Couched within a relatively narrow register, his vocal shading nevertheless allows him a fair breadth of tonal contrast. In particular his falsetto range is usually characterised by a nasal tone that results more from a head tone than that found in his middle to lower range where a more breathy and chest resonance is detectable. Like Paul McCartney, David Bowie and Sting, Morrissey strains to pitch notes in his falsetto register. It is in these moments that pitch inflection becomes most pronounced, especially in upward intervallic leaps such as those that are targeted at major sevenths. Importantly, the effect of vocal straining evokes a sense of increased emotional intensity for the receiver through the sheer effort invested on the part of the artist.

Thus the codes of pitch control, register and dynamic intensity are responsible for shaping vocal timbre. Certainly these properties of vocal production are determined by how the voice resonates through bodily control. In Morrissey's case, it is the mellowness in tone produced through a certain physical exertion that captures the full range of his moods. Above all, his broad mid-range span, with occasional slides into falsetto, is aligned in physical terms to the control of the expansion and contraction of his diaphragm, throat and lungs, in a manner that displays the degree of effort being invested. Motivated by the significance of his words, the exertion invested into his vocal control shapes the subtleties of emotion he exudes. And, in this way, his singing style solicits an intimacy through the calculated effect of the voice's bodily signification.[33]

Another pertinent code of vocal expression is located in the rhythmic inflections of his melodic lines. Pronounced delay and anticipation of rhythmic phrasing in the vocal lines results in a particular tension. Seldom do his melodic elaborations adhere to the regularity of the metrical divisions found in the instrumental backing. The effect of this is to set up a musical tension which undermines conformity. Often a kind of linear independence is generated by the elongation and floating of pitches over the regular phrase structures that control the instrumental flow. This form of musical treatment tends to stress the extent of Morrissey's ambivalent purpose. The point here is that the delay and anticipation of beats run parallel with his style of characterisation. For example, a propensity of rhythmic independence in the vocal line of 'Satan Rejected My Soul' liberates the singer from the strict quaver figure of the guitar part. Flirting with the beat, it seems as if he never yields to it.

So far, I have attempted to draw on features of vocal technique to illustrate how the voice is crucial to our interpretation of musical texts. As a direct expression of his body, it is the distinctive approach to singing that evokes empathy in pop texts. In this respect, the pleasures derived from Morrissey's songs rely on the challenge of his vocal address and *how* we respond to it empathically. Always the voice functions as the prime carrier of a specific attitude, relaying to the listener what the singer is all about. And, although the singer might assume a range of positions in his texts, it is the consistency in his characterisation through the codes of vocal production that arguably mark out his 'authenticity'.

My conception of empathy is that pop artists are aware of their dependency on audiences and accordingly measure their voices through the complex channels of communication. This is central to the way in which identification makes us *feel* for the artist. In this sense, Morrissey's musical traits become statements on their own and therefore represent the trademarks of his identity.

In the heated press releases that accompanied the launch of the album *Your Arsenal* in 1992, the mixed sentiments concerning Morrissey's references to national identity could not have been more controversial. No British artist during this period was at the centre of such political and social controversy as much as Morrissey. With the song, 'The National Front Disco,' some of the harshest responses ever from the music press threatened to ruin his career. Prompted to write this song by the much publicised and condemned tactics of the extreme right British party, the British National Front (BNP), Morrissey's objective was to explore the vulnerability of a young suburban boy seduced by the sentiments of this racist organisation. Morrissey's characterisation of the boy's parents, in lines such as, *Where is our boy? We've lost our boy!* is offset against the contentious line, *England For The English*. Interestingly, the intentions of such stark nationalistic sentiment were interpreted as Morrissey being condemnatory of racism (at least by his fans), especially with his scornful references to 'banal' disco, a style of music he intensely disliked. Yet, with all the awkward juxtapositioning of ideas of political sensitivity in his references, the underlying intent of the song could be construed as deliberately ambiguous. In many ways, the song subverts, confronts and offends on many levels. By unpacking its problematic innuendos, important questions concerning motive and the musical realisation of sentiments need to be considered.

One could hardly have been surprised that when Morrissey walked on stage at the Madstock event, Finsbury Park, on 8 August 1992, he was pelted with anything the 30,000-strong audience could find. Clad in a glittery gold lamé shirt and large Union Jack flag draped over his shoulders, he would have been well aware that a large BNP demonstration had been held earlier that day with a small-scale representation of right-wing skinheads at this event. Moreover, Morrissey knew that his forthcoming Your Arsenal tour concert at the Hollywood Bowl, Los Angeles, had just been sold out and that Mozmania in America was escalating. In fact, all the seats for his two-night gig there had vanished in 23 minutes, smashing the sales record set by the Beatles. Going to the US on the wave of such immense popularity for the biggest tour of his life made his supporting act to Madness at this event feel almost humiliating. That the press was fuelled by Morrissey's openly blatant flirt with racism, of course had a lot to do with his non-commital position on the performance of this most controversial song. Years later, in an interview with *Mojo* he would explain his relationship to the English press:

... and then in the early '90s they accused me of everything from extreme racism to other extremes, which has always been crap. And you can't really go cap in hand to people and say, 'Oh please accept me – not racist, really.' It just doesn't work. So you have to retain your dignity and step away ... [in Uhelszki 2001]

I have referred to Morrissey's awkward relation to songs like 'The National Front Disco' for two main reasons: first, to highlight that the nature of his performance is dependent on an ongoing game between himself, the press and the audience – one always has the impression that the pleasure in his texts result from a kind of friction between ironic political reflection and emotional response. Second, I want to suggest that Morrissey's songs are cultural activities that describe how groups and artists go about assimilating music as part of a local discourse.[34] On this issue, Andy Bennett (2000) stresses the cultural significance of understanding musical style – in this case *bhangra* – as a local resource. He makes the important argument that the appeal of specific categories of music are often positioned culturally within contexts where identity is compressed into musical performance. In terms of working out the construction of nationalism in English music, Bennett notes how the issue of definition is something that needs to be continually addressed: 'Such differences in the definition and application of the term "English music" relate back to and must be understood within the wider context of the relationship that exists between locality, identity and the politics of musical taste' (2000: 115).

It would seem from this that questions of racism and nationality result from 'a locally constructed social sensibility' (p. 127), through which a territorialisation of space defines precise social relations. We know that historically musical expression has involved the communication of categorisations and classifications that are emblematic of national identity. Thus, the problematics attached to this issue are obvious in Morrissey's 'The National Front Disco', as he confronts the frustrations inherent in reactions to the propagation of the nation-state. Notably, his lyrics not only refer to the exclusionary practices that characterise state control through political intervention, but they also highlight the embattled attempts by ethnic groups to assert their Englishness. So, in songs such as this, it is as if Morrissey sets out to put his own spin on the complex and contradictory values of national identity. And, within a local context, he tracks down some of the key social turbulences linked to ethnicity and nationalism in Manchester during the 1980s and 1990s. Not unexpectedly then, such songs cannot fail to drive home highly charged sentiments that function as controversial at the same time they are delusive.

Possibly what comes most to light when *explaining* the communicative processes that engage our political responses in such a song are the problems associated with the process of identification. On this note, McClary has also pointed to how social groups instinctively 'know how to detect even minor stylistic infractions and to respond variously with delight or indignation,

depending on how they identify themselves with respect to the style on hand'
(McClary 1991: 21). Yet, how exactly music affects us is fraught with difficulties in clarification. Indeed, the challenging task in working out one's
responses to musical style lies in deciding *how* to account for why music is
experienced in the way it is. Invariably, pop songs involve the activity of
working out what the performer is saying to us. Enjoyment often lies in the
interplay between address and response, and in taking in the personality of the
star. If how a performer affects us forms an integral part of musical evaluation,
Morrissey strives to negotiate his position with a range of markers that play on
controversy. It is as if he recognises that 'playfulness' is situated in relation to
the listener's understanding of the artist's codes of expression.[35] Such positions
of identification cannot be construed as deterministic in any sense. This is
borne out by one fan's perspective:

> Morrissey remains an enigma, though with the passing of time he has become
> tougher, more cynical, and less tolerant of that undistinguished but sadly power-
> ful group of bigots who by deliberate misinterpretation continually attempt to
> destroy his career. Any fan – and any detractor who is being *really* truthful –
> would, of course, maintain that he is indestructible! Such is his power, and his
> ability to give out and accept love, that these people are more willing to forgive
> his every indiscretion. *Only* Morrissey could get away with cancelling *two* ele-
> venth-hour concerts at the prestigious Carnegie Hall for a reason other than
> sudden death!
>   Some critics, too, have stated over the last year or so that his career may be
> on the wane simply because not all his records get into the charts. The albums
> *always* do, but the singles vary, a fault which lies squarely with the record
> company for trying to stretch what is taken from the albums far too far .... In
> this respect, and without wishing to compare him with anyone (simply because
> he remains incomparable in his own one-star sphere), one may hope that Mor-
> rissey's *true* career as an All Time Great has only just begun ... so long as the
> ink continues to flow from that Wildean quill, so long as this is his wish. [Bret
> 1994: 201–202, original emphases]

I have quoted this at some length to underline the importance of the relationship between the fan and the pop celebrity. For pop fans, such as David Bret,
it is clear that biography plays an essential part in the understanding of music
through the characterisation of the *real personality* behind it. This also serves
as a mechanism for discovering one's own sense of cultural identity. Note
Bret's manner of description when he describes Morrissey's power as 'indes-
tructible', and his standing as 'incomparable'. This clearly demonstrates the
operative empathy that exists between performer and fan. Of course, as with
any pop performer, Morrissey is reliant on the support of fans who can believe
in him. For Bret, although Morrissey 'remains an enigma' and is thus prone to
'misinterpretation' by the media press and others, he acknowledges the pop
star's 'ability to give out and accept love'. More specifically, the cause of
Bret's above response might be explained by Morrissey's ability to cajole him

knowingly in a way that flatters the fan's social competence. From this, it seems to be a two-way empathic process in the fan's engagement with the pop artist that shapes a variety of positions for further exploring the issue of musical signification, not least through strategies of irony.

Interpreting ironic markers in pop texts

Up to now, the focal point of this chapter has rested on some of the markers that alert us to the resonances of musical signification. If our experiences of pop texts involve a desire to become engaged with the subjectivity of the artist, what interests me then is the strategy with which Morrissey constructs his affective charge. And, it is this point that ushers in the final theme I want to consider in this chapter: the effects and intentions of *irony*. As a starting point, I want to return to the question of reception by further considering the internalisation of norms that confer meaning through the artist and his performance.

Understanding how *attitude* is mediated through musical performance constitutes a salient part of working out meaning in pop texts. My proposed method is to examine how irony functions as a *relational strategy*. By this I am referring to the way in which it pulls together diverse meanings in order to create something ambiguous. To conceptualise ironic meaning in pop texts surely involves reading the effects of the musical codes in term of their relationship with words. Using this as our frame of reference, I would suggest that ironic function be comprehended as something which is *inferred* by the ironist's intentional actions. The premise for the interpretation of irony here is predominantly dependent on the interpreter within the context of her/his membership of a social group. In this respect, the audience-enhancing function of irony in pop music is entangled with strategies that draw fans together while driving others away. Most importantly, irony reinforces the fact that meanings are only created within specific contexts as a result of social practice.[36]

By stating this, however, I am not suggesting that Morrissey's appeal is only based around an attitude that can be interpreted as ironic or that this is what he intends. But, rather, that there is a measure of playful pretence to his delivery that might set up ironic distancing. Further, emphasis on detachment as an entity allied to self-reflexivity, provides us with evidence that Morrissey seeks to address and moderate levels of excess in stardom status. This becomes most pronounced in a deceptively simple musical style that diffuses lyrical cynicism through the inference of ironic retort.[37]

At this stage I want to expand this idea a little more by focusing on the general nature of cultural specificity in ironic intent. Dependent on the conditions that link the interpreter (fan) to the ironist (performer), the will to be ironic can be determined by a set of rules that require a shared awareness of the communicative assumptions that differ from everyday discourse. As I emphasise at various points in this book, it is the fusion of musical and contextual codes, with their respective markers, that result in the problematics of ironic interpretation. Often one encounters an oversimplification of context to denote a set of cultural and social conditions that are perceived as fixed and unchanging. This specific issue is dealt with by Jonathan Culler, who insists in his book, *Framing the Sign*:

> ... context is not fundamentally different from what it contextualizes; context is not given but produced; what belongs to a context is determined by interpretative strategies; contexts are just as much in need of elucidation as events; and the meaning of a context is determined by events. Yet when we use the term *context* we slip back into the simple model it proposes. [Culler 1988: ix]

Culler's suggestion is that context cannot be evaluated positivistically as an element in itself. If we accept this, what seems more relevant is an identification of the unstable quality of contextual markers. It is the interactionary nature of markers, with all their textual signifiers, that signal the occurrence of irony within an *intertextual* context or transpersonal space where any acts of self-expression exist as a cultural-specific markers.

Indeed, an intentionalist approach to theorising irony would seem to suggest that its codes are only recognisable within a framework that is specific to a certain form of communication.[38] An indication of this is found in the exclusivity of such a property, which, in fact, makes ironic identification so personal. To this extent, what might function ironically in one context might easily offend in another (Hutcheon 1994: 155). Thus, to identify codes or markers of irony in a song,[39] we can only *assume* their function within a specific setting that denotes meaning for us. But how then does irony connect to non-verbal markers such as musical codes? And what makes a text ironic through the juxtapositioning of musical codes with linguistic citation?

Within this framework of debate, I will now turn to a number of markers within Morrissey's songs that infer ironic meaning. In terms of their function, it is the non-verbal markers – the musical codes – mainly also delineate ironic intent. Clearly, in considering the relationship between musical markers and lyrics, it seems that we cannot detach the music from the structural implications of the words themselves.[40] As markers of verbal expression, lyrics are inextricably linked to the syntactical meaning of the music which provide us with an insight into the intentions of the artist.

In effect, Morrissey's style draws on traditions of English popular song that can be experienced as ironic. The album *Vauxhall and I* (1994) contains an array of ironic markers that occur in many different forms.[41] Among the most prevalent markers are fluctuations in voice register, emphases of specific words, stylistic referents, and instrumental gestures in the overall musical material. A close look at the song 'Billy Budd' reveals a number of ironic markers.

In Herman Melville's short story, *Billy Budd* (also adapted by Benjamin Britten for an opera with the same title first performed at Convent Garden in December 1951), the narrative is based around a relationship between a sailor and the first mate. This illicit love affair ends in tragedy as the sailor is betrayed by his lover and subsequently hanged. Apparently Morrissey's inspiration to draw on the Billy Budd story was the film version, in which his idol, Terence Stamp, plays the beautiful sailor. One can hardly avoid the sheer mocking style in Morrissey's song, 'Billy Budd' as he sounds his dismay at the demise of Budd as a result of a death sentence. Hyperbolic gestures in the guitar solo and fills function as markers in parallel with the inferences of the lyrical lines *Things have been bad yeah, but now it's 12 years on.* During this passage, the frenetic guitar solo harks back to the Smiths, soliciting a nostalgic reading of the beginning of Morrissey's fraught love-hate relationship with Johnny Marr, twelve years prior to the release of *Vauxhall and I.*[42] Notably, the restless guitar gestures are reminiscent of Johnny Marr's legendary solos on tracks such as 'The Queen Is Dead'. Not only does this stylistic code echo the Smiths' sound, but it also functions as an ironic marker. Effects, such as the wah-wah pedals, add an amusing flavour to the overall pull of the song's story, in a fashion diluting the pain of reference as Morrissey vows that he would *lose both of his legs* if it could mean Billy Budd could be freed from his fate. A most powerful empathy results from the full force of vocal intensity, as the lyrical emphasis falls on the protagonist's promises to save Billy Budd from his fate.

Now when Morrissey delivers these lines, the music is structured around simple harmonic patterns set against an up-tempo, cheerful, regular rock groove. With a superficiality underlined by the very stylistic features of these musical codes, the protagonist's enunciation is sarcastic while deadly serious, and certainly succeeds in its aim. The pleasure derived from this song, as with all his others, lies in how Morrissey highlights his choice of words through musical expression.

In the song 'Hold On To Your Friends', the lyrics are set to a pleasant ballad which conveys the following painful sentiment: *A bond of trust has been abused, something of value may be lost, give up your job, squander your cash – be rash, just hold on to your friends.* Codes such as the undulating guitar arpeggios, the melodic phrasing, transported by a gentle, slow rock rhythm figure, appear uncomfortably light-hearted and superficial alongside the paranoid intensity of verbal expression.

Once again, the influence of the Smiths' style on Morrissey is highly conspicuous in this track, especially in the guitar part, which infers with bitter-sweet sentimentality the inner torment of the performer. Immediately the wash of guitar sounds enter – nostalgic in their encoding – there is a sense of satirical charge as Morrissey emphasises his feelings of persecution. While the story-line is arguably facile, this song abounds with an energy which is captured in the imaginative production and recording of Morrissey's performance.

Similar feelings of *angst* surface in another song from the album *Vauxhall and I*, 'I Am Hated for Loving', during which Morrissey eloquently describes how he can't belong anywhere because he is always under attack from the *anonymous call, poison pen, brick in the small of the back again*. The type of instrumentation employed, in particular the guitar backing, helps evoke the mood Morrissey sets out to achieve. Remaining within his comfortable mid-range register, Morrissey's distinctive vocal style involves pronouncing the words with exaggerated clarity, reminiscent of Noël Coward's camp style. Such mannerisms prepare the ground for the inference of irony as they inter-mesh with the instrumental harmonic/melodic/rhythmic gestures. In terms of the sensitivity afforded to this song's arrangement, as well as it's convincing performance, the overall effect of the textures within the audio image of the recording greatly enhance the gist of the lyrics. For instance, the emphasis on wanting to be unloved or unwanted – *I still don't belong to anyone-I am mine* – allows Morrissey the distance to address his fans with remarks that he knows will be 'felt'.

Perhaps most significant in the above example is the lyrical resistance to any fixed categorical position through musical treatment. For instance, the melodic contours of *I still don't belong to anyone* are edgy in their intervallic structures as they conflict with the flow of the harmonic progression. Here, an avoidance of vertical alignment contributes to an ambiguity that relies on a musical provisionality that acknowledges uncertainty is always there. This is also borne out by the artifice of role-playing whereby Morrissey adopts a particular position in order to test his own ideas and goad responses from his audiences.

Another interesting indication of the structuring of musical codes in relation to the words is found in the song 'Used to be a Sweet Boy', the ninth track of *Vauxhall and I*. As Morrissey agonises over the uneasy, allegedly real-life relationship he has had with his father, the compositional organisation works at maintaining a sweet vacuity, not least as the instrumental comp dispenses with a triple-meter rhythmic feel. Harmonic structures, dominated by bland I-IV-V progressions, with the occasional diminished seventh, provide a degree of predictability as they become secured by their resolution to perfect cadences. Texturally, the song builds up into an effective fabric of sounds, which is characterised by a pretty piano riff providing an instrumental thread throughout. Towards the end, the utilisation of effects on the vocal melodic accompaniment (without lyrics) opens up the spatial image, blending all the instrumental and vocal timbres into a quirky yet evocative passage of pastiche schmaltz. Enhanced by the heavy use of reverb, the constant kit and bass sequence (in corny waltz-time), accompanying easily memorable melodic segments, helps draw out a blandness of style, which functions as an antidote to the pain felt in lines such as *Used to be a sweet boy and I'm not to blame but something went wrong* (Example 3.4). Trivialising, almost to the point of overkill, the music in this ditty alienates the subject from the affective charge of his lyrical enunciations. While, yet again, stylistic codes of voice-leading function as agents in diffusing the intensity of the words.

Example 3.4   'Used to be a sweet boy...'

As in this song and others, Morrissey's refusal to be tied down to the explicit terms of his emotions becomes a main factor for exploiting oppositionality through music. In more general terms, a form of detachment boosts the sense of irony to the point that its intent can become enshrined in blatant indifference and superiority (see Hutcheon 1994). In other words, Morrissey's ambivalence through ironic intent demonstrates how the passively aggressive character operates.

Indeed, what persists in most of his songs is a satirical approach to performance where ironic retort is not only teasing but also assailing in its manner. This is exemplified in the last track of *Vauxhall and I*, in the song 'Speedway', where Morrissey combines inferences of satire, parody and travesty to ridicule traditional social values. With its title derived from the fashionable coastal resort of Santa Monica, this song is teasing through its seductive ambiguity.[43] Stylistically, there is little shortage of aggressive purpose in the shocking, deafening sound of a chainsaw sample that violently disrupts the atmospheric textures of the introductory rock groove. The sheer musical intensity in 'Speedway' sets this song apart from the others on the album as Morrissey pulls together all his forces to direct his anger toward the tabloid press who attempt to destroy him. From the heart of the pop celebrity, lines of anguish are delivered, such as *You won't rest until the hearse that becomes me finally takes me*. Little sentimentality is permitted, as satire and burlesque go a long way in dictating toughness and constraint. As Morrissey's penchant for poetic satire takes on a strategy of oppositionality, his entire performance becomes a vehicle for scorn. Again, a wide range of possibilities within this corrective mechanism are located in a wealth of ironic markers, not least in a crooning style of singing that harks back to the late 1950s and early 1960s with British singers, such as Adam Faith, Bill Fury and Cliff Richard. And, in Morrissey's case, his specific vocal style conveys an intention that opposes the over-sentimentality of lyrical expression. More specifically, it is the combined effect of harmonic and melodic gestures, timbral flavourings, and blends of effects through studio processing that prescribe the conditions for receiving meanings on a number of terrains. When experienced ironically, these markers frame our interpretive expectations. In such instances, we are reminded of how musical codes are always organised around procedures linked to experience.

In 'Speedway', Morrissey's playfulness is identifiable through a spate of striking cross-references. For example, the deadpan sentiments of the lyrics are offset against the menacing sound of a chainsaw and the whining, sliding guitar riffs – the 'assailing' function of which can be experienced as both aggressive and distasteful in its caustic wit. From this, I would suggest that a framing of irony regulates discrete modes of interpretation that expose its very own arbitrariness. Of course, this idea might support the argument that there is no possibility of a marker that guarantees the presence of irony. However, on the other hand, such a position cannot insist that markers do not exist or function to signal or attribute irony. In other words, reading irony can only draw together a range of markers that describe how musical structures are received by the interpreter on a personal level. It is the links in the chain of ironic markers that are most relevant, especially in terms of the context of their interpretation. Indeed, this emphasises once again the extent to which the reception of a text is dependent on its social context. Moreover, it is the *phatic* function of songs that involves specific formulaic gestures (riffs, grooves, melodic fragments) which establish immediate social contact. Here, we could say it is the musical gestures that refer to the 'function of solidarity, cultural recognition and subcultural contact' (Middleton 1990: 242), which, in turn, govern the intricate process of communication.

As in earlier Smiths songs – 'Margaret On The Guillotine', 'The Queen is Dead', 'Meat is Murder', and 'Suffer Little Children' – the song 'Speedway' gives way to political retort through Morrissey's offensive attack on a range of social conditions of the period.[44] A common feature in all these songs is Morrissey's rich sense of musical imagination in terms of vocal expression. I have already pointed out that he only rarely aligns his vocal lines to the regular subdivisions of the beat as his melismatic style picks up on the speech patterns of his lyrics.[45] As a rule, he sings against the current of the rhythmic pulse to punctuate the words and their spoken meter. At the same time, the specific control of discursive repetition he employs, helps shape the vocal lines into larger structures of narrative flow (Middleton 1990). While the lyrics expound upon politically and socially important issues, the indifference of musical gesture negates their intensity and imaginative profundity. In this way, the music affords the listener light relief at the same time as ironic recourse.

All this centres around a significant issue: that musical structures contribute directly to the juxtapositioning of signifiers that function as ironic markers. As I have discussed above, Morrissey's texts depend on their specific environments of social reception where they will be understood and enjoyed. The implications here are that ironic meaning resides in an understanding of the broad process of communication and degree of intentionality, where the musical text forms part of that intimate interrelationship between audience and performer. In effect, Morrissey's regulation of such intimacy draws to our attention the wider issues of social and political commentary in relation to musical expression in popular song. Above all, it seems that the exclusivity of his utterances rely on a purposive musical enactment which is only detectable when we access his ironic intention. In this sense, Morrissey taunts us with the many shades of his musical expression, from the ethically suspect to the tacitly positive. And, in the final prognosis, there is always a double edge to his strategy that make readings of him culture specific.

Conclusion

The assumption I have worked with in this chapter is that Morrissey's texts are representative of a type of performativity that opens up new spaces for considering identity in a culturally defined setting. For me, the nature of Morrissey's social space is one of crisis where the shifts and rearrangements of masculinity in the 1980s and 1990s exist in a permanent state of tension. The effect of his performance lies in the emotions that are evoked when we experience his music. In this sense, it is the combination of responses to musical expression that highlight the pleasures of specific performance style. It might seem somewhat paradoxical that through the pain, despair and sheer misery of his songs the greatest pleasure is derived. But what is at issue here is the modelling of a position of ambiguity and indifference within a site of potential social and political conflict. I am referring to a site that is characterised by the young male of the 1980s within a social space where the crisis in rigid categorisation continues to provoke angst-related reactions.

In the course of this study, I have set out to discover how musical expression contributes to the appeal of Morrissey's identity. It is not only an emphasis on a fluidity in melodic linearity and vocal delineation, but also a recognition of dramatic irony through musical articulation that provides meaning to his songs. Often he fantasises about difference in a world where the pain of oppositions exist all around us. Yet, amidst all the incongruities of Morrissey's texts, we are reminded that he is singing about his desires, which are about *male desire*.[46] Although displays of vulnerability in male identity are nothing new to pop culture, it is *how* Morrissey self-defines his that becomes most compelling.

In this chapter, we have also seen how music can operate as an important part of the process that advances the idea of characterisation in pop songs. Music can tell us an abundance of things about how artists regard the narratives being sung about and how they would like us to regard them. That is to say, music channels the artist's persona by generating a kind of commentary on matters with which the individual is concerned. In this sense, music, with all its stylistic and technical codes, offers up a wealth of narrative information. And, even if a fan fails to recognise fully the significance of every intended musical code, the music's overall impact imports expressive features that are contextualised. Thus, it is in its full force of connotation we are reminded of the remarkable persuasive strength music possesses as a signifying entity.

Now into the early twenty-first century Morrissey continues to thrive on a controversy that is ingrained in the oppositional complexities of his persona. Yet, notwithstanding the naturalness of his construction (at least when positioned in a local context), he still conforms to the demands of an industry embedded in commercial gain. A Nietzchean sense of power underpins Morrissey's creative agency as his songs and videos promote a style which is unmistakably dogmatic in its rhetoric. Yet, his texts function as condensed ideas and reflections on the changing role of the pop artist. And, this explains how his performances develop a range of social and political statements that articulate an ideology that can be experienced as fragmented and contradictory. Indeed, while Morrissey may be considered as politically engaged, there is always speculation as to his intentions when it comes to issues of self-promotion and commodification.

Clearly, the central problem facing any study of this nature is the ongoing issue of how one interprets popular song.[47] In my experience of Morrissey's songs, it is predominantly his articulation of a certain Englishness that promotes his texts as intriguing signifiers of artistic expression. With his performances mounting to unified moments of deep self-reflection and empathic poignancy, Morrissey always has a political agenda which is communicated through his characterisation. Thus, his marking out of difference revolves around the construction of a specialised individuality that is often portrayed as vulnerable in the need of support on the parts of his fans. Above all, he is aware that only through our nurturing of his ego and consumption of his texts can his identity survive. Through a reflexive approach to performance then, he demonstrates that much of the success of marketing pop songs lies in the uniqueness of the voice. Indeed, it is this quality that affirms the expressive impulse behind his mediation of sincerity and concern – a vital component in the construction of authorship in pop and rock texts.

Finally, in the readings I have provided in this chapter, it is the specific counterpoint between identity and a personal musical style that throws into question the relation between the pop celebrity and his music. Morrissey's performances are a challenge to attending to the issue of how the anti-hero is positioned through an attitude of self-distantiation. Most signifantly, it is the double-sidedness of his act that embodies a potent rhetoric which articulates the social lives of people. Considered in this way then, his musical style infers the many voices that can be attached to sites of identity through time and space which dictate the enjoyment of pop music.

Acknowledgements

This chapter first appeared in the form of working papers at the Britpop Conference, Department of Music, University of Leeds, April 1997, organised by Steve Sweeney Turner, and, at a symposium at the Department of Music, City University London, 'Music, Television and Postmodernism', October 2000, organised by John Richardson. In addition, special thanks go Robynn Stilwell, Bengt Olav Hansen and Jone Frafjord for their enthusiastic encouragement.

Notes

1   Morrissey in David Bret (1994: 79).
2   Also of Irish parents, Johnny Marr was born John Martin Maher at Chorlton-on-Medlock, Manchester on 21 October 1963.
3   Julian Stringer (1992) considers in some detail the question of racial identity in the Smiths as important to his analysis. In his critique of their music, Stringer situates the issue of white ethnicity within a national context which is predicated upon a heritage of racism. However, there is an important distinction here: while their songs might concern expressions of white music, they are, he claims, in fact not explorations of being white. Clearly, Stringer's position opens up important debates on ethnicity within a political and social context.
4   Tony Mitchell (1996), in his discussion of aspects of British nationalism, suggests that the rise of national pride might be a result of some Britons feeling 'threatened' by the US and Europe. In addition, he points out that it is largely the British press who are responsible for building up notions of nationalism through the music scene. On the wider implications of this in terms of subcultural identity, see Hebdige (1985).
5   This included artists such as Sandie Shaw, Cilla Black, Rita Pavone, Marianne Faithfull, Petula Clark, Patti Smith, Marc Bolan, David Bowie and Alice Cooper.
6   See Johnny's Rogan's very personal account (1992) of Morrissey's sexuality and David Evan's more general analysis (1993) of sexual citizenship in the 1980s and 1990s.
7   I would suggest that the choice of the Smiths name could be read as ironic, especially for a group of distinctly Irish extraction. On this issue, Rogan has pointed out that Oscar Wilde commented 'Surely everyone prefers Norfolk, Hamilton and Buckingham to Jones or *Smith*...' (1992: 143, emphasis added).

8   Stringer (1992) has pointed out how in Morrissey's style there is an avoidance of the inflections one associates with African-American popular music. This trait clearly distinguishes Morrissey's vocal technique from that of many other English pop singers. The straightforward and semi-spoken quality of his delivery accentuates the words in a manner that ironises their meaning. In one sense, the musical style of the Smiths rejects the idiomatic nuances of Black American music for a construction of a type of indigenous Englishness.

9   Traditionally, British audiences have not responded easily to demonstrations of self-adulation and taking oneself seriously in popular song. This can be traced back to songs of the mid- to late nineteenth century, where self-mockery and ironic retort was often discernible (see Frith 1996; Scott 1989).

10   Ruud has argued that through music we preserve important biographical memories; music functions as a central organisational framework for both the spoken and unspoken topics that have to do with our identity (1997a: 209).

11   As Victor J. Seidler has observed, it is only through 'critical self-awareness' that men can become aware of the 'different traditions and ideas that help form our sense of ourselves and our relationship with others' (Seidler 1994: 53).

12   We know that from an early age he resisted the pressures of conforming to be one of the lads, but this had a price. This point is dealt with in detail in biographical accounts of his growing up in Manchester and attending the all boys' St. Mary's Secondary School in Renton Road. See, for example, Rogan (1992); Bret (1994).

13   The postmodern move to materialise the body through discourse theory and reject any natural reality, as suggested by postmodernist feminists such as Judith Butler, is indeed problematic. Note that Butler's description of identity subversion has been described as an example of 'elitist individualism' by Neil Nehring (1997).

14   Stringer (1992) also picks up this on point by insisting that Morrissey's image is very much constructed in the English 'gent' vein. In fact, Morrissey's method is to crisply articulate his words and to bring out his English diction to a point that emphasises the specialised traits in the voice that suggest indulgence. In addition, there is a tendency for him to exaggerate his vocal intonations, a strategy that draws out the ironic and camp intent of his performance style.

15   This is discernible in a legacy of English artists, not least Robbie Williams in his notable spoof-take performances at the end of the millennium.

16   Note that Brackett (1995) investigates the connection between authenticity and the historical construction of a Romantic ideology through pop expression.

17   Middleton (1990) describes how words function as 'shifters' in a way that musical features can be experiences as social actors whose identity varies according to genre and social context. In his theorisation of social voices, Middleton draws on the theoretical position of the Prague school and their approach to semiology which involves the exploration of 'semantic' gestures in music.

18   As I stress in Chapter 5 in my readings of the Pet Shop Boys, a shifting in representations of masculinity in the 1980s impinged on the sexual politics of the marketplace. Especially pop music styles became a focal point for gay culture and cultural diversity. Moreover, youth-oriented representations of identity started playing on an aesthetic that was ironic in its disorientation of sexual meanings. In his analysis of Morrissey and the Smiths, Stringer makes a reference to Morrissey's 'fragile, quasi-gay sexuality' (1992: 17) when discussing his Englishness and point of appeal. Clearly such an evaluation of Morrissey's sexuality is problematic especially given that it is not explored thoroughly or theorised by Stringer. I therefore prefer to employ the term 'sensibility' to describe the overall effect of his intentions in embracing aspects of gay culture. On the basis of many of the

Morrissey interviews I have come across, I would emphasise that there are certainly difficulties that arise in his appropriation of the Other through the dubious act of gender tourism.

19   This point of course distinguishes Morrissey, and for that matter, the Pet Shop Boys, from other quintessential English figures, from Wilde, W.H. Auden, and Coward, to George Michael and Elton John, whose sexual rampages at various stages in their lives were subjected to great condemnation and speculation thanks to the British press.

20   This is borne out by the countless interviews he has endured where the issue of his sexuality becomes a major point of speculation. Furthermore, the homoerotic content of his image and songs tend to conflict with his claims to asexuality.

21   *Viva Hate*, released in March 1988, moved quickly to the top of the album charts. For this recording, Morrissey enlisted the help of the producer Stephen Street and the Mancunian guitarist, Vini Reilly, to write and produce the material for the twelve songs on this album which marked a significant point of departure for the artist.

22   Musically, the song is more commercial in its flavour than most of the Smiths' songs, with the influence of Stephen Street coming through the catchy melodies, not least of all in the guitar part. This song was also rated as commercial at the time of its release through its state-of-the-art production values and the use of a drum machine.

23   Of course one of the difficulties in identifying the exact nature of Morrissey's vocal style is underscored by his apparent straightforward mode of delivery. Note that Stringer has referred to the 'ironic edge' which Morrissey's voice possesses, which, in a sense, compounds his status as a conventional rock star (1992: 20).

24   For a detailed discussion of the analytical premise I am referring to here, see Norwegian musicologist Rolf-Inge Godøy (1997). His study is based upon the multi-dimensionality of timbral modelling as a paradigm for modelling musical objects.

25   I would suggest that his approach to singing and emphasis on clear diction parodies a certain recognisable pretentiousness that has its origins in British music hall, whose traditions are found in artists such as Gracie Fields, Marie Lloyd and Noël Coward.

26   It is worth noting that with indie bands, such as the Smiths, the emphasis on sounding English (and not just Northern) became an important strategy in reworking of English pop during a time when most bands had been swept away by synthesiser-based New Pop, which aimed for the MTV market. This certainly explains the Smiths' popularity with the bulk of their fans who were from college and university backgrounds. Not only was it their clever and witty lyrics that appealed to a more educated group, but also the Englishness and indirect anti-American idioms within their sound and use of language.

27   A similar point is raised by Frith (1996), who claims that protest songs function as 'slogans' rather than ideas. This would explain why political intent is often misconstrued during the reception of slogans.

28   In terms of defining our reactions to the artist, it is really how we respond to the artist's musical delivery that constructs notions of the artist's 'credibility'. Brackett expands on this concept by stressing the function of self reflexivity: '...self-reflexivity implies that there is no "outside" from which to view the "authentic," that the "authentic" is always already in play, and that "truth to one's feelings" may be recuperated at any moment for financial gain' (1995: 82).

29   Note that Moore (1993) does concede that in older styles of popular music traits of the 'trained' voice can be found which avoid the embellishing techniques found in rock.

30   This might be read as a reaction against the New Romantic artists of the early 1980s who tended to adopt a more 'trained' approach to vocal technique in contrast to traditional rock singers (Moore 1993; Brackett 1995).

31   See Wishart (1977) for one of the earliest, concise discussions of the impact of sound recording on the foregrounding of aural-based praxes, which, certainly in the case of most pop music, circumvent the idealisation of discrete fixed pitch.

32   Register refers to the range of pitch which is determined by its low, middle and high sounds.

33   Explorations of the physical properties of the voice by Roland Barthes (1977) have opened up the debates surrounding the relationship between music and sexuality, especially in terms of the voice's erotic charge. See Dame (1994), Frith (1996) and Middleton (1990) for different critiques on Barthes's work. On another related point, which I owe to my friend Robynn Stilwell, Morrissey's adaptation of a speech-sung style could be read as a denial of his body through his overt manner of singing, especially with regard to the way in which he recoils from the more physical properties of singing.

34   I have found no evidence, for example, to suggest that this song gained any popularity amongst National Front supporters. Its general meaning, one of political scorn and anti-racism, is verified by the responses by Morrissey's fans to the tabloid music press (see Bret 1994). In addition, I would not read Morrissey's slant on disco as a homophobic reaction.

35   Cf. Sontag's pathbreaking analysis (1964) of camp artifice.

36   Gibbs (1984) points out that what linguists refer to as 'usage' has resulted in the argument that all language can function as ironic. In other words, that readings of meaning are not necessarily the meanings intended by the writer.

37   In Hutcheon's critique of irony she refers to this same point by employing the term *operative* to signal her interest in how irony functions. She maintains that inferred motivations result in a variety of reasons for attributing irony (Hutcheon 1994: 45).

38   See, for example, Hutcheon 1994; Warning 1982; Allemann 1956.

39   In this context I define the ironic marker as a sign which is dependent upon recognition within a discursive community. Markers, in this case, function to warn the interpreter of the possibility of ironic intent which is always culture specific. Therefore, any element of speech or musical utterance is potentially an ironic marker which the interpreter needs to identify (or notice) in order to carry out its interpretation. Given this, ironic markers might be considered as signals attributed to the suggestion of the possibility of ironic intent.

40   For a detailed exploration of the relationship between musical markers (musemes) and their paramusical context, see Tagg (1991). Through an exhaustive analysis of Abba's song 'Fernando', his analytical approach seeks to demonstrate how musical structures correspond to context

41   Whether intentional or not, it is interesting that the word 'Vauxhall' conjures up connotations of music-hall songs. At venues like the Pleasure Gardens, it was in such halls like Vauxhall that the first comic-style songs were performed during the early nineteenth century.

42   I owe this valid point to one of my former Oslo postgraduate students, Bengt Olav Hansen, an ardent Smiths fan whose perception of their music has been very informative and useful to this study.

43   The name, Speedway, is derived from a place in Santa Monica where Morrissey has allegedly escaped to, in order to avoid the British press and his staunchest critics.

44 During the song 'Margaret on the Guillotine' he politely asks Thatcher, *when will you die?*, pleading to the public not to *shelter this dream*, but *to make it real*. As the songs opens, Morrissey sings *The kind of people have a wonderful dream ...* over a chord progression reminiscent of the sweetest of all romantic ballads. Perhaps it is no coincidence that the release of this song was at the same time that the Conservative government introduced Section 28 of the Local Government Act 1987–8 – a poor moralistic law that prohibited local government from promoting homosexuality. The significance of this law can be measured alongside the increasing concern by the New Right for the tighter control of censorship and curbing of minority sexual identities. While in practice Section 28 had little impact, in symbolic terms it heralded an attempt to undermine the civil rights of gay and lesbian citizens through British law.

45 See David Laing (1969) for a detailed discussion on how lyrics become transformed through musical treatment. Laing suggests that while lyrics only hold the *key* to the context, musical signification should be represented in a meta-language.

46 Cf. Suzanne Moore's discussion (1988) of the postmodern male and the shifting positions of masculinity.

47 As with the other artists I have presented in this book, Morrissey's strategies cannot be easily categorised as modernist or postmodernist. I should stress that while the deployment of irony is often construed as postmodern, we also need to recognise its modernist properties. See Kellner (1995) for an in-depth discussion of this issue.

Chapter 4
Annie Lennox's 'Money Can't Buy It': Masquerading Identity

Introduction

While Madonna was breaking into the pop mainstream in the US, and Morrissey was stirring up trouble for young fans in Manchester, surprising changes in the representations of certain female pop stars were taking place in the UK. Perhaps no pop star quite challenged stereotypical gender roles to the extent that Scottish-born Annie Lennox of the Eurythmics did. Instinctively, she understood how to exploit the music industry in the 1980s and utilise the powerful medium of the pop video to develop the androgynous look. By frequently opting for gender disguise, she went out of her way to establish new standards for women in the music industry (see O'Brien 1995). And, in the aftermath of punk, her look gradually slotted into the fashionable fetishising of the queer look employed by many 1980s British pop bands.

By 1983, Lennox had achieved international stardom with the Eurythmic's first hit 'Sweet Dreams Are Made of This'. Not only did this group display a freshness in musical style, but their legendary videos captured the ongoing transgression of identity boundaries taking place in early 1980s pop.[1] Lennox's choice of wearing men's clothes was a calculated move in appropriating and parodying the most corporate of all business attire, the suit. Moreover, her cropped, red-dyed hair, heavy make-up, alongside the 'attitude' she exuded, appealed to millions of fans worldwide, so much so that by the mid-1980s the Eurythmics were recognisable as much through their new look as their sound.

With the release of their seventh album, *Savage* in 1987, the Eurythmics were secure in their experimentation with a colourful range of images and musical style. In particular, the group's unique approach to the pop video was crucial to their popularity: 'Instead of seeing videos as just another promotional tool, Eurythmics used the medium as another avenue of artistic expression, learning to manipulate their image instead of being manipulated *by* their image' (Gaar 1993: 329). Clearly it was the advent of MTV during the early 1980s that emphasised the importance of image, and, like Madonna, Lennox was able to exploit pop promos to her advantage. As one of the first major female MTV stars, Lennox played about with a repertoire of gendered roles – prostitute, angel, young girl, housewife, drag artist, male rock star – to challenge the traditional representations of females found in rock. For example, in the video of the song 'I Need A Man', her guise turned to the vamped-up drag artist, which not only targeted an enchanted gay male audience but also satirised an entire rock culture intent on stereotyping and denigrating women. In particular, the gender confusion of her act corresponded to questions concerning her real intentions. Was Lennox 'playing a man in drag who's impersonating a man-eating vamp, or a "real" female vamp, or what?' (Reynolds and Press 1995: 296). Or were her acts of impersonation merely strategies for cashing in on an industry fixated on the fetish of image-based representation?

Shortly following the release of their final album in 1989, with the somewhat misleading title, *We Too Are One*, Lennox and Dave Stewart decided to part company to pursue solo careers. Nobody would have believed then that ten years on they would join up again and gain as much popularity as they did in the 1980s. Such is the unpredictability of the pop industry. Meanwhile, by the time Lennox released her first solo album, *Diva*, in 1992, as a mature mother, she had already established herself as a pop diva who could expertly manipulate her identity. With the launch of *Diva*, she opted for a range of disguises which would still prioritise masquerade. In one sense, she further capitalised on the spectacle of the drag queen which continued to defy fixed notions of identity. Throughout the video of the album *Diva*, aptly called *Totally Diva*, references to drag oscillate between more stereotypical representations of the female, which, as we will see later in this chapter, raise all sorts of questions concerning the conditions of masquerade and the dynamics of performativity.

Opting for gender disguise

So far in this book I have been arguing for a position that locates the interrelationships between musical texts and identity. In this respect, musical interpretation needs to be conducted through identifying the *specific localities* within which music is realised and contextualised. In the case of Annie Lennox, her manipulation of image works together with her music to form the basis of her appeal. At the heart of her video performances she manufactures a sense of gender confusion as part of her masquerade.

Throughout this chapter I have decided to concentrate on the analysis of one of her songs, 'Money Can't Buy It', from her solo *Diva* album. My intention here is to discover how various musical codes convey, organise and construct narratives through video performance. Underlying this investigation is the notion that social meanings are constructed within the communicative framework of the technologies that produce the music.

The narrative of 'Money Can't Buy It' derives its meaning from the prevailing ideologies of late twentieth-century capitalist consumerism, through its blend of narrative connotations and musical production. High-quality digital recording, sampling techniques and the choice of instrumentation (mainly keyboards) within the production of the *Diva* album instantly reveals its period of conception as that of the early 1990s. The technological dimension of the recording captures a distinct aesthetic associated with the employment of state-of-the-art, fashionable timbres. Middleton has argued that the techniques employed in pop recordings have 'increased the variety of possible configurations, and the sense of specific physical space that can be created has enormous potential effects on the power and types of gestural resonance which listeners feel' (Middleton 1993: 179). The configurations of production are a key to understanding Lennox's sound and performance techniques. And while her gestural resonances might be read as intentional, they also exist as a means to another end. As well as being entertaining, Lennox's stress on fluidity in identification elicits a broader meaning when it comes to taking into account the effects of her performance on the listener. From a historical perspective, it was her now-familiar image of androgyneity that helped shape a discourse based around the question of not only spectatorship but also gendered gesture in performance.

During the early part of her career, the destabilising effect of Lennox's representation was bound to provoke strong reactions, as she would very soon discover. The following incident is documented by Lucy O'Brien:

> Before her appearance at the 1984 Grammy Awards, MTV demanded a birth certificate as proof that Lennox was a woman and not an impersonator. In response she appeared at the Awards show disguised as Elvis, with fake side-burns, a pocked chin and greased-back hair. Despite guffaws from the stage manager, the celebrity crowd greeted her with a stony silence, her masculine edge interpreted as hostile chic. [O'Brien 1995: 255]

Amusing as this might read, it does highlight a more serious point, namely that of the representation politics surrounding pop artists at the dawn of the MTV era; a period where pride and prejudice defined the cultural context for many female artists involved in making it in the pop world.[2]

Upon establishing a partnership with Dave Stewart and their formation of the Eurythmics in 1981, Lennox's image became wrapped up in an array of teasing images of sexual ambiguity, which, as Reynolds and Press put it, 'brought masquerade into the mainstream' (1995: 294). Strongly influenced by the display of sexual ambiguity in 1970s rock, by artists such as David Bowie, Bryan Ferry and Lou Reed, Lennox's strategy was to extend the plethora of gender constructions into a parodic performance of masquerade. In fact, through the visual medium of MTV, Lennox parodied conventional gender roles on an unprecedented mass scale.

With their first hits, the Eurythmics quickly discovered the extent to which they could benefit by such widespread media exposure. The impact of this British duo, with their rotating line-up of supporting musicians and quirky name, spelt out what they really wanted to be: *rhythmic* and *European*.[3] Now determined to play a more prominent role in the Eurythmics than she had in her previous band, the Tourists, Lennox pushed the display of gender-bending to new heights through her unique mode of dress. The impact of this is summed up by Gillian Gaar: 'Lennox [also] played with androgyny in a manner no female performer had really explored before, a trend dubbed "gender bending," and popularized by other performers, such as Culture Club's Boy George and the cross-dressing singer "Marilyn" ' (Gaar 1993: 325).

Dwelling on the issue of gender-bending a little longer, it is worth stressing that in contrast to the colourful geisha-look of Boy George, Lennox's play on androgyny was much more unsettling for its time. Acutely aware of the music industry's tendency to stereotype women artists and to prioritise white male stars, Lennox went out of her way to disrupt clichéd representations of femininity through a determined provocation. There was no better channel than the pop video for manipulating her music and image in a manner that would open up new possibilities for masquerade. In fact, the video era of the 1980s gradually replaced the stage as the fantasy world through which the female artist could now seek liberation in the formative power of an active politics of representation. To a degree, the apparatus of music television helped secure the visual gestures and empower the female body in popular culture (see Kaplan 1987).

In effect then, Annie Lennox's look as much as her sound became the inscription of her difference. Her play on androgyny and impersonations of both women and men was frequently couched in a narcissistic display of personal performance. Her femininity could be interpreted as a deconstruction of traditional reference points which embodied an aesthetic that satirised the authenticity of rock music. In terms of her performance, by transcending the restraints of gendered determinism, she entered a postmodern space where androgyneity would challenge the voyeuristic masculine gaze. Flaunting her femininity, Lennox instinctively learnt how to put on and discard identity through masquerade – this helps explain her fluidity and ambivalent positioning within the context of pop music of the 1980s and 1990s.

Questions of musical coding

If masquerade be granted its own discursive moment in the consideration of Lennox's performance, the constituted sound patterns of coding attribute a significant effect to the mediation of her musical expression. The focus there-fore must fall on the organisation and manipulation of specific musical codes which embrace a set of practices responsible for conveying meaning within the pop text. A number of important musicological questions arise in relation to the material effects of musical meaning. How might we identify signifiers of performance and gender through the construction of a musical discourse? And what is the function of identifying musical codes and processes in the interpretation of an artist?

The song 'Money Can't Buy It', set within a simple formal structure, consists of a multitude of components which encode themes of pleasure, greed, love, narcissism, passion and vulnerability. As a starting point, I have concentrated on two areas of stylistic coding: harmonic organisation and vocal timbre, which contribute to defining the aesthetics of this song. Clearly, the control of harmony is exceptionally important in pop songs, the significance of which rests on its ability to embrace established codes (technical and stylistic) of Western musical practice that communicate much about musical meaning. That is to say, harmony can make cultural references possible in its inferences to traditional patterns of musical organisation. To a certain extent, at least in the case of this song, I therefore see the reductive analysis of harmony as most relevant to the discovery of what the music signifies on a broader level.[4] Moreover, the relationship between melody and harmony is an important factor when considering the overall aesthetic of harmonic flavouring in music. Similarly, melodic pitch content has significant ramifications for the working-out of harmonic formulae. This is conspicuous in the modal functioning of harmony in the song under scrutiny, which, as I will argue, is determining in its ability to characterise and implicate the protagonist.

In 'Money Can't Buy It', the regulation of harmony is deceptively subtle and ambiguous throughout. This is borne out first and foremost by the avoidance of any conventional diatonic closure through the use of modality. On a macrolevel, its harmonic codification in 'Money Can't Buy It' involves a gradual progression from the minor-flavoured C dorian mode in the chorus (constructed around Cm7) up by an interval of a third to the brighter E♭ lydian, and then followed by a stepwise move to the subdominant chord of F major (see Table 4.1).

In the six-bar instrumental introduction, a contemplative, dreamy mood is established through the gentle harmonic oscillation. This prepares us for the vocals which enter with the hook, *Money can't buy it, baby,* as Lennox insists that neither money, sex or drugs can buy *it*. Transporting the central sentiments of the song, these lyrics are cushioned by the melancholic mood of the C dorian mode, consisting of chord shifts by the interval of a fourth in each bar, from Cm9 (i) to F (IV). The effect of the repetition of these two chords is to set up a sense of stability through their structuration. Leading into the verse within the same modal vein, Lennox claims that *love alone might do these things for you ...* and proceeds to describe how to *... take the power to set you free, kick down the door and throw away the key....* At this point, the harmony refutes any variation, retaining a pensive mood with the chords gliding over a C bass pedal. While the harmony resists change, the rhythmic pulse becomes more strident in its setting-up of a regular groove.

Table 4.1   Modal organisation in 'Money Can't Buy It'

PITCH CENTRE:	C	E♭-F	F
MODAL CENTRE:	C Dorian	C Aeolian/ C Dorian/E♭	F Mixolydian
CHORD TYPES:	Cm7(9) F7(9)	E♭ Fm F	F
SONG STRUCTURE:	intro A B A1 B1	C A2 B2	Coda
EFFECTS:	tension searching	release finding	tension questioning/ responding

By the time we enter the second verse, a release of harmonic tension is afforded by the resolution to E♭ major chord (III of C aeolian/dorian). With the brightness in this shift to E♭ major, from the doleful C dorian mode, the strength of Lennox's convictions are embodied in the lyrics: *I believe that love alone, might do these things for you ... I believe in the power of creation, I believe in the good vibration....*

Throughout this nine-bar passage, some respite in harmonic tension is built up before E♭ major resolves to Fm (iv). The modal excursion from C dorian to C aeolian and its resulting modal-minor duality (established by the regular oscillation between chords Fm9 and Fm6) heightens the intensity of Lennox's words: *Won't somebody tell me, what we're coming to?* One final reference to the E♭ major chord occurs in the coda, before this chord progresses to an F chord (in F lydian mode), evading diatonic closure as a result of its modality. A sense of ambiguity soon arises from the shift from C dorian to F mixolydian in the coda, with the modal centre F assuming prominence. The effect of this is to reinforce the stacking-up of emotional energy in the music/lyric relationship.

A general regulation in levels of tension and release within the harmonic organisation (see Table 4.1) plays an important role in communicating to the listener a variety of nuances that relate to the song's central message. Harmonically, the effect of moving from C dorian through C aeolian/E♭ lydian, and then resolving to F mixolydian, symbolises Lennox's struggle to discover *why* money can't buy it. In their combination with other musical codes, it is these harmonic codes that contribute significantly to stretching out the song's affective charge.

Among the many other musical structures that contribute to the song's overall modal flavour is the synth bass line. This is driven by a funky dotted figure against a regular, straight figure in the kit line. Influencing our perception of the harmony as much as the melody, this line is developed from a simple idea consisting of single pitches forming a double-unisoned melodic riff as accompaniment to the vocal melody (see Example 4.1). Transformed timbrally by the additional layering over of piano and guitar parts, riffs such as this serve to enhance the chordal progressions and also add weight to the gestural impetus of the song.

As the song reaches its conclusion, the bass part undergoes further alteration by shifting to an E♭ pitch centre, as it acquires a higher profile within the mix. The rhythmic motion of the bass line focuses on an active figure on the first two beats of the bar, with a release and break in movement on the third and fourth beats. In terms of musical gesture, such details in musical process heighten the sense of a strong downbeat, thus creating a tension throughout most of the song. Furthermore, the effect of the bass figure is to underpin the rich and sensual quality of Lennox's voice, especially by enriching its timbral quality.

Example 4.1   Bass riff in 'Money Can't Buy It'

Next, I want to turn to the question of timbre. The wealth of contrasting shades, textures and tonal colours found in the vocal part emphasise the physicality and sensuality of Lennox's singing. In songs of all genres the detail in vocal tone colour is one of the most expressive features that we experience. Within the self-contained framework of the sound recording, vocal production in pop music is usually contingent on many different effects, such as flanging, filtering, artificial chorus, and analog and digital manipulation. As already suggested in my studies of Madonna and Morrissey, the production techniques behind vocal delivery – phrasing, inflection, dynamic shadings – constitute some of the prime carriers of technical coding. My purpose here is to try to demonstrate how differences in qualities of timbre can offer the listener a way into understanding the musical meaning within a song.

Commencing with the first line of the lyrics, the hook, *Money can't buy it, baby,* Lennox's nasal vocal tone is quite detached, evoking a sense of dreaminess and melancholy. This establishes the mood for the first two sections of the song. A more rhythmically accented passage (lines 8–15, Table 4.2) then follows, marked by a broadening-out of vocal tone which underlines the lyrical message: *take the power to set you free, kick down the door and throw away the key.* Through the location of the vocals in the foreground of the mix, with

Table 4.2 Timbral spectrum: 'Money Can't Buy It'

1	Flanged Warm Rich sonorous melancholy soothing	stronger inflected strident more emphasis	passionate richer tone conviction more forceful	innocent pleading 'little girl voice' nostalgic	strong – rap style positive excitasble aggressive	elated confident decisive emotional with feeling	dreamy contemplative cool detached
2	mp	mf	f	sub.pp cresc	f–ff	f	pp
3	1–7	8–15	16–22	23–30	31–43	44 k	
4	A B	A1	B1	C	A2	B2	coda

1 = timbre description 2 = dynamics 3 = lyric lines 4 = formal sections

a marked intensification of dynamics, a definite shift in mood takes place. Here, the increase in levels of ornamentation (inflections and embellishments) within the vocal part are anchored by an emphasised, quantised rhythmic groove in the bass and kit parts. Later on, the piano line, doubled with the bass, reinforces the contour of this counter-melodic line (see Example 4.1). From lines 16 to 22, the vocal part becomes more rhythmically profiled through its positioning within the mix, as Lennox stresses the verse's hook, *I believe that love alone might do these things for you . . .*, while still sustaining a richness and warmth in resonance. During this section her timbre undergoes further change by taking on a more passionate, determined edge; the sound is now shaped through a concentration of fuller resonance in the chest tones.

In the next passage (section C), *Won't somebody tell me what we're coming to?*, Lennox's tone starts chilling as her voice transforms into a pleading, innocent, vulnerable 'little girl' voice, with the thin, flanged vocal timbres capturing the fragility and searching quality of the lyrics. Here the focus of vocal exertion moves to a more strenuous head tone – the effect of which is enhanced by the flanging of the vocals in the mix without reverb. At this moment in the song, a special sense of intimacy with the singer is attained through the very control of vocal execution. Then, by fading into the background of the mix, the groove virtually disappears as the harmonic rhythm decreases and becomes grounded on chords Fm9 and Fm6 (see Table 4.1).

From lines 31 to 34 of the chorus hook, the mood changes once again, now regulated by a more strident vocal edge. Enriched and sensual at this point, Lennox's vocal articulation is projected once again from the chest tones and phased into the foreground of the mix and strongly reinforced by the backing parts. Even more changes are introduced in the passage (lines 35 to 43) that follows, such as the stylistic alteration from a ballad feel to an angry rap. Lennox's tone now undergoes further change in terms of its physicality and sensuality, assuming an aggressive, excitable and emphatic edge amidst the vivid interplay of vocal colours that underline the hard, cool message: *now hear this, pay attention to me, 'cause I'm a rich white girl, and it's plain to see I got ev'ry kind of thing that money can buy*. This point signals the moment of transcendence in the song when Lennox determinedly draws on all her resources to proclaim her empowerment. Importantly, the effect of this is achieved not only through the shift in range and physical exertion of the voice, but also through the displaced accents and increase in rhythmic complexity of melodic contour.

Then from line 44 onwards, her vocal expression returns to that of its original colour found in the opening bars of the song. Finally, when drawing to a close, one final timbral change occurs on the hook in the coda section of 'Money Can't Buy It' as the voice is flanged and phased around in the mix through use of a delay unit and pitch harmoniser – this provides a mechanical, desensitised and contemplative conclusion to the song.

So far, in this inspection of musical codes, what stands out is Lennox's affirmation of the song's message through an array of expressive techniques and rich textures linked to vocal technique. Breadth in register, singing methods, and manipulation of timbre all contribute to the construction of a rich tapestry of moods (see Table 4.2). Predominantly, it is the flexibility of her vocal gestures that confound timbral interchangeability. Indeed, Lennox's singing style in 'Money Can't Buy It' raises questions concerning how timbre incorporates what John Shepherd has described as 'mediations brought on by gender' (Shepherd 1987: 164).[5] Most discernible is her vocal elasticity, which I would argue adumbrates a type of musical androgyneity. Here I am referring to a quality in her vocal sound that comes about through a special virtuosity that is self-conscious. Her almost exaggerated use of melodic embellishment and timbral expanse demonstrate not only an awesome flexibility in technique but also a form of empowerment which radiates through her vocal pyrotechnics.[6] This seems to be in direct contrast to aspects of Morrissey's style of singing that we examined in Chapter 3. Continuously harnessed by the measured extremities of her approach to articulation, it is Lennox's voice that correlates to a range of gendered intentions that are concerned with masquerade. For instance, the gestures of the restrained girlish voice (section C) are vividly contrasted against the fuller sound of the mature, sensual, confident woman (section B2). Features such as these mobilise a whole set of interchanging connotations attached to attitude.

Most of all, Lennox's wide range of vocal nuances generate constantly shifting layers of *Klangfarben*[7] that relay specific sets of musical shades which fortify the degree of self-reflexivity in the song. Here we are reminded that our responses to vocal nuance are undoubtedly influenced by sets of factors that relate to our immediate associations with gendered identity. On this note, we cannot ignore the fact that her performance – stylistically classifiable as pop-rock – is situated in what has largely been a male domain (Frith and McRobbie 1989; Moore 1993; Wood 1994). For me, it seems as if Lennox appropriates the male singer by parodying the serious world of rock – this becomes most evident in the more aggressive moments of the song. Yet moments like this are fairly short-lived, as she switches over to an imitation of the high-pitched female voice. To put this differently, it is as if she parodies the woman or girl she certainly does not want to be. Thus, as her different voices connote the effect of her authority, we are faced with moments of exchange that convey the multiplicity of the gendered body.

I would argue here that vocal gestures constitute the most important part in the process of masquerading. Time and time again, Lennox, through her singing style, indulges in brashly virtuoso gestures of ornamentation that can be experienced as gender-transgressive. Indeed, the wide span of one single voice is able to produce an ambiguity which Elizabeth Wood (1994) has referred to as 'Sapphonic'. Wood suggests that the extremity in compass of the female range, with its break across register borders, results in an effect of 'sonic cross-dressing': the merging of the male and female through synthesis rather than separation. In general the destabilising quality of the Sapphonic voice embodies a range of desires that refute the simplistic categorisation of female voice-types. And, in her capacity to cross-dress sonically, Lennox challenges the very polarities of her own gendered identity, a pertinent feature I shall now investigate in my consideration of the video promo for 'Money Can't Buy It'.

Visualising sound through videography

Another approach to interpreting the tonal shadings of Lennox's voice can be invoked by considering its technological juxtapositioning in the confines of the sound recording and the video. I should emphasise that the results from my investigation in this section demonstrate a wealth of information concerning the question of the artist's musical imagination and the role this plays in her expressive impulse. In this respect, how the codes of musical materiality convert into visual representation obviously depend on what level the sounds are read. I would suggest that the starting point for modelling responses to visual representation lies in the notion of sonic configuration. With reference to the video of 'Money Can't Buy It', I am particularly intrigued with how the visual narrative of a song interacts with the effect of compositional processes, such as repetition, groove gestures, and melodic and harmonic sequence-types. To explore these issues in close detail, I have devised a table (see Table 4.3) as part of my method for exploring the events produced in the video clip of 'Money Can't Buy It' alongside the musical effects and lyrical content of the song.

Inevitably, numerous events, reactions and emotions occur when we experience the kinetic energy of musical processes in tandem with representations of visual imagery.[8] As with music compositional processes, the repetitions found in the large-scale structural organisation of visual events function as unifying devices in the song's narrative. Comprising a selection of facial shots, the central visual hook – Lennox's face – maintains a level of interest by continuously undergoing changes in expression that correlate to the musical text. Effectively, this hook reflects a variety of moods linked directly to the gestural layers of the musical movement. Functioning as the predominant mode of visual emphasis within this video clip, Lennox's iconography (her body, facial expressions and gestures) holds a vital clue to our reception of the music. Sensual, 'feminised' and erotic dimensions of the visual performance are captured by the musical elements, as articulated by the soft synth lines, the sustained lush chords, the gentle, undulating rhythm tracks, the cascading glissandi at the end of keyboard phrases, as well as the general arrangement and production of the mix.

Generally, it is the full effect of vocal and visual tonal connotations that articulate the song's aesthetic. This is implicit in the vivid contrasts between visual codes – Lennox's physical features, plus her red dress, white towel, fluorescent yellow mimosas – and the richness of musical codes – the lush dorian and lydian harmonies, the moody instrumental sounds, the gestures of the sparse groove. From the moment the song begins, its appeal is rooted in the serene, swirling effect of the synth sounds which accompany the visual framing of Lennox in regal splendour before a massive mirror amidst opulent surroundings. In particular, the acoustical setting of this opening shot is enhanced by the artificial effects of studio production, such as phasing and reverb within the mix of the recording. Close-up details in the facial features (smooth, flawless complexion, dark red lipstick, large made-up eyes), with constantly changing shades of musical expression, provide a link between the lyrical and musical structures of organisation. Additionally, the technique of employing mirrors in the video clip, serves to repeat Lennox's image in tandem with the repetition of musical ideas through the 'mirroring' effect of sequencing and recording. This is further borne out by the recurrence of familiar timbres, doublings of melodic and riff lines, and shapes of vocal phraseology.

In section C, Lennox's dramatisation of vulnerability and fragility is captured by her overtly seductive pose; a position which can easily be read as satirical. Here, the tearful, downcast look of Lennox is boosted by the flanged vocals, the noticeable drop in dynamics, and the subdued rhythmic motion. Moreover, a range of technical and stylistic codes in the music are depicted within the visual representations of the clip in a variety of ways. I will now turn to a number of these features in closer detail:

1. In terms of the technological processes employed, the manipulation of sound imagery within the context of the recording often correlates directly to the angle shots and positioning of the visual image within the frame of the video clip. Stereo imaging, the foregrounding, mid and backgrounding of musical codes correspond to similar processes in the visual text. In the final chorus (A2), Lennox's voice is multitracked with pitch shifts to enhance a wider, chorus effect. Here the clip includes a variety of rapid, interchanging middle-range and close-up shots of the performer, which directly interact with the general increase in density of the musical text.

2. Musical tempo in 'Money can't Buy It' corresponds in a number of ways to the visual sequence of events. Visual tempo is regulated by camera movement and editing, which involves alternating speeds of splicing. For example, in the introduction the rate of visual cuts is relatively high in contrast to the steady groove denoting the musical tempo, which heightens the overall level of anticipation. Once the vocals enter with the lyrics,

Table 4.3   Visual, lyrical and musical structures in 'Money Can't Buy It'

FORM	lyrics	musical effect/aesthetics	video shots/visual narrative
INTRO		Smooth, swirling synth lines over long, sustained chords creating a mood of tranquility and relaxation. Subdued rhythmic motion, with percussion sounds prominent in mix. Repetition of chords, richness of timbres are homologous with the mirror effect in the video.	Long shot: opulent surroundings, Lennox framed seated in front of a huge, ornate mirror -. dressed in full-length blood-red evening dress, white towel draped around head, clasping a large bunch of yellow mimosa flowers.
			Mid shot: Lennox stands up, moving languidly and sensually in time to the music, her reflection is juxtaposed by mirror images.
			Ten shorter duration fast mid-shots follow, framing her in a variety of different poses in front of the mirror.
A	1. Money can't buy it, baby 2. Sex can't buy it, baby 3. Drugs can't buy it, baby 4. You can't buy it, baby.	Voice becomes foregrounded in mix, striking up a balance with Lennox's facial image which is foregrounded in the clip. Minor quality of D Dorian and the blues melodic line highlights the pensive, resigned quality of the lyrics.	Close shot: Lennox's face, with its reflection in mirror, becomes the centre focus. First full-eye contact with the camera/viewer, with gaze shifting flirtatiously from her own image in the mirror to the cameralviewer. Image depicted is luring, seductive, confident and narcissistic.
INSTR. BRIDGE		Repetition of musical ideas! timbres from intro passage, capturing luring and contemplative mood.	Close shot continues throughout this instrumental bridge, with Lennox shutting her eyes for the first half of passage, thereafter opening them slowly.

Section	Lyrics	Musical commentary	Visual commentary
		Open voicings on chords Cm9 and F9 serve to heighten the level of tension and expectation within this passage.	Emphasis is predominantly on changes to facial expression.
B	5. I believe that love alone 6. Might do these things for you 7. I believe in love alone yeah, yeah.	Vocal lines more rhythmically emphasised, highlighting the positive nature of the lyrics in this section.	Close shot: Lennox's face and reflection in the mirror continues, with the gaze shifting continuously from camera to herself.
INSTR. BRIDGE		Build up in musical intensity, with introduction of piano/ bass tiff, accenting 1st and 3rd beats.	Close shot: facial expressions continue to dominate, now enhanced by slow, gestural hands movements which enter the frame, emulating the pleasure in the music.
A¹	8. Take the power 9. To set you free 10. Kick down the door and 11. Throw away the key. 12. Give up your needs, 13. Your poisoned seeds, 14. Find yourself elected 15. To a different kind of creed.	Dynamics in vocal parts increase, with voice more foregrounded within the mix. Vocal line more embellished to accent words. Build up in instrumental layers, with guitar fills inserted at the end of line 11.	Close facial shot of Lennox continues, hands now moving out of the frame as verse starts. Lennox's gaze is directed towards herself in the mirror. Facial expressions become more varied and animated throughout this sequence.
B¹	16. I believe that love alone 17. Might do these things for 18. I believe that love alone 19. Might do these things for you, 20. I believe in the power of creation, 21. I believe in the good vibration, 22. I believe in love alone yeah, yeah	Verse is further developed by doubling in length. Dynamics increase, emphasising vocal line and lyrics. Piano/guitar fills included to intensify overall musical interest. Noticeable embellishment of last two words, 'yeah, yeah,' which suspend and prolong final cadence.	Continual close up shots of Lennox's face, with her singing/mouthing the lyrics throughout.

	Lyrics	Music	Visual
C	23. Won't somebody tell me 24. What we're coming to? 25. It might take forever till 26. We watch those dreams come true, 27. All the money in the world 28. Won't buy you peace of mind. 29. You can have it all 30. But you still won't be satisfied.	Flanged treatment of the vocals create blurred, dreamy mood, which captures essence of the lyrics. Dynamics are kept low throughout, with changes to the percussion part. A certain fragility in the sound is maintained during most of this section until the end when a drum roll crescendo leads into the …	Continuation of close-up shot of Lennox's face, this time more pronounced changes in the expression, e.g. eyes cast down, vulnerable look, plaintive, pleading, with a hint of tears. Mirror mists up from the closeness of her breath in front of her mouth, as she looks into the distance. Hands reappear within the frame, gently and sensually caressing her face. Towards the end of this section there is an imprint of her lips evident on the glass of the mirror. Entire effect is erotic.
A^2	31–34. Money can't buy it, baby … 35. Now hear this, pay attention to me, 36. cause I'm a rich white girl, 37. And it's plain to see 38. I got ev'ry kind of thing that the money can buy, 39. Let me tell you all about it, 40. Let me amplify, 41. I got diamonds, you heard about those, 42. I got so many that I can't close my safe at night, 43. In the dark, lying awake in a sick dream.	Chorus returns with loud dynamics, multi-effects. Chorus extended into improvised-rap section. Vocals multi-tracked to create large chorus-type effect within this seciton.	Rapid sequence of fast shots during this section with regular alternation between long and close shots. Frame begins with Lennox tossing back her head, wrapped in white towel. Rap section: close-up shots of face throughout, with variety of expressions – selfish, greedy, mean, conceited, confident, etc. Exaggerated use of facial expression,

			especially with reference to eyes, which flash wickedly and knowingly as the lyrics are emphasised. Overtones of camp style.
B²	44. I believe that love alone … – – – – – – – (instrumental)	Musically, this denotes as an arrival point in the song. Harmony resolves to E/$flat$ major centre, vocals are multi-tracked to create spatial feel and the mix is rounded and filled.	Long shot: upbeat at the beginning is synchronised with upward motion of Lennox throwing her head back wrapped in the white towel – a recurring, cliched gesture. Close shot of face with back to the mirror, eyes face upwards for first time in the video clip. Towards end of section eyes fix firmly on camera/viewer, before looking away.
CODA		Recap of intro material. Hook line repeated ad lib, with effects, voice and fades into background of mix.	Mid shot: Lennox clutching flowers – image linked up with the first frame of the clip. Close shot: Lennox faces herself in mirror, then looks into the camera, mirror mists up in front of her mouth, upon which she traces $ dollar signs repeatedly as the clip reaches its conclusion.

editing is reduced, so as not to detract from the image of the performance and the musical tempo. Rate of change in musical gestures and the formal sections of the song (Table 4.2) appear to be coordinated directly with the singer's mode of expression and apparent control of the image.

3. Rhythmic pulse, groove or 'feel' is expressed in a variety of visual processes throughout the clip. Percussion and kit tracks set up the main groove that activate the performer into motion in the first few frames. However, the visual images frequently assume an independent rhythmic flow of their own, at times out of sync with the musical rhythm. Lennox sways in time to the rhythm of the music during the beginning of the clip, but thereafter for most of the song performs without much physical response to the beat. This might be explained through the nature of the slow, undulating ballad style. Jody Berland throws further light on this issue by discussing the significance of rhythmic movement in the context of music video. She has argued how images are teased out by the beat which helps determine the 'rhythm of the experience' (1993: 40). When we watch pop videos, it is as if 'the rhythm conquers all', first us as the viewers, and then the protagonist of the song.

4. Perhaps the most powerful expression of rhythm is captured through the compelling image of Lennox herself, which includes variants of physical movement intensified and amplified by the clever and deceptive use of mirrors. This functions to emphasise the obvious narcissistic and hedonistic representation of Lennox as diva. Her flirtatious yet detached performance is mirrored by the links between the range of visual and sonic images (see Table 4.3).

The task of ascertaining the correlations between visual and sonic processes of motion is of critical importance when considering how we respond to Lennox's characterisation. In fact, it is the rhythmic gestures of both the musical and visual structures of 'Money Can't Buy It' that frame a constantly shifting kaleidoscope of rich timbres. The various combinations of sonic and visual images absorbed into the video clip also provide the viewer/listener with clues for understanding the political constructs of the performance. In this sense, the star's performance, it might be argued, with all its signifiers negotiates strategies of sexuality, style and gender within the transpersonal confines of the pop text. This returns us to the musical processes, gestures and techniques employed in the realisation of the video performance and how they connote specific notions of identity.[9]

Significantly, lyrical connotations and musical codes clearly constitute an integral part of reading visual narratives. It follows that the intimacy in the mode of address in pop videos is articulated as much through gestures as words, which carry with them the impressions of their meaning. With the body operating as a prime visual hook, the viewer/fan/spectator is compelled to concentrate on the star's physical expression as a means for gaining access into the narrative. At a structural level, it is the merging of musical codes with iconography that constitute the syntax of the pop video. In other words, the stylistic and technical codes, in their juxtapositioning with the visual codes, sustain a special kind of meaning. Even in an apparently straightforward song, it is the micro-gestures, textures and somatic properties of musical performance that are responsible for regulating continuity in the visual narrative, thus establishing the intricate rituals that we perceive as compelling within pop texts.

Being *Totally* Diva

Of course, debating the reception of pop texts is clearly a personal process as music is based upon multiple responses to the dialogues that take place on many levels. During the 1980s, feminist criticism insisted on the urgent exploration of the Subject's position and the plurality of its discursive location. The result of this was that within the domain of a broad politics of representation, aspects of female power started to be addressed as a counter-response to the assumptions that had supported dominant ideologies. In this terrain, the conditions of the female Subject in performance gradually became negotiable in a range of disciplines, not least musicology. Feminist theorist Sue-Ellen Case (1993) has worked out a masquerade theory that she applies to the butch-femme subject on stage. From a theatrical position, she has argued how female roles can assume a quality of construction that lends agency to the historically passive Subject. This often occurs through a strategy that draws on the ironic modes of camp, satire, sarcasm and parody. I will return to this point later on in my discussion.

Meanwhile, the performativity of star iconography and storytelling in pop texts can form a useful pathway into discovering how gender politics function in music.[10] As a case in point, Lennox's masquerade reminds us that constructs of female identity provide important social points of reference. Indeed, we can assume that her performances presuppose the engagement of the listener who is prepared to identify with and appreciate specific qualities of representation.

Up to now, I have attempted to demonstrate how the video clip of 'Money Can't Buy It' volunteers various readings of the sound recording and video text. As I have already described, musical structures in the video are transposed into facial expressions which include the mouthing of words, eye movement and contact, head rotation, smiles and pouting. Through the synaesthetic imposition of these codes of representation, the viewer's sense of imagination soon exceeds the boundaries of the visual image (see Cook 1998). In other words, musical perception becomes shaped through visual imagery in a manner that enhances and even detracts from our experience of the music on its own (see Goodwin 1993a). Because there is always a relationship between musical codes and gesture, which, in the case of the pop song is manifested in the visual spectacle of the artist performing, we are left with multiple possibilities for interpreting musical data.

It seems to me that the *Totally Diva* promo video, with its nine clips, positions Lennox in the role of successful diva within a highly introspective, narcissistic and self-critical context. From the opening shots of the video of 'Money Can't Buy It', Lennox is positioned as the central focal point. Clasping a large bunch of bright yellow mimosa flowers, we can see her mannerisms are highly affected. With a clever use of mirror effects to create various juxtapositions of Lennox's face, the close-angle shots amplify her play on narcissism as she inverts the focus of her own gaze. One's first impression of this scene might be that the artist wants us to know that she has chosen to be characterised through specific codes that emphasise a conventional (and arguably patriarchal) positioning of femininity. Yet, quite the inverse of this occurs in the song's narrative as Lennox exercises her power through a no-nonsense characterisation of the narcissistic and successful self-made prima donna.

Throughout the video, Lennox parodies the spoilt, rich woman – the kind she claims who *supposedly* possesses *every kind of thing that money can buy*. For myself, this prompts two distinct readings. First, the portrayal of some fictional character, classically feminine, beautiful and greedy, aspiring to everything money can buy – there is clearly a satirical touch to this blatant construction. Second, the foregrounding of Lennox as she really wishes to portray herself – a self-reflexive character who, in 'reality', has become the rich, lonely, unhappy figure of economic empowerment.

In fact, the dominance of the pop star in such a traditional mode of representation tends to satirise the pop diva in all her glory. Yet, seen within the wider context of the video *Totally Diva,* we need to bear in mind that this constitutes only one of many constructions we are presented with. Significantly, in each video clip, Lennox positions herself within a broader range of identities which display her gender fluidity at a symbolic level. From this, the various representations of identity we witness in Lennox's act need to be evaluated in relation to the promotion of the star within the record industry. Goodwin has addressed this aspect closely by considering the functional role of stardom in music videos:

> ... the creation of character identities for pop stars provides a point of identification for the listener-spectator – a necessary one, given the lack of characterization or narrative depth in song lyrics ... the construction of star identities is central to the economics of the music industry ... Thus, stardom, while it may have varied meanings for the consumer, is always functional from the perspective of the music industry. [Goodwin 1993a: 103]

As Goodwin's observation insists, the focus rests as much on the function of stardom as on characterisation within the confines of a multiple text. In analysing star imagery in pop music, we therefore need to be alert to how the precise packaging and designing of album covers (in addition to video and other promotional material) reveals the specific codes of meaning in the creation of the actual genre.

And this returns me to the question of spectatorship. How does the artist construct varying levels of pleasure in the spectacle offered up? The depiction of Lennox on the CD cover of *Diva* and the video *Totally Diva* tends to fetishise the drag artist. Looking into the camera seductively, Lennox's face is framed within an elaborate, over-the-top, multi-coloured feather headpiece (Figure 4.1). On a number of counts her look sets out to challenge the hetero-normative gaze. By sporting such an overtly drag image, her imagery in this pose certainly invites varied readings. For example, does the striking image of

Figure 4.1   Annie Lennox on the *Diva* album cover

this pose parody Lennox as masquerader of the carnivalesque body, or does it rather, paradoxically, play on a blurring of identity in the form of what could pass as a male posturing as drag artist? The overall interpretation here could be one of distantiation, where the Subject sets out to keep femininity at a distance. This problematic position, as Sue-Ellen Case argues, 'offer[s] the female viewer a way to be the spectator of female roles while not remaining close to them … attaining the distance from them required to enter the psycho-analytic viewing space' (1993: 301). In masquerading, does Lennox set out to create a spectacle of herself *for herself* through *her* assimilation of drag culture?

From this it would seem that what Case describes as an 'excess of femininity', becomes visualised through Lennox's strategy of gender parading, something which bridges the gap between drag queen and classical femme. Here I would suggest that such representation becomes a series of masks for distancing the artist from the stifling side of gender binarism, and, thus, challenging the very definition of drag itself. In popular culture, displays of drag are made explicit through the fictionalised role-playing of the Bakhtinian carnivalesque body, especially in the guise of the transvestite look. In further theorising the unhinging of gender binarisms, it is significant that Case's vision of the active masquerading woman is one freed of 'biological determinism, elitist essentialism, and the heterosexist cleavage of sexual difference' (1993: 305). In breaking with the narratives of closure that, in Case's words, 'choke women to death', Lennox, in foregrounding her masquerade as a distancing strategy, appears to transform all the well-worn normative realities of gender into a dazzling semiotic play. This is framed by the imaginative space of the pop promo – a space where identity can easily be interpreted as queer.

Based upon a strategy of queering, it seems that Lennox dons the mask of the drag artist to blur the divide between her 'womanliness' and masquerade. This occurs through a cunning process of renegotiation. Yet, casting aside for a moment, the potency of the female artist in drag, there are implications here that are problematic. For imitation transports with it the meaning of the 'derivative' or 'copy' in order to confirm the original of itself. Particularly in gender imitation, simple inversions never, in reality, take place. Arguing the case for this, Butler maintains that drag should not be perceived as the appro-priation of a specific gender role because in actuality 'gender is not a perfor-mance that a prior subject elects to do' (1993: 314). Rather, because it is always performative, gender exists as an entity the subject sets out to articu-late. In other words, the reality-effect of gender practice is that it is a display of compulsory performance because, as Butler insists, 'acting out of line with heterosexual norms brings with it ostracism, punishment, and violence, not to mention the transgressive pleasures produced by those very prohibitions' (1993: 315). Thus, the problematics of Lennox's transgression are located in a logic of inversion where she replicates a femme role for the more androgynous role she knows her fans are familiar with. Intent in making her position crystal clear, Lennox sets out to emphasise her pose on the album cover. As a snap shot from the opening promo video of the song, 'Why', this image seems to brilliantly thematises the female diva bent on playing with drag in all her glory (Figure 4.1).

How then might we interpret the kind of identifications that Lennox presents us within her videos texts? I would suggest that multiple characterisations of her construction as diva are expressed through what Butler describes as a set of 'psychic identifications' (1993: 316). These identifications set out to destabilise any fixed notions of gender and sexuality. Seen in this light, Lennox's identification makes explicit the loss of some kind of identity. It may well be that the very categories of identity she produces are intended to disrupt the repetition of compulsory heterosexuality. Yet the effort to differentiate oneself from that by which one is formed is in reality impossible. In other words, the representations of fluid identification that Lennox actualises carry with them the confirmation of her own heteronormativity. Ultimately what appears to stylise Lennox's iconography most is a range of identifications whose imitation provide us with an insight into how the pop performer can structure and manipulate her own persona. Herein lies the teasing qualities attached to gesture and pose, which in turn are central to the experience of postmodern pop texts.

Indeed, it seems that Lennox's characterisation in 'Money Can't Buy It' posits an obvious strategy of irony which her fans can hardly miss. During the 1980s, she insisted that she did not want to appear as a 'girlie' singer wearing pretty dresses. And, as Gaar has pointed out, since the late 1970s Lennox consciously shaped her image in a way that set out to confront stereotypical notions of femininity, voicing her concern that videos should be used for more than just promotional purposes, and viewed as a channel for artistic expression (Gaar 1993: 329). Commenting on the construction of her androgynous look, Lennox has explained: 'I don't want to change sexual labels – I want to sidestep them, and to confound people a little bit with something fresher and less cliched' (quoted in Gaar 1993: 329).

Interestingly, the obvious displays of gender-bending can also be bypassed in 'Money Can't Buy It' as Lennox shrewdly masquerades the character she seeks to reject. And here we can read the core of her ironic intent. With reference to the employment of her femininity in the video 'Money Can't Buy It', set against the drag-like representation on the *Diva* album cover, her look becomes part of an intentional statement of masquerade and sexual mobility. In my view, the greatest achievement in this performative positioning rests in the transient quality of Lennox's femininity – a construction that embodies and affirms a sense of Otherness by parodic practice.

As if forcibly denunciating the patriarchal control of women by the music industry, Lennox draws on a range of counternarratives that empower her

personalised politics of expression. This is particularly evident in the construction of the pretty-girl image in the video clip magnified by the 'little-girl'
vocal timbres in Section C of 'Money Can't Buy It' (see Table 4.2), all of
which evoke impersonations of a more standardised, conventional and safe
femininity (read: non-threatening). Yet, such visual references also set up a
confrontational rhetoric of seduction through the flaunting of femininity to an
excessive degree.

Of course the ambiguity of such codes are bound to prompt far-reaching
reactions. Lennox's fetishised image might well be perceived to be confusing
while at the same time exhilarating and challenging. Male sexual fantasy,
female empowerment, and erotic desire surface as the prime constituents of an
idiom that taunts the gaze. And it is through the mix of our responses to this
aspect of performance that the politics of power and pleasure are received or
rejected in pop songs. Thus, encoded through the range of her musical ideas,
Lennox's power of expression is situated within a carefully regulated style that
draws upon the cultural resources of her identity.[11]

Returning then to my introductory point in this section, the significance of
musical expression in videos needs to be understood in relation to the social,
cultural and political dimension of the artist's address. That aesthetic responses
extend to the impact of the performer's body in pop texts grounds the possibilities of representation we are faced with when experiencing the links between
music and identity.

Conclusion

During this chapter I have attempted to problematise a number of issues
concerning the characteristics of female address and the nuances of *jouissance*
afforded by performance in pop videos. In concluding, it seems that the
different displays of identity in Lennox's texts are integral to our negotiating
musical signification. For the practice of deciphering sound ultimately relies
on readings from a variety of perspectives. In 'Money Can't Buy It', Lennox
offers us a critique on the prevailing ideal of pop for many – getting rich and
famous as quickly as possible in order to gain freedom and empowerment –
all of which is made clear through the song's cynical narrative and its glossy
musical production. Certainly for a generation of artists (and many of their
fans) intent on high financial returns, the message of the song could not be
more explicit.

Without entering into the well worn debates of economic determinism in
popular music studies – others have laboured this point frequently – it is worth
bearing in mind that 'Money Can't Buy It' has a clichéd, albeit relevant, moral
overtone. In an overt way, the song serves as a sober reminder that while
money might purport to buy everything – one of the most ubiquitous sentiments

in commercial pop songs – it cannot ever achieve this. Obviously this is a hackneyed theme that runs through decades of pop songs, and one which Lennox decides to bring to light in an introspective video that portrays herself as disenchanted by all she has achieved.

Yet, by confronting the glaring truth of greed, hedonism and loneliness, this pop diva seeks to inform her fans, as much as the industry, that she is intent on survival and making it as a solo artist. Very much like Madonna, she longs to escape the confines of socially defined gendered identity by journeying into a world of unlimited guises and masks. Generally one has the impression that Lennox goes out of her way to control the gaze of the viewer to her advantage. And this is most borne out by her spectacular manoeuvres of masquerade that seductively entice us into a visual space where gender constructions are playful. The visual text, however, cannot alone construct identities or spectator positions – music plays a most vital role in this process in countless ways, as I have argued.

Ultimately it is through the production and performance of musical texts that we are reminded that pop offers us wide-open opportunities for self-identification. The values encoded by the aesthetics of 'Money Can't Buy It' – slickness, gloss, sentimentality, playfulness – operate simultaneously with an ideology that celebrates and confers distinctions in identity. In this regard, Annie Lennox, as a white, Western, proponent of the Anglo-American music industry, functions as a symbolic and highly provocative construction for the changes facing the female pop figure in the music industry during the 1980s and 1990s.

Acknowledgements

The main part of this chapter first appeared as 'Perspectives in popular musicology: music, Lennox and meaning in 1990s pop' in *Popular Music*, 15/1, eds Lucy Green and David Laing. I would like to thank Cambridge University Press for their assistance in the editing of this article and for two of the examples I have used in this chapter. Very helpful feedback in the revision of this chapter was provided by John Richardson, Derek Scott and Anne Danielsen.

Notes

1   In the video of the song, 'Love is a Stranger', for example, levels of gender transgression are exceptionally visible. In fact, the sight of Lennox playing around with male and female roles and blurring rigid gender divides led to this video being banned on cable television.

2   Note that for female artists in the 1980s, such as Cyndi Lauper, Madonna, k.d. lang,

Sade, Joan Armatrading and Queen Latifah, respect was a major issue given the perpetuation of stereotypes in mainstream pop. The autonomy and control of these artists contrasts sharply with that of the more mainstream representation of female superstars such as Whitney Houston, Mariah Carey and Janet Jackson.

3   With the name, Eurythmics, according to Stewart, the band was exactly what they wanted to be seen as 'European' and 'rhythmic'.

4   For two of the best problematisations of music analysis, with reference to approaching harmony and its application to Western forms of music from both a musicological and sociological perspective respectively, see McClary (1991) and Frith (1996). Also see Everett (2000) for a broad range of music analytical essays that deal with the relevance of harmonic and pitch-based analysis in pop and rock texts. Throughout this collection, convincing yet problematic arguments are linked to the reductive approach to harmonic and pitch analysis in popular music.

5   On this issue, Shepherd (1987) has identified how male and female timbres, hard and soft, evoke specific readings and responses of gender in pop music. In Lennox's music, however, the issue of reading 'female' timbres would appear more complex than Shepherd's rather essentialist approach suggests.

6   My friend John Richardson has contributed the relevant point that the outrageous virtuosity of Lennox's voice functions as a highly gendered form of transgression. In a sense, Lennox's voice is not dissimilar to that of Joni Mitchell's in terms of its virtuosic charge and sheer excess.

7   I borrow the term *Klangfarben* from *Klangfarbenmelodie* as suggested by Schoenberg in his *Harmonielehre* (1911), to relate directly to timbre as a structural element with equal importance as pitch, duration and rhythm. Directly translated into English this term would be 'sound-colour'.

8   Nicholas Cook (1998: 57–97) makes a useful study of this feature and theorises on the various ways in which music embodies movement. He concentrates especially on forms of kinesis that correspond to the relationships between the combination of musical structures with other elements. In addition his identification of a kinesis of genre and kinesis of structural processing provide models for analysing the associations of music with movement.

9   Also see Alf Björnberg's video studies (1993, 1994) into the structural relationships between music and image in commercial pop.

10   I have taken my formulation of performativity throughout this book from the work of feminist theorists, such as Judith Butler, who have been influenced by de Beauvoir, Bourdieu, Foucault, Lacan and Derrida. That gender can be performative implies that the body has no ontological state besides the acts and events that structure its reality. When considered as performative, gender is a dramatic construction – a project that has a cultural strategy as its means. Hence, the action of sexuality and gender is produced through a stylisation of the body as a performative achievement through which an audience can begin to believe in this as a norm. My own position on this is: that notions of gender credibility can be sustained through the repetition of video performances, and thus form part of a strategy that reveals the performative character of gender. But, performativity can never be a single entity as it is a ritual that is of temporal duration, achieving its effect within the context of the body. While the debates surrounding performativity call mainly into question gender, the status of performative construction through other elements of identity, such as race, should not be treated simply as analogies to one another. And, as Butler insists time and time again, no single accounts of construction are acceptable because multiple categories of identity always find their articulation through one another. See Butler (1999): vii–xvi.

11 By tapping into the new pop synth-based aesthetic of the 1980s, her musical influences are also wide ranging. As well as a strong rock base to her sound, the influence of African-American styles are prevalent in her work, especially in the forms of soul and Motown.

Chapter 5
'Call it Performance, Honey': The Pet Shop Boys

Introduction

'For me, being in the Pet Shop Boys has always been a struggle between total embarrassment and total shamelessness,' said Neil Tennant in his coming-out interview with Paul Burston in 1994.[1] Cool, ironic, and very camp, the Pet Shop Boys have always presented themselves as shamelessly English and, according to them, completely misunderstood, which partly accounts for their appeal and success as mainstream pop stars from the mid-1980s onwards. Endeavouring to understand the Pet Shop Boys is a useful continuation in our evaluation of the links between music and identity within pop texts. 'Obviously, people are going to look at our songs and read things into them.'[2] lamented Tennant in the same interview. But, it is precisely the process of how we read things into songs at many levels that interests me. Through the very artifice that constructs pop texts, these artists remind us that music is a key vehicle for constructing identity in everyday life. I am therefore concerned with interpreting the relationship between the music of the Pet Shop Boys and their identity and exploring how this offers a pathway into problematising the implications of performance practice in synth-based pop.

This chapter also takes into consideration the issue of authorship alongside the questions of reflexive display in musical performance. As I have set out to demonstrate so far in the case studies of Madonna, Lennox and Morrissey, the fan's personal identification with the artist can elicit feelings of disclosure through musical expression, an important process in the decoding of pop texts. In the various styles of performance we have examined so far, creative practice is entwined with a sense of agency that is mediated through the medium of the production. Moreover, the communication of songs and authorship via media and music technology is a process that emphasises the historical shifts in the music industry.

It was an agreement in 1981 between musical instrument manufacturers, such as Yamaha and Roland, for a common Musical Instrument Digital Interface – MIDI – that probably represented the most momentous phase in music-making during the last two decades of the twentieth century. Musicians became programmers of musical-event information that could digitally link any number of machines of different makes. The fusion between programmer and musician would become manifested in all sequenced pop tracks where the step-time programming of musical events through electronic commands were congruent with formal and aesthetic characteristics. In many ways the dedicated synthesiser revolutionised the dexterity of keyboardists as step-time programming enabled the recording of events in new ways. Most significantly MIDI-based approaches to composition eradicated any distinction between technician and musician. Crucially, this flexible apparatus of musical production reshaped the music industry as the user-friendly and low-cost MIDI set-ups marked a change in the direction of music-making (Kempster 1996; Theberge 1997; Rietveld 1998; Toynbee 2000). Producing and programming music soon took on new forms with the performer engaged and reimagined in different ways. The impact of this can be traced through the developments in dance music and commercial pop artists, such as the Pet Shop Boys.

Rapidly, post-disco British dance music spread out in many directions in the mid- to late 1980s, instigated by the adaptation of black American styles originating in Detroit techno and Chicago house. Almost instantly, DJ culture had a direct impact on commercial pop forms, not least in its influence on stylistic change and ideology (see Langlois 1992). From this point on, the ingredients of dance music would feed into the tracks of countless commercial artists, such as the Pet Shop Boys, whose output over a span of twenty years encapsulates the advances of musical production. For all this, their texts occupy a sonic landscape that embraces the interrelationships between gendered identity, stylistic progress, and technology in many exciting ways.

What emerges during this survey is the recognition of how musical expression intersects with details of representation found in the body and gender. A key point to surface from examining the repressed nature of the Pet Shop Boys' delivery is that their performance style introduces elements that are attached to many different sites. Above all, their identity is disseminated through a myriad of somatic properties of musical style that can be charged for sexing the groove and getting us onto the dance floor. In this sense, we could say that the pleasure derived from the Pet Shop Boys' texts is modelled by the seductive nature of their sound, not least the danceability of their grooves.

I am particularly interested to explore in this chapter the general changes in the position of masculinity in the 1980s and 1990s which can be traced through pop texts. What has always struck me about the Pet Shop Boys is the plurality of meaning articulated through the diversification of their expression. Situated within an English context, their style has been characterised by a sultry camp sensibility common within the British marketplace. The reception of this indeed raises questions as to how these pop artists have captured the essence of the changes in masculinity in the 1980s and 1990s, and the extent to which their songs have offered up new possibilities for constructing discourses of meaning. How then might a critical approach to the Pet Shop Boys serve to enhance our awareness of sets of differences in style and identity?

Indeed, to initiate such an inquiry, it is necessary to search beyond the formalist restrictions of musical coding to explore how their musical processes are communicated. One of the central arguments here is that to interpret pop music we need to enquire into the nature of musical rhetoric as inferred by the various 'voices' inherent in the pop text. Underpinning such a premise is the need to challenge the binarisms that have historically categorised gender and sexuality by 'revealing that they are not in fact symmetrical' (Solie 1993: 19). Again this returns us to the numerous useful studies engaged in gender identification within musicological scholarship.[3] Starting in the 1970s, the broader debates of feminism finally filtered into many of the discourses conjoined to popular musicology in the late 1980s (see Chapter 1). Importantly, music feminism helped expose the necessity for disclosing the pluralities in the representation of the body and its modalities of desire through music and dance. In this respect, not only have concepts of gender-transgression in musicology been approached as an outgrowth of feminist theory, as we have seen in Chapter 4, but the complex forces of male identity, in terms of its categorical inversions, have absorbed much critical attention.

For scholars involved in feminist and mens' studies, the exploration of sexual ambiguity has inevitably illuminated problems in normative ideals of masculinity. And, in the broader field of popular music, scholars have begun to acknowledge the extent to which musical style impinges on gendered expression. The serious engagement with subjectivity is already evident in studies by a number of male musicologists, who have accessed the musical text from a variety of perspectives by closing in on rhetorical modes of address that are linked to gender and the body.[4]

In appending the question of male identity to the aims of textual analysis in pop music, two points for consideration stand out. The first concerns the developments in the politics of representation that have influenced stylistic expression – I will take the case of the Pet Shop Boys to demonstrate how the ambiguity inherent in their musical codes defines their subjectivity. The second point concerns the communicative possibilities of synthesiser-oriented pop and its arguably artificial mode of address. By the same token, the politics of artistic identity lead straight to questions of authenticity and authorship (Grossberg 1987, 1992). Of course the commodification of the pop star produces a critique inextricably bound up in authenticity. As I argue in this chapter, this point is central to theorising the question of performance alongside identity.

The discussion that follows therefore attempts to tackle these issues by exploring how the Pet Shop Boys' identity is played out in a variety of ways. In one sense, defining their identity can be seen as a mechanism for contesting authorship in popular songs. Obviously, the connection between the songwriter and listener varies considerably, depending on both listening competence and listening situations. Moreover, it seems that all facets of our identity shape our subject positions as listeners. In other words, they are influenced by the attitudes that imply that a type of 'multiple listening' stance exists, something that is always endemic in the experience of music (Brackett 1995: 22-23).[5] In terms of the connection between musical text and social context, I would suggest that pop texts such as the Pet Shop Boys' songs invoke discourses that revolve around a whole range of cultural and political inflections. This chapter then explores how working out the organisation of musical structures and evaluating them aesthetically can contribute to our understanding of other texts. The basis for my readings is to indicate the importance of the homologies that exist between types of musical rhetoric and identity, which, in the end, help to account for the Pet Shop Boys' popularity.

Masculinity in the 1980s

It was from a distinctly postmodern English culture that the Pet Shop Boys[6] emerged during the mid-1980s in the aftermath of the British New Pop scene, 1981–83 (Straw 1993). Having met in a music shop on Kings Road in London in 1981, Neil Tennant and Chris Lowe started working together on writing pop songs. But it was in New York that the HiNRG[7] producer Bobby 'O' Orlando would produce their first hit single, 'West End Girls'. Until March 1985, the Pet Shop Boys held a contract with Bobby 'O' who played an influential part in launching their rise to fame. Somewhat paradoxically, it was only after cutting their ties with Orlando and signing up to EMI that 'West End Girls' became a top hit in the USA and Europe, rocketing them to fame.[8]

Right from the beginning, these English dandies thrived on a certain ambiguity, one of their most distinctive features that contributed to their popularity. If we locate this historically, it was during the 1980s when masculinity underwent significant changes that there was a 'rush and a push in English Style Culture ... to make dandyism and technology the pop accessories for the end of time' (Bracewell 1998: 206). And, as the Pet Shop Boys were making their name, the new male in the UK was being rapidly accessed and 'getting an airing at the popular end of the market' (Mort 1988: 202).

Increasingly, fashion became more popularised for males and blurred in its gender-orientation: Gaultier drew on street style and gay culture, Next was launched, Nick Kamen stripped down to his boxer shorts in a launderette for the famous Levis ad, *Arena* became an outlet for male hedonism, and the marketplace boomed with young male consumers. Frank Mort describes the new bricolage of masculinity to emerge in Britain during the 1980s:

> Images of affluence, the first teenagers, rock 'n' roll, are handled with a distinctly 80s sensibility. The Levis ads were a tongue in cheek parody of 50s style. Young men in launderettes – not a common sight then in Britain or the

US! Mean and moody looks on inner-city streetscapes reference, albeit in sani-
tized and glamorized form, unemployment, making one's way in a world in
which the young – and now unusually young men – are short on the crucial
element it takes to get by in a capitalist society – money. They have only their
looks, their style, their bodies to display and sell. These are the cultural images
framed both by recession and by the more fluid sexual scripts of the 80s, rather
than 50s affluence and tight gender roles. [Mort 1988: 199, 201]

From Mort's above account, we are reminded that the cultural politics of the
marketplace form crucial narratives on identity within any specific period of
social development. But, not only changes in the representation of male
identity should be accounted for in this case, but also the causes for it.

Deeply rooted in Thatcherism and Tory popular capitalism, materialistic
consumption in the 1980s was hegemonically foisted on the population with
'an orgy of tax cuts and consumer durables' (Mort 1988: 215). Furthermore,
the Thatcher decades of political struggle were underpinned by a powerful
right-wing, think-tank that was situated outside the predominantly left intellectual establishment. At the same time, free-market policies gave rise to a boom
in media publishing, leading to a form of journalism that elevated 'individual
opinion to the level of social commentary'. Equipped with 'the power of the
anecdote', newspaper columnists translated 'the prejudices of politicians into
the commonplace of daily discourse' thus providing their readers with a sense
of community (Frith and Savage 1997: 11–12). Under such circumstances, it
seemed as if the columnist's job was to save readers from thought rather than
make them think.

Within such a social setting, a politically ambiguous sensibility emerged in
English pop as artists and groups were critiqued 'at both ends of the political
spectrum' (Bracewell 1998: 208). And, it is worth bearing in mind that the
new breed of pop stars to emerge in the 1980s were commodified through the
bombardment of media technology into an aesthetic which was constructed
around fluid constructions of identity. From such a turbulent environment of
social disruption, the songs of the Pet Shop Boys emerged. Expressing a kind
of defiance, they distanced themselves from authority by ironic detachment.
By rejecting the overt sentimentality found in more serious popular styles, they
opted to pursue an escape route out of punk into a rejuvenated strain of disco.
Their songs thus signalled texts of understatement, disguising any sense of
emotion through the most nonchalant, camped-up delivery imaginable.

Accepting that the thrill of music is wrapped up in the exploration of
identities, positioned not only in proximity but also at a distance from our
own, the pursuit of escapism and pleasure in pop music is about rediscovering,
rejecting or even reconstituting personal concepts of identity. Now it was
through a distinctly ironic attitude that the Pet Shop Boys appealed to the in-
groups of a wider community.[9] This duo also offered up new readings of
masculinity within a cultural context where the politics of the image were

steadily substituted for reality. And, into the 1990s, the Pet Shop Boys, like Steven Morrissey, continued to satirise what their identity meant to them and their community.

Ever since the early 1980s, when the eroticisation of the male body within popular culture moved gay erotica[10] into the mainstream marketplace, pop music has exhibited an array of disparate and conflicting localised narratives. Historically, this needs to be measured against the normative representations of males in rock of the 1960s and 1970s, where phallic imagery and sexist lyrics constituted a main part of its expression (Frith and McRobbie 1978/9; Shuker 1994; Whiteley 2000).[11]

Again it is important to emphasise that in the New Pop mainstream of the 1980s, notions of difference functioned effectively alongside the generation of new electronic musical equipment and the production culture which emerged. In a sense, the unlikely fusion of HiNRG disco with the serious, impassive, lyrical lines of the Pet Shop Boys' songs established a rhetoric that was often self-parodic and indifferent. Notably, in their first videos the image collided with the musical event, which, when interpreted as an element of playfulness could be seen to function as subversive. In the video of the song 'Domino Dancing', for example, nuance and connotation underlie the intentions of the narrative.

The sequences throughout this video position a romantic narrative at the centre, with the concentration on the boyfriend/girlfriend scenario occupying the main focus of attention. A beautiful Mediterranean girl occupies a foreground position in the visual narrative, with two boys fighting over her for love. However, as the sequences progress, the camera becomes more engaged with the two boys, who finally end up jostling with one another in the sea, stripped to the waists wearing tight-fitting jeans. The girl is left alone as onlooker, while the two boys are shot wrestling and falling numerous times into the water. However, they never quite fall down, as the camera cuts and repeats the sequence four times. Interjected with this narrative are scenes of dancing taking place in a club, again with both boys competing to dance with the girl. A reading of the video 'Domino Dancing' takes place on at least two levels: one, a heterosexual narrative of romance, sun, love, beautiful young people, idyllic surroundings, images of healthy bodies, all of which articulate a straightforward narrative. However, a second queer reading exposes a more subtle interpretation of where the focus of the gaze centres. Here, both the compelling homoerotic visual and lyrical narratives contest love 'of a different kind'.

Considering the second point in more detail, I wish to turn to Ian Balfour's reading (1991) of this video which emphasises the camera's insistence in watching two half-naked men fall into each other's arms in the closing frames. Notably MTV refused to show the video without editing the ending. Importantly, Balfour's interpretation opens up the space for inspecting aspects of queer identification within a social context. As his reading reveals, marginalised identities exist as sites of receptive openness that oscillate between straight and gay. In this sense, reading the text as queer certainly need not be perceived as gender specific (Butler 1990; Case 1991), as pleasures are often located in overlapping social spaces of reception. Understood in this way, the cultural reception of pop videos extends far beyond the essentialist confines of everyday definitions of sexual identity.

Another point worth considering here is that while queer readings can include a wide range of responses outside the essentialist categorisation of identity, they should not necessarily be positioned as alternative or wishful misreadings. Alexander Doty's position on this underlines the point that queer readings 'result from the recognition and articulation of the complex range of queerness that has been in popular culture texts and their audiences all along' (Doty 1993: 16). Arguably, the mobile trajectories of queering operate in destabilising further what is already an uncertain domain. And, in terms of musical expression, it is the Pet Shop Boys' disco riffs, with superimposed simple tunes on synthesizers that help capture the romantic frankness and exuberance of the expression in 'Domino Dancing'.

Constructed around the lyrics *All day, all day, watch them all fall down, Domino Dancing*, the chorus section consists of a descending broken minor seventh chord, symbolic of the 'falling down' reference in the lyrics (see Example 5.1). Interest also centres on a Latin-style chordal riff in the piano part, as well as a typical 1970s disco two-bar riff that is an embellishment of the first three notes of the chorus. Characterised by the falling and rising motion of a perfect fourth and fifth, this 'disco' riff functions as a unifying thread as it weaves in and out of the mix. As a distinctive feature in the song, this riff forms one of the various layers of the mix. And, in addition to functioning melodically, it also contributes to the harmonic, textural and rhythmic fabric of the song.

Shrouded in nuance and connotation, 'Domino Dancing' is just one in a series of songs that registered the Pet Shop Boys' sentiments on AIDS. Repressed emotions of shock, anxiety and pain at having to deal with the death of friends by AIDS are emphasised by the relentless repetition of the song's hook, which functions as a metaphor for dancing with danger before falling down in domino-like fashion. Yet, such metaphorical representation in the lyrical address is set against the blissful, escapist, party-time musical texts, thus constituting one of the most compelling forces inscribed in the Pet Shop Boys' songs.

My argument through this interpretation is that the poetic scope of their lyrical content should not be taken lightly even when '[t]heir bland insouciance seduces us with the promise of low-risk disco'. For all along, we are confronted with a sense of social commentary in 'Domino Dancing' as the beat functions as the disciplinary baton, with the bass lines 'sheathed and numbed by a prophylactic irony' (Hughes 1994: 155). The song's intertexts

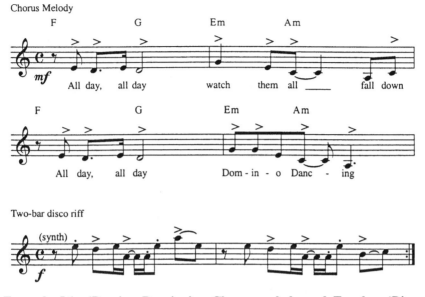

Example 5.1   'Domino Dancing' – Chorus melody and Two-bar 'Disco riff' fill

provoke the communicative act of playing off one meaning against the other. In the end, it is the interplay of an array of meanings – kitsch Mediterranean sun-drenched package holidays, ambiguous sexual desires, AIDS, blissful disco, homoeroticism – that provide this video with both its critical edge and ironic charge.

If we accept that it is the relationship between contextual and textual markers that delineates meaning, the overarching issue here is one of under-standing how communication and reception involve a range of interlinking dialogues. Clearly contextual overtones determine the aesthetics of musical expression, especially when it comes to receiving humour in musical dialogics (Bakhtin 1981). For example, in flouting the conventions of live performance, by not playing or singing in a traditional manner, the Pet Shop Boys manage to introduce elements of parody into their texts that challenge the conception of sex roles and modes of address. To consider the wider implications of this, let us turn to the question of mannerism and attitude.

Constraint gestures within fashionable oversize suits, stylish jackets and designer clothes soon became the cool trademark of the unsmiling Pet Shop Boys by the mid-1980s; a sullenness in attitude blending with the new face of the 1980s man, irrespective of sexual orientation. Through the 1980s into the 1990s, a camp sensibility emerged as part of the acceptable face of mainstream pop, with new mannerisms and gestures all becoming 'part of the repertoire'

(Mort 1988: 205). In fact, the art of being cool in 1980s UK pop was certainly not about looking straight in a 'normative' manner.

In this regard, narcissism had started to dominate the urban male's perception of himself in no way more visible than through the emergence of the New Romantic pop artist of the early 1980s. Sophisticated patterns in marketing became responsible for inducing significant changes in gender roles, as shopping steadily became a recreational pastime rather than merely a household chore. In broader terms, by the 1980s shopping had become as much part of the male's domain as the female's (see Chapman 1988). Indeed what seemed pertinent to much pop music during this period of hyper-consumerism was that gender stereotypes ceased to function as the prime transmitters of ideology.

Clearly the task of debating issues of gender ideology in pop texts is not without its difficulties. On this matter, Chapman has discussed how an uneasiness crept into society with the transformations in masculinity aligned to new trends in advertising:

> With its emphasis on artifice, on style over content, it caused a fragmentation in the image that the new man presented to the world. A narcissistic interpretation of the new man, with its stress upon style and personal consumption, could more easily and more usefully be assimilated into the prevailing consumerist ethos. [Chapman 1988: 230]

The effects of this, as explored by Chapman, led to the fragmented identity of the 1980s male, which consisted of an amalgamation of conflicting historic traditions. An emphasis on hedonism, extravagant consumption and fashionable lifestyle through the countless channels of advertising undoubtedly affected constructs of identity in Western society in the last decades of the twentieth century. Yet, within this same historic period it is important to recall that a certain ambivalence had started to permeate English culture, as the politically correct man learnt to modify, if not conceal, his attitudes.

Naturally this helps flag up the changes in male attitude during the 1980s and how these might be attributed to processes of modification rather than as a resistance to patriarchy. From a cultural perspective, theorists have regarded the postmodern male as having evolved into a more slippery creature still fully in control of all structures of social and political power (see Moore 1988). In this connection, Chapman observes the new male as a 'patriarchal mutation, a redefinition of masculinity in men's favour' (Chapman 1988: 247), still grounded in assertions of physiological difference. While a flaw in her argument might be a leaning towards biological deterministic readings, Chapman's studies are useful for assessing a range of contradictions inherent within a 1980s social climate. This indeed becomes relevant when examining the rhetoric of male-performed pop texts as they either withstand or challenge ideological change.

Being boring and clever: style as rhetoric

> This, too, was the age of clever pop, from Paul Morley's wittily intellectual sleeve notes to Frankie Goes To Hollywood's *Welcome to the Pleasure Dome* LP, through to Scritti Politti's breathy pop song 'Jacques Derrida' and the lyrically nimble and authorially self-aware songs from Prefab Sprout and Momus. Posing as makers of commercially-minded perfect pop, the sub-textual cleverness of Nick Currie (aka Momus), Paddy McAloon (of Prefab Sprout) or Green Gartside (of Scritti Politti) was both whimsical and knowing, suggesting a tertiary-educated sensibility that was equally related to the techniques of literary composition and the manipulation of pop glamour. [Bracewell 1998: 215]

During the last decades of the twentieth century a clever breed of English pop was produced by the 'metaphysical poets of early middle-age' (Bracewell 1998: 215) whose cynicism was matched by a voracious self-obsession. Fitting into this framework, the Pet Shop Boys' music articulated a distinctly English rhetoric whose irony appealed to the tastes of an increasingly varied mainstream popular culture.

Notions of sincerity and ironic reflexivity often seem at odds with the simplicity, superficiality and accessibility of the Pet Shop Boys' music. On closer inspection, what stands out is an intricate blend of social politics that functions as a main transmitter of musical style. Monotonous and void of dynamic colour, the act of playing out 'being boring' vividly captures not only the cynicism and despondency but also the coolness in attitude of a generation living through the Thatcher years. In this way, the authority of the Pet Shop Boys' texts underlies a political intent, which unmasks preconceptions of identity.

As with many pop artists of the day, they wielded power to different ends. Marketed on a packaging of male identity skilfully confounded by an embarrassed-looking, grey, sulky image, they resorted to satire. And, connected to an English obsession with class and rigid gender classification, their narratives elicited a broad range of responses that played on conflicting messages. For instance, while an openness to claiming love of an alternative nature might have been apparent to some through their texts, their narratives remained intentionally ambivalent.[12] Commenting on this frankly, Neil Tennant has linked their music to a broader understanding of sexual expression: 'Our music is, and always has been, fuelled by a strong sexual undertow. Pop music is partially about sex. The two things can't be divorced.'[13] What emerges from this statement and others is a particular attitude that (un)comfortably blends into a postmodern discourse.

Interpretations borne out of musical sound, lyrics, production techniques and visual images, however, are ultimately constructed around the identities and experiences of the fans themselves. This means that the pleasure and power located in the 'sexual undertow' that Tennant refers to can never be rendered fixed; everything is left open for negotiation, redefinition and reinterpretation. Of course, differences in the paradigms of sexual articulation have always been inherent in pop music, and while the sombre and pensive mood of their lyrics might appear heartfelt, the wit and ironic ambiguity of the HiNRG, euphoric musical charge of their songs functions as an effective strategy of sexual oppositionality.[14]

In an interview appearing in *Out* in 1993, Tennant was keen to acknowledge the strong gay subtext of their work, while he nevertheless felt obliged to emphasise that they have always disliked being categorised. Relating this to features of creativity (note, rather than marketing), he explained that 'when you do anything creative, you give away of yourself what you want to give away.'[15] Understandably, such guarded comments have evoked sharp attacks from scholars and journalists in the gay community, who have refuted the Pet Shop Boys' cautious stance. Arguably, in the wake of gay pop groups, such as Frankie Goes to Hollywood, the Communards, Soft Cell, Bronski Beat, Culture Club and Erasure, which enjoyed immense popularity in the 1980s, many have felt that the Pet Shop Boys had no cause to conceal their sexual orientation. Whatever their reasons for holding back what they might not wish to give away may be, John Gill (1995) is unprepared to buy any of this. In his book *Queer Noises*, he sets about questioning their motives for so-called discretion by exploring the issue of identity:

> The Pet Shop Boys may fall short of Coward's wit and sophistication, but they very much fit the bourgeois English tradition of discreet perversion and collusion with the establishment. The Pet Shop Boys may give a lot of money to AIDS charities, but they also feel an overwhelming need to keep quiet about it. This may be modesty, for they distrust the ostentatious compassion of Live Aid and other such charity events. But this modesty, if modesty it really is, has become a hostage to their refusal to make a simple statement about their sexuality. [Gill 1995: 9]

Gill contends that the Pet Shop Boys represent a new type of post-Thatcher conservatism through the compromising stance they take with respect to their sexuality. Yet, what Gill does not acknowledge directly is that in pop music it is such a contrived construction of modesty and sincerity that builds up the popularity of artists. This would explain why rather than having a marginalising effect, the appropriation of codes of sexual difference often transports gay culture into the centre of mainstream pop for access by all its fans. Undoubtedly, the merits of this strategy are contentious not least when it comes to the question of marketing constructs of gender and sexuality. For such a duo then, it was hardly surprising that the song that launched them, reaching Number 1 worldwide in 1986, was entitled 'West End Girls'.[16]

Banality: political discourses of pleasure and power

> They also did something unthinkable: they wedded the euphoric sound of gay disco to lyrics which sounded very serious. Before the Pet Shop Boys, disco records were noted for the vacuity of their lyrics. In many instances, the words provided little more than verbal echoes to the all-important beat. The Pet Shop Boys were keen on the beat too, but they weren't prepared to surrender everything to it. Even now, it is hard to imagine Neil Tennant ever completely surrendering himself to a typical disco lyric like, 'oooh, love to love you baby'. For one thing, it's too passionate.[17]

This above account helps explain why, having heard it just once on the radio, Frith, like other intellectual pop fans, rushed out to buy the record of 'West End Girls' which became the first British Number 1 of that year. He describes their effect on him in 1986:

> [The] Pet Shop Boys are, after all, just another British pop group, showroom dummies with electronic equipment and a memory bank of old club and disco riffs. There are hundreds of duos like this. Pretty packages, synthetic centres, they roll off record company assembly lines like new sweets from a candy factory. What makes Pet Shop Boys special is their sense of tacky drama. [Frith 1988: 146]

Frith's first impression of the Pet Shop Boys is revealing, as he concentrates on the role of drama and packaging in transmitting an array of social signifiers. For me though, the prime source of pleasure is derived from a lot more than just this. It is especially their musical reworking of old club and disco riffs through banal features, such as easily memorable melodies, simple chord progressions, overkill glittering orchestral arrangements, catchy bass lines and flirtatious rhythmic and lyrical hooks that really capture the thrill in their expression.

Asked on one occasion whether their material was just fun music, Tennant acknowledged '[i]t *masquerades* as good time party music.'[18] Undoubtedly, into the late twentieth century, dance culture, and the technological innovations that go with it, have had a major influence on the emergence of their style. Openly, Chris Lowe has stated that their aim has always been to write songs that reference a contemporary dance context. And over the past ten years, their material has served to document substantially some of the main trends in dance music as well as music production.

Searching for musical meaning in the Pet Shop Boys therefore involves an enquiry into how emotions of pleasure, desire and enjoyment convert into the urge to dance. One of my aims here is to demonstrate how the compositional features of their songs form the basis for working out their texts. To pursue this, let us take a look at the song, 'Yesterday, when I was mad', off the *Very* album.

Opening with a catchy cross-rhythmic (duple vs. triple) riff in a compound duple metre, the groove provides the main driving force behind this song. Picking up speed, this riff converts suddenly into a straight, quadruple HiNRG groove, enhanced by the entry of more percussion samples. Characteristic of most dance music, the hi-hats are foregrounded in the mix, with the bass parts accenting each main beat. Heightening the anticipated entry of the lyrics, this introduction passage firmly establishes an upbeat feel.

The lyrics of 'Yesterday, when I was mad' air numerous sentiments, in particular the frustrations of being famous and constantly in the public eye. Nostalgia, insincerity, regret, loneliness and anger are just some of the feelings wrapped up in the song, with the chorus hook, *yesterday, when I was mad and quite prepared to give up everything, admitting I don't believe in anyone's sincerity*, preceded by a sweeping synthesised string glissando, consisting of a memorable chorus repeated gratuitously (see Example 5.2). While the narrative of the song wallows in a wave of self-pity, and, as Tony Mitchell puts it,

Example 5.2   'Yesterday, when I was mad' – chorus hook

'laments an absence of sincerity' (Mitchell 1996: 18), the music is charged with energised house riffs, cushioned by easy harmonic progressions (I-III-VI-V-I-IV-V in the chorus) and simple melodic tunes. Despite the simplicity of the chord progressions and the chorus melody, it is significant that the song never resolves in a traditional manner. Instead, the last chord, B♭ major, subdominant of the home key F dorian, denies any such teleological outcome.[19]

For the more traditionally minded music scholar, it is quite possible that songs, such as 'Yesterday, when I was mad' might signify little more than a retreat into banality in terms of musical simplicity and blandness. For example, the vocal delivery might seem unassuming, introspective and boring, the melodies, harmonies and rhythms, trivial, with the synthetic effect of the production and instrumentation holding little interest whatsoever. But simplicity and banality in pop texts should not be underestimated. Robert Walser makes this clear when he emphasises the point that popular musicians often invest great craftsmanship to produce material which conveys a high degree of simplicity: 'The musical construction of simplicity plays an important part in many kinds of ideological representations, from the depiction of pastoral refuges from modernity to constructions of race and gender' (Walser 1993b: 128).

Functioning as an integral feature of the Pet Shop Boys' music, banality is contingent on its grasp amongst a range of intersecting social, political and sexual subject positions. In fact, musical banality functions to underpin the inference of irony. And, incontestably predicated on a sense of musical understatement, the Pet Shop Boys' style emerges in a variety of interesting and clever ways. To expound on this, I want to discuss four musical parameters – rhythm, vocal style, tunes and production.

Rhythm tracks

Implicit within all their songs, the rhythm tracks articulate an array of compelling grooves articulated by the expert programming of kit and percussion samples. By activating somatic responses, the grooves heighten the levels of desire to escape through music. Blissful rushes of rhythmic gestures, exchanges of meaning via the beat, communicate the discursive power of their musical style. Most of all, it is the high energetic drive of their rhythmic riffs that create their aesthetic. And, it is the programming of the beat that holds the clue to their style. In other words, the rhythmic syntax of their grooves communicates their musical identity.

In striking contrast to African-American derived stylistic idioms, many of the Pet Shop Boys' gestures can be best categorised as tacky Europop, although the origins of their style are traceable in black American disco traditions. Possibly their musical references to Euro-electronic dance music styles are most discernible when it comes to the rigid control of the on-beat pulse and mechanical precision of their unsyncopated rhythmic patterns. Indeed, a reliance on new electronic and digital technology has always distinguished their rhythmic signatures. And, timbrally, the effect of synthetically generated drum and percussion sounds shifting on countless levels has slotted their music into mainstream four-on-the-floor Eurodance culture.

Vocal style

So far, I have been arguing that the rhetoric of the Pet Shop Boys' songs lies in the manipulation of an array of musical codes. The banal, albeit profound, quality of the lyrics is intensified by the often expressionless and flippant quality of Tennant's singing style. Here a controlled, cool, and detached delivery resists any dynamic variation, which is often in contrast to the colourful exuberance of the instrumental backing. Indeed, Tennant's vocal style functions as a central ironic marker. To be more specific, his affected contours of intonation, syllabic inflections and general vocal expression function to underpin an ironic subtext. Often the stylistic codes found in the stressing of words, the lowering of register, the effortless slides up large inter-vals, set up a series of expectations that are both culture and language specific. In terms of Europop, the vocal sound of the Pet Shop Boys demonstrates the strong influence of Kraftwerk through the 'disembodied' voice and the mechanical, cool and detached manner of singing. Stylistic coding is produced through the positional connotations of the vocal tracks alongside the technolo-gically derived instrumentation, while all the time the mannerisms of their musical vocabulary are accentuated by their vocals, which are delivered with the lackadaisical effortlessness of someone reciting prose.

Tunes

Of course, vocal style is inextricably linked to melodic shapes and patterns (Example 5.3). In effect, the Pet Shop Boys are brilliant tunesmiths. Easily memorable, their tunes are simple, banal and sometimes downright silly. Their pitch range mostly falls within the octave with few large intervallic leaps. This makes them catchy and easy to sing or whistle along to, with little technical demand on the singer. Furthermore, the intervallic structures of their melodies are frequently characterised by downward and upward triadic or broken-chord motion in either major or minor keys which functions to reinforce the harmonic flavourings of the key centres (also see Stefani 1987b).

In their rendition of the Village People's gay anthem of the 1970s, 'Go West,' intervallic movement is most pronounced, serving to provide a sense of cushy resolution (read: banal) within the context of harmonic tension. In parti-cular, their use of the cycle of fifths and obvious quotation of Pachelbel's *Canon* in 'Go West' is just one of many instances whereby the Pet Shop Boys resort to musical clichés to ironise their musical gestures (Example 5.3).

Example 5.3   Melodic constructions in the Pet Shop Boys' songs

Above all, the melodic clarity of their tunes discloses a subtlety, which on close examination reveals many surprises, including quirky gestures, unexpected modulations, and irregular middle sections.[20] Furthermore, melodic structures and fragmented phrases are seldom repeated note for note. Rather, subtle variations and adjustments in melodic figures are frequently discernible, the result of lyrical insertion and inflections of certain words and phrases. Importantly, it is the intricacies found in the compositional manipulation of tunes, rhythms, textures and harmonies that hold the listeners' attention and challenge their expectations. There is always a sense that their tunes masquerade as carriers of traditions through the clichés they exhibit. In this way, they are imbued with an innuendo that spells out a Cowardian-type sardonic wit.

Production

Finally, the most crucial clue to the Pet Shop Boys' style lies in the technical wizardry of their productions. Their ultra-clean productions celebrate a certain European aesthetic that is aligned to a romantic approach to technological sophistication. Indeed, it is in the aesthetics of their mix that their distinct sound is characterised. For example, this is discernible in the foregrounding of the kit sounds, the specific blend of the vocal parts, the predominant use of new electronic/digital equipment in terms of keyboards, samplers and drum machines, and the creative articulation of studio effects. Moreover, the innovative spirit of their productions depicts the advances in music technology. Always at the cutting edge of production techniques, their sound is determined by an original use of music technology. Essentially, their commercial success is dependent on their adaptation of new technologies that provide the interface between them and their fans.

Musical (dis)pleasures

Now in attempting to tie the musical codes described above to my proposed concept of banality, I am led to consider how (dis)pleasures are linked to musical expression through political engagement. The aim here is to demonstrate how many of the compositional features that constitute the Pet Shop Boys' musical flavour resist the tendency to take themselves too seriously. From the above list of musical features two things become clear: first, most of the musical ideas, at least when positioned within a traditional musicological context, appear crudely simple. This is especially relevant when the category of production is removed from the list. Second, the musical codes I have identified only achieve full signification when working in dialogue with the other texts (lyrics, performance style, generic references, gender correlatives). What creates the satirical impulse in the Pet Shop Boys' songs seems to be harnessed by a play on oppositions, a feature which has characterised intellectual pop styles since the 1960s (see Brackett 1995). By this I am referring specifically to the manner in which musical clichés are located next to gestures of parody. Assuming that banality in musical expression has the potential to mock the original, and even cast ridicule on those who do not wish to receive it, the very possibilities of its pleasure are heightened for the listener who is tuned into the social motives behind the musical gestures. In other words, the critical moment of enjoyment is when one recognises how parody turns on musical style, a characteristic obviously tied up with interpreting constructions of identity.

In the end, all this sheds light on why responses to banality in pop are often greeted with mixed reactions. In fact, when parody is perceived as void of humour it quickly converts into a Jamesonian 'blank parody' (1983: 113–14). For many critics, the aesthetic dilemma of postmodern forms of expression is instituted in a stark blankness that strips away at depth and meaning in artistic materiality. Seen from this perspective, the disappearance of artistic content can only result in a type of crude, meaningless banality. We know that in the wider field of popular music, Jameson-type reactions are not uncommon in their disassociation with the so-called triviality of pop acts that oppose serious expression. But, in the case of the Pet Shop Boys' texts, I see the denunciation of being original musically as a move towards not only resisting modernist ideals of artistic expression, but also the naturalism of rock authenticity. Of course it is the inverse of their strategy that spells out the credibility of their postmodernist authorship (see Toynbee 2000: 31). This is a problematic position that I will return to later.

By pitting their inauthenticity against all notions of artistic seriousness (read: 'Call me an artist, honey'), it is as if they set out to accentuate the slush of commercial hype and triviality through musical performance. And out of this emerges a mannered style that calls into question their own sense of authenticity as artists.

On the tricky issue of debating artistic virtue within commercial pop, Neil Nehring (1997) has stressed that ideas of non-commercial authenticity only exist in the minds of aesthetes bent on nostalgia. In his sharp rebuttal of academics bent on denouncing postmodernism, Nehring points out how even the 'most difficult experimental works of modernism' have frequently 'fed right into advertising' in order to survive (1997: 65). The importance of this observation exposes the well-oiled arguments in music scholarship to politicise certain genres over others in a bid to make claims for authenticity. We know, for example, that the politically based arguments centred around commerciality also stem from a pessimistic claim that youth culture has been more engaged in hyperconsumerism than political opposition since the early 1980s. But, I would rather suggest that the political differentiation between the banal and the meaningful, at least for the MTV generation, is firmly rooted in the fun of both

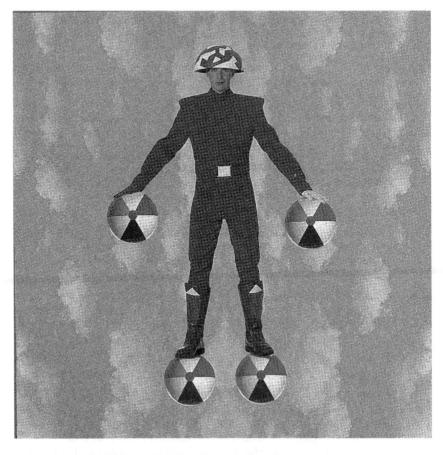

Figure 5.1   Neil Tennant on the *Very* album cover

observing and partaking in musical performance. My central point is that banality can all too easily be overlooked when music is measured against the criteria that fit the qualitative remit of traditional musicology. Yet, as I have attempted to argue, the banality of the Pet Shop Boys can direct our attention to a difference in attitude by mobilising the socially encoded qualities that determine taste and preference historically. Thus, allowing ourselves to identify with and even enjoy such texts is all about gaining access into a range of emotions that negotiate the riskiness yet playfulness of desire. Through parody then, musical performance invokes pleasures that disempower the primary pillars of authentic artistic judgement. Most of all, parody acts as a reminder that pop texts are never self-determining in any tangible way. From this, one thing seems certain: acknowledging banality in any form demonstrates the necessity for probing further into pop expression and the notions of (in)authenticity it evokes.

'Disco-Tex and the Sexelettes': satirical musical address

Towards the middle of the song, 'Electricity', off the *Bilingual* (1996) album, Tennant parodies their roles as artists: *Call it performance, call it art, call it disaster, If the tapes don't start, I've put all my life into live lip-sync, I'm an artist honey.* At this stage in the song, the whole dimension of pop performance is given the most hilarious send-up, as Tennant's voice is foregrounded in the mix while the lyrics are delivered in a nonchalant, camp manner. The audio scope of the sound-box at this moment is distinguished by an array of synthesisers, phased in over a pounding bass line, punctuated by powerful off-beat snare shots, all arranged within a tightly compressed mix.

As with all the Pet Shop Boys' songs, musical pleasure is negotiated through a satirical employment of sampled and synthesiser sounds and disco riffs, often with the bass part fusing with the kit lines at a slow grinding pace, sexually suggestive and erotically charged. A main part of the appeal rests in the gestural content of their productions, with their lyrics, choice of instruments and style of performance negotiating an exchange of meaning between performer and listener. In 'Electricity', the musical emotions peak at a point where the bass line, coupled in unison with a Hammond organ, picks up the central melody, transporting the chorus hook *Disco-Tex and the Sexelettes*, thus lifting the overall mood to new heights of blissful engagement. Polyphonically, the interweaving synthesiser lines are enhanced through the arrangement of the vocal lines (flanged, spoken, sung and chorused), all of which are filtered into the insistent disco riff.

The Pet Shop Boys' appeal is embedded in the production as much as in the arrangement. Frequently, their musical mood is retrospective, not only in its absorption of disco styles but also in its reference to other artists, whose influences are frequently discernible in Tennant's vocal style. It is virtually impossible to ignore the striking references to David Bowie here, whose influence has had a profound impact on the Pet Shop Boys ever since he first became visible in pop culture. As Jon Savage puts it, Bowie 'touched every suburban heart' (1996: 113) by promoting the message that everyone could change their look in order to be an entirely new personality. Above all, the Pet Shop Boys' song 'Electricity' can be read as a commentary on exactly this dimension of Bowiean theatricality, through the superficial, showbiz entertainment world of urban bourgeoisie: *Costume changes, performed with poise, Dancing in formation with a couple of boys, I take them on the road, with my reels-to-reels, I'm an artist honey, You know how that feels?* Elegantly conveyed through the camped-up representation of their identity, it is always the satirical lyrics that highlight the discursive community to which the Pet Shop Boys know they belong. In fact, the social critique imposed by their lyrics makes their ironic intentions possible.

Stylistic address in 'Electricity' alerts the listener/interpreter to a variety of markers that ritualise identity in different ways. Moreover, the plot of this song conflates social politics and erotics as Tennant satirises the role of the camp artist. In keeping with an English sense of wry understatement, the affected dimension of his lyrical aphorisms underscore the charge of mocking intent. In this instance, the Pet Shop Boys' rhetorical and political strategy is to displace rigid structures of male identity.

It is this edge to their attitude that clearly opens their texts to a multiplicity of readings. If we pursue the question of identification to include the issue of sexuality, the idea of contradictory or multiple constructions is a compelling one. As Evans and Gamman suggest, such multiple identifications can become 'extended into the metaphor of genderfuck where the freefloating signifier, biological sex, is detached or cut loose from its signified, cultural gender' (1995: 41). Picking up on this, I would suggest that experiencing constructions of sexuality in musical performances offer us the opportunity to float around in imaginative cultural contexts. With the Pet Shop Boys, their very recordings and videos reflect the 'freefloating' signifiers of their gestures while their camped-up imagery fools around with the cool passion of their musical exuberance. As in the case of Morrissey, we cannot ignore that such displays of contradictory retort form a crucial component of an English sensibility, as once again we are reminded that it is through pop culture that the sentiments of British youth have traditionally exposed the flaws of their own national landscape (see Bracewell 1998).

Historically, irony has occupied a special position in English popular song as a form of protest. In the case of the Pet Shop Boys, theirs is imbued with much the same wit found in Noël Coward and W.H. Auden's work, yet, however, extended into the unlikely genre of 1980s disco. Functioning as a mechanism for liberation, their theatricality refutes and ridicules the constraints of everyday life, including pop culture, in various ways. This seems blatantly obvious in songs, such as 'Saturday Night Forever' from the *Bilingual* album, with its pumped-up tempo, irresistible disco pulse and joyous repetition, all of which communicate a sense of shared meaning.

Of course, pop aesthetics are located on many different levels. In 'Saturday Night Forever', I find the Pet Shop Boys' appeal to be wrapped up in the mesmeric structuring of an almost over-produced mix and cheesy lyrical hooks, all of which promise instant gratification, as Tennant sings: *Forever forever, Saturday night, Saturday night, I go where I go and I get there fast*. In this song, the liberating quality of the groove seems to be stamped out in the lyrics in much the same way we saw in Madonna's song, 'Don't Stop' (Chapter 2), as Tennant cries out *Don't stop me, I know that it's not gonna last*. In every conceivable way possible, the music unleashes the desire to participate physically through the thrill of dance.

Now reading songs in this manner obviously involves countless responses to a range of musical codes the groove, the beat, the melodic and harmonic structures, the vocal delivery, the lyrics – all of which transport the listener into a world where the urge to escape is captured by the blissful charge of the disco style. Yet, decoding the politics of 'Saturday Night Forever' is a complicated task as the text challenges and ingratiates, thrills and repels, unites and separates. All this ties into the realisation that pop aesthetics are culture specific, always relying on that intimate link between the musician and listener.

Fully aware that they can meet their fans on any number of terrains, it is as if the Pet Shop Boys set out to evoke a range of different responses. With little doubt, their intention is to exude ambiguity, as they themselves explain: 'We have always preferred to be enigmatic. Part of the Pet Shop Boys' image has always been to be enigmatic and not define things. I think in pop music that works very strongly, because people imagine things about you ... you are a creature of their imagination. And I like that.'[21]

Most importantly then, the Pet Shop Boys remind us that we can exist in numerous discursive communities at the same time. That these contexts offer up contradictory and confusing settings is indeed part of the complexity of understanding how music works. The general principle I am promoting here is that the reception of pop texts triggers off the construction of complex relationships between music and identity. And it is the organisation of sound structures that present us with useful starting points for examining how performance delineates our preferences and dislikes.

As slickly produced disco riffs and pumping bass lines typify the Pet Shop Boys' style, they also contrast vividly with the monotony of the chord progressions and melodic lines. In fact, the essence of their musical flavour is located in the familiar brand of campness we have come to associate with the Pet Shop Boys. Entrenched in the very contours of their melodies, it is, in the end, the infectious disco beat that forms a basis for parodic delivery. Layered over the HiNRG groove, the special delivery of banal tunes in 'Saturday Night Forever' help discharge the energy of the musical underlay as the rhythmic exuberance promises us instant abandonment. In such moments, the poignancy of melodic phrases and catchy chord progressions underscore a sensibility that discloses this duo's identity. And this brings me back to the politics of performance. In the case of the Pet Shop Boys, this might well be interpreted as a strategy for shaking music loose from the pretentiousness it possesses when trying to take itself too seriously.

Towards a PSB discourse

So far I have constructed this chapter around two premises: first, that the Pet Shop Boys' music offers up sets of questions that warrant an investigation into the diversities of identity within an English context; and, second, in being grounded culturally, their musical codes engender a specific rhetoric which constructs their own sense of authenticity through sheer banality. Of course any claims to extracting musical meaning, as I have suggested in my analysis of all the case studies in this book so far, depend on identifying the performers and their music within their social and cultural context. As we have seen, pop texts signify an outgrowth and appropriation of various styles, images and modes of expression that are situated ideologically. Ultimately it is within the creative space of the studio production that notions of authenticity and artifice arise. The artifice of pop has been widely addressed in pop scholarship,[22] and in his critique, Lawrence Grossberg has demonstrated how ideas of aesthetic authenticity centre on notions of style in pop: '[It] becomes a self-conscious parody of the ideology of authenticity, by making the artificiality of its construction less a matter of aesthetics and more a matter of image-marketing. The result is that style is celebrated over authenticity, or rather that authenticity is seen as just another style' (1993: 202–3).

In his mapping of pop aesthetics against questions of authorship, Grossberg claims that when linked to dance, music positions authenticity in 'the construction of a rhythmic and sexual body', which leads to any number of impressions, such as those of fantasy, romance and sexual mobility.

Significantly though, in pop, when authenticity is no longer measurable in terms of the natural live performance, it is relatively unimportant that musicians, such as the Pet Shop Boys, might lip-sync and simulate a performance. What seems more pertinent is their 'ability to manipulate the presentation' which results in the 'measure of affective power' (ibid: 205).

Continually, the Pet Shop Boys' mode of expression suggests a confession of inauthenticity, and as Tennant puts it, an admission of shamelessness. Yet, as Grossberg indicates, 'the only possible claim to authenticity is derived from the knowledge and admission of your inauthenticity'. Grossberg's critique highlights the problems of reading authenticity in popular music and calls for ways of understanding it alongside performance styles. In the Pet Shop Boys' case, it is the attitude to performance that most confounds the problematics of categorisation. Their use of spectacle, in terms of fashion and design, as seen in their concerts as much as their videos, together with gesture, both musical and bodily, all contribute to a constructed sense of artifice. For all this, their frequent mocking of trend-setting norms in Anglo-American popular culture is often taken to extremes, thus heightening the flippancy of their parodic address.

Like Madonna, Lennox, Morrissey and Prince, the Pet Shop Boys tailor their image to suit the pluralism of their style. Their emphasis on look and mannerism, in one sense, epitomises the postmodern direction of their work, as exemplified in video clips, such as 'Go West', 'Liberation' and 'Can You Forgive Her?' (off the *Very* (1995) video compilation). Absorbing a wide array of visual codes in much the same way that they draw on numerous musical styles, they manage to manipulate their identity in ways that parody social conformity. This is bound up in their approach to technology. Again I wish to emphasise that the influence of old and new production styles have had a most significant effect on the shaping of their sound – a sonic trademark which, while always adapting to technological innovation, still remains distinct through these artists' attitude and musical gestures. Yet, the Pet Shop Boys' sound also becomes a mixture of genres that trace the advances of digital technology and, most significantly, production techniques.

Inspired by the technologies that create relationships between body and machine, their sound surfaces as inimitable. Théberge has explored the significance of this special type of relationship between sound and inspiration. In his studies he points out how sounds in pop extend further than prefabricated sounds to include the '(c)omplex special effects, such as multiple delays, phasing, and gating available in digital signal processors and applied to virtually any acoustic or electronic sound' (1997: 199). Above all, the aesthetic characteristics of pop production have signified new directions and tendencies in the definition of styles and genres.

Clearly, questions of musical value and inspirational source need to be positioned within the wider debates of appropriation and authenticity.[23] In this respect, the stylistic dimension of the Pet Shop Boys' expression cannot be ignored. According to Tony Mitchell, their creativity signifies 'a shift from perceived postmodern expressions of stylish surface ambiguity towards a more modernist, even realist concern with social issues' (1996: 18). Mitchell sets out to problematise the reconfigurative nature of their music in a critique that attempts to legitimate their standing as creative artists. He describes the extent to which the Pet Shop Boys might be categorised and even utilised as follows:

> The Pet Shop Boys' continuing commercial success, and increasing fascination for highbrow commentators on pop music, suggests that the multiple forms of post-postmodern pop music have regenerated themselves into modernist manifestations which are best considered discretely in a case-by-case approach. While many of the regenerative qualities of pop music largely involve appropriating a succession of different styles as they become fashionable, the Pet Shop Boys show that the inbuilt obsolescence and inherent ephemerality of pop can be utilized in intelligent and socially meaningful ways. [Mitchell 1996: 18–19]

Mitchell's position on post-postmodern pop as a return to a modernist manifestation of creative virtue is difficult to sustain on the terms of such categorisation. If one agrees that the postmodern subject is characterised by a superficiality and emptiness, then the Pet Shop Boys do, in a sense, fit this agenda, not least in terms of their strategies of irony and camp. Indeed, if one theorises postmodern expression in pop as a series of practices that combine the traditional with the new, the modern with the postmodern, then the Pet Shop Boys' identity emerges as very fragmented. To be sure, their texts induce many contradictory readings that are grounded in a complex blend of cultural effects. But to assume a modernist (or post-postmodernist positioning) on the basis of intelligence (read: condoned creativity) seems rather trouble-some.

Which returns me to the question of banality in expression. For many fans there is little doubt that the Pet Shop Boys' music stands for pop at its best as it functions as a powerful catalyser against many of the styles of hardcore metal, rap and ladrock. Seeping out of every musical moment of their songs is a gendered sensibility that taunts the rigidity of binary empowerment often found in the oppressive modes of many patriarchal texts of pop culture. In this manner, notions of difference in identity are always thematised, explored and turned over in their texts.[24] From this then, we might interpret the Pet Shop Boys' appeal as being grounded in an ironic vision of their sexuality, nation-ality and class. Often their gestures can be read as an attack on the normative values of white, middle-class, English males, as well as on the kind of authori-tative modernist representations Western music history has brought about. Their texts, when seen in this light, are a celebration of a new-era of postmo-dern pop that cunningly sets out to defy easy categorisation.

Conclusion

As I have suggested earlier in this chapter, any evaluation of the Pet Shop Boys needs to take into account the context of their particular social and political positionings, with their stylistic codes linked to a full array of conflicting effects. For my part, their songs signify important narratives of male identity within a pluralistic cultural landscape. It is as if their preoccupa-tion with themes of social decline and political mourning transports their texts into similar historic spaces of nostalgia as found in the work of Wilde, Larkin and Auden.

Consistently, they have striven to capture the mood of their specific locality through their songs. Jon Savage insists that the Pet Shop Boys have managed to sing about London with conviction in a way that

> ... acknowledges that the city is in recession after the febrile boom of the
> 1980s, and that recession does terrible things to people. Neither are native
> Londoners. Just think of the PSB's 'Kings Cross' and 'The Theatre' – the latter
> written after a reported comment by a Tory MP that the homeless were the
> people you stepped over on your way to the opera. [Savage 1996: 345]

Through a blend of wry intellect and resignation, their texts function as signifi-cant social landmarks of Britain at the end of the twentieth century, with their celebration of pop consumerism working as a compelling snapshot of this period.[25]

On the one hand, their mannerisms of witty eccentricity might be interpreted as typically English, while, on the other hand, as Frith points out, they are also 'continentally European', especially with regard to their adaptation of new technology. Their effectiveness as musicians and their appeal stems from an approach to songwriting where 'computerized instruments [have] freed sounds from a performance context' (Frith 1996: 6). There is little question that an Europop dance aesthetic (reminiscent of Switzerland's Yello and Germany's Kraftwerk and Neu) permeates all their songs. And, significantly, during the 1990s, the Pet Shop Boys have felt compelled to emphasise their internationalisation. Commenting on their album *Bilingual*, Neil Tennant emphasised this point in no uncertain terms: 'We always wanted to make a record that spoke to some other people outside the United Kingdom ... British music has been so insular that we wanted to make an album that went out into the world and could be popular in Russia and Latin America and East Asia' (Firth 1996: 6).

From this we might conclude that the Pet Shop Boys' texts stress the transnationalistic nature of their Englishness within a European context, even if this might be interpreted as a crass market ploy. On the track 'Single', such sentiments are endorsed as they joyously proclaim: *Single bilingual, In Brussels Bonn or Barcelona, I'm in demand and quite at home there 'Adelante!'*[26] Such mannered language and style of delivery can only denote the laconic wit that has its roots in English music-hall songs and traditions. In addition, an air of camped-up seduction, threatening to heteronormative politics, is inherent in all their texts. Of course, to pull any of this off successfully, 'you have to be shameless,' insists Tennant.[27] And, shaped by a vibrantly passionate energy, it is such rhetoric that ultimately liberates them from the repression of their mannequin-like posturing. Moreover, it is in musical performance that an assured sense of self-reflexivity rests. Discernible in every one of their songs, self-reflexiveness shines through the lyrics, the tunes, the chord sequences, the trashy synth riffs, the vocal style, and, most importantly, the coolness of their productions.

Finally, while it might be Tennant's delivery that works in a way that invokes consensus amongst fans, Chris Lowe's role as instrumentalist, programmer and controller of production is of equal importance in balancing their performances. All in all, it is their shared cynical attitude and theatrical disposition – a quality found in other English artists such as Bowie, Costello, Morrissey, Damon Albarn, Marc Almond, Brett Anderson, and, most recently, Robbie Williams – that becomes a matter of unspoken understanding which cuts across a range of categories and appeals to a wide audience.

Of course, unpacking one's identity through musical performance rests on personal interpretation and the fan's own discursive community. Fully aware of this, the Pet Shop Boys have flirted with a variety of contrasting identities which surface with delight in contexts drenched by ironic artifice. As in Morrissey's songs, a playful encoding of male identity is manifested in the spectacle of satirical performance. Thus, slotting into some wider framework, all this seems to draw on a multiplicity of styles and texts that bring to mind that the pleasures we experience from musical sound are after all politically and culturally charged.

Finally, the intertextual nature of their songs points to the fact that musical codes cannot be analysed on their own as primary texts. Rather they need to be measured through their proximity to and in dialogue with other texts. From the outset, the Pet Shop Boys have always been mobile in their references. This is a result of the full dimension of their production, something that is always changing while simultaneously remaining identifiable through its cultural context. Their recordings are located at the point where consumption and production fuse and where the intermingling of pleasure and meaningfulness becomes part of our own identities. In this sense, their sound becomes a metaphor for many different kinds of identities. But, if this all seems too bewildering, perhaps we should afford the Pet Shop Boys the last word when they remind us, somewhat ironically, that as long as *the music plays forever, it's gonna be all right.*[28]

Acknowledgements

A large portion of this chapter is a reworking of an article in *Popular Musicology*, Vol. 2 (1993), and a chapter in *Sexing the Groove* (1997), ed. Sheila Whiteley, entitled, 'The Pet Shop Boys: Musicology, masculinity and banality'. Special thanks go to Jonty Stockdale and Derek Scott for their encouragement and support, which directly led to writing this chapter.

Notes

1   'Honestly', interview with Neil Tennant by Paul Burston in *Attitude* 1994.
2   Ibid (emphasis added).
3   In particular, see McClary 1990, 2000; Green 1988, 1997; Whiteley 1997b; 2000; Bayton 1997, 1998.
4   I am referring to the work undertaken by male musicologists, such as Shepherd 1987; Walser 1993a; Richardson 1999; Scott 2000; Middleton 1993, 2000.
5   Again, I want to stress that the views expressed here relate on a personal level to how I perceive representations of the Pet Shop Boys' authorship as a process of my reception. Yet, my interpretation of their music is also largely influenced by the diverse responses of female and male fans I have encountered over the years.
6   Christopher Sean Lowe, born 4 October 1959, first studied architecture before meeting Tennant. Active as a pianist, he worked with one of Blackpool's cabaret groups, One Under The Eight. Neil Francis Tennant, born 10 July 1954, graduated from North London Polytechnic before working as an editor for Marvel comics and writing for the British pop paper, *Smash Hits*. Interestingly, both Lowe and Tennant originated from the North of England.

7   Hi-NRG – an abbreviation for high-energy – can be viewed as a style of pop that has emanated from disco. It is thought to have started in the mid-1980s with Evelyn Thomas's smash hit, although there are strong traces of its conception some years earlier. Hi-NRG owes its success to the vibrant gay music scene, with its style formed by artists, such as The Weather Girls, Sylvester, Two Tons of Fun, Village People and Donna Summer. One of the first recordings of Hi-NRG is 'Hit 'n' Run' by Carole Jiani from 1981. Other notable recordings in this style have been made by Alison Moyet and Suzie Q, whose 'Computer Music' in 1985 was heralded as a standard of Hi-NRG.

8   The duo's albums span more than ten years, a period during which they have provided a string of hits and remixed versions of their singles. Amongst the numerous artists and producers they have worked with are Dusty Springfield, Liza Minnelli, Boy George, Trevor Horn, Patsy Kensit and Cicero. In 1992 they launched their own record label, Spaghetti, and produced other artists as well as themselves.

9   This becomes a particularly complex strategy in the construction of identities through pop texts. The potential exclusion of playing to in-groups by the Pet Shop Boys is a defining quality of their seductive charge.

10   See Edwards (1994) for a detailed critique of gay sexuality from a historical, social and political perspective.

11   It needs to be emphasised at this point that performers during the pre-1980s, such as the New York Dolls, T. Rex, and Bowie – the gender-bending glam rockers – were very much the exception to the rule.

12   Burston (1994) has noted that references to gay culture can be read within the lyrics of the Pet Shop Boys. Burston maintains that they played a major role in establishing new codes in gay culture during the 1980s. It is worth emphasising that in the UK their popularity reached a mainstream audience that was not gay, and not necessarily aware of the subtexts and levels of difference running throughout their songs. As the Pet Shop Boys entered the pop scene, so gay eroticism started filtering into pop mainstream, not least through dance music.

13   *Melody Maker*, 27 November 1993.

14   In direct contrast to the flamboyancy of 1970s gay culture, which Neil Tennant claims to have disliked while growing up in Newcastle upon Tyne, the Pet Shop Boys offer a more modest face in terms of style. Most notably, Tennant has openly declared an unwillingness to be identified specifically with one single community: 'I don't want to belong to some narrow group or ghetto. And I think, if they're really honest, a lot of gay people would say they felt like that as well' ('Honestly', *Attitude*, 1994).

15   *Out*, 'Pet Shop Boys, Frankly', interview with Larry Closs, December 1993.

16   It was from this point onwards that Neil Tennant and Chris Lowe continued to experience growing success with the following discography, *Please* (1986), *Actually* (1987), *Introspective* (1988), *Behaviour* (1990), *Discography* (1992), *Very* (1993), and *Disco II* (1994).

17   Paul Burston in 'Honestly', *Attitude* 1994.

18   *Melody Maker*, 27 November 1993 (emphases added).

19   Notably in a later remix of 'Yesterday, When I was Mad', off the *Disco II* album, the emphasis and euphoric quality of the music is even more intense than the original recording, detaching itself even further from the lyrics. Also see Mitchell (1996) for an analysis of 'Yesterday, When I was Mad' in which he discusses the Pet Shop Boys' own perception of irony in this song as well as their reference to Noel Coward.

20 For an engaging discussion of the Pet Shop Boys' 'simple' pop-form structures, which provide a basis for their appeal, see Frith (1997), whose reference to irony is situated alongside references to a number of songs from their album *Very*.

21 *New York Post*, interview by Lisa Robinson, 6 September 1996.

22 Here I am referring in particular to the studies carried out by Frith 1983, 1987, 1996; Laing 1985; Middleton 1990; Nehring 1997; Toynbee 2000.

23 For Bourdieu (1984, 1990), the theorisation of popular culture inevitably entails an intellectual exercise on the part of those *within* the academy and their relationship to the outside world. This, though, leads to certain contradictions as discoursing on popular aesthetics affirms the differences between high culture and vulgar, populist culture. It is significant that Bourdieu's position also underlines the resistance of cultural studies to the symbolic domination of conservative, 'official' cultures. Also see Toynbee (2000) on Bourdieuian theory.

24 See especially 'Young Offender', 'To Speak is a Sin', 'One and One Makes Five', as striking examples of songs that thematise issues of difference on many levels.

25 Significantly, their texts are in opposition to much mainstream popular culture that has continued to absorb virulent machismo and latent violence in all forms of entertainment. An example of a spate of films dealing with notions of machoistic manhood in the 1980s were the *First Blood* movies starring Sylvester Stallone as Rambo, who sets out to conquer all that is evil through violent action.

26 Insistent that they do not wish to draw or cash in on world music, the Pet Shop Boys nevertheless set out to fuse the energy and rhythmic colours of Latin American with their characteristic disco sound in their album *Bilingual*.

27 'Honestly', *Attitude* 1994.

28 From the famous Pet Shop Boys song, 'It's Alright' (1989).

Chapter 6
Subversive Musical Pleasures in 'The Artist (Again) Known as Prince'

Introduction

Just two years after the launch of MTV in the US in 1981, his image was beamed to millions worldwide when he appeared on MTV with the song 'Little Red Corvette'. Since then, the Minneapolis-born musician, Prince Rogers Nelson, has become legendary within pop history. And, with over 22 albums behind him, his prolific status as songwriter and multi-talented performer has assured his ongoing commercial success well into the twenty-first century. Significantly, he is one in a line of African Americans to have reached superstar status in the pop world, alongside Michael Jackson, Whitney Houston, Janet Jackson, Tina Turner, Lionel Richie and Lenny Kravitz.[1]

Exploring the ways in which the politics of performance pull together issues of ethnicity, gender, sexuality and race, this study further concentrates on the concept of identity as an integral part of musical meaning in pop texts. I have found that Prince's music testifies to the potential of his ethnicity within a specific historical and social period. In conjunction with the issue of race, the focus of this study rests on the shifting positions of Prince's ambivalent identity through musical performance. While his mode of performance introduces musical ideas which are bound up in diasporic music cultures, the stylistic references he draws on display the agency of a most reflexive performance. It seems to be that Prince's reflexivity has always enabled the extension of musical idioms into transpersonal spaces through crossover. As a style and process, crossover in Prince's music marks both the differences and stylistic developments in new social spaces. Clearly, the cross over of African-American music into the white mainstream market inevitably raises questions linked to institutionalised racism and ethnic particularity. In this chapter, I see this as a complex phenomenon, whose debates have already been extensively addressed in numerous studies (George 1988; Tagg 1989; Middleton 1990; Brackett 1995; Frith 1996; Cashmore 1997).

What I also want to look at here is the kind of gender tourism one commonly finds in pop music of the MTV era, where artists explore constructs of gender on their own creative terms. While in earlier studies I have stressed the importance of the creative agency of Prince through devising various models of musical analysis (see Hawkins 1992a, 1992b), in this chapter the emphasis falls more on the ways in which one might connect his musical codes to a range of identity constructions. The ideas presented here thus extend my musicological position into a more discursive framework where the matter of gendered performance is situated culturally in a context where a multitude of identities articulate the power and desire of the artist and the record industry. Of particular significance to this study is a consideration of the kind of performativity that arises from new technologies in musical production.

Prince's career spans momentous developments in the consumption and production of music, and, like the Pet Shop Boys, his texts draw our attention to the positioning of the artist in relation to the developments going on in music technology. In taking up this debate, I want to suggest that by exploring the relationship between the performer's body and aspects of production it is possible to reveal important elements connected to questions of musical meaning.

What counts most here is that recordings can capture pop performances in diverse and thrilling ways. The status of the composition, for example, can be measured by the recording which, in the case of most pop, is realised through a blend of live performance, multiple takes, overdubs and mastering. Significantly, the recording is disseminated through different kinds of media: music videos, radio broadcasts, home playback systems, live concerts, club mixes, live gig broadcasts. Although the pop score is fixed by the recording, it is important to bear in mind that, in a sense, it represents just the final stage of one set of musical ideas within one performance rendition. The implications of this point have been discussed by Toynbee, who cautions us against perceiving recordings as if they were 'the great works of great authors' because, importantly, they only form part of a 'continuous process of performance and creation' (2000: 56). At any rate, for pop artists the structuring apparatus of performance does not end in the recording – performance is an ongoing process that is extended by its mediation through different contexts into different dialogues.

Implicit in all the discussions that follow then is the idea that performance can be measured through strategies that arise in relation to the artist's awareness of himself as a performed act within a given context at a specific time. In a dialogic state, the performer speaks through the recording in multiple voices that are socially circumscribed. I have always considered Prince as a fitting example of the artist who marks out his territory by drawing together an amalgam of voices and traditions. By positioning himself at the centre of a creative field, he integrates musicians and audiences through the musical possibilities attached to race, locality, sexuality, gender and social sphere. Above all, his performances express the ambiguities inherent in a transitory space. Hence, his creative agency can be associated with a profusion of styles that simultaneously articulate the conditions of authenticity and artifice in musical expression.

Dialectics of music and imagination

Born in 1958, Prince grew up in north Minneapolis. Both parents were musical – his father, John L. Nelson, was a black jazz pianist, while his mother, Mattie Shaw, was a singer of mixed race. A troubled childhood made him shy and withdrawn. We know that at the age of seven, Prince experienced grief when his parents' marriage ended and his father left home. Just two years later his mother remarried, to a man whom Prince could not get along with, which culminated in him running away from home at the age of twelve. His being bullied at school due to his slight build, short height, and ethnic background certainly added to a range of childhood problems.

From an early age, Prince played the piano and guitar, as well as writing his own material and band directing. He has described how this provided him with a vital outlet: 'I realized that music could express what you were feeling and it started coming out in my songs – loneliness and poverty and sex' (in Nilsen 1993: 6). Music thus formed an integral part of his life as a child and teenager, so much so that by 1974 Prince had started his own instrumental group at junior school, Grand Central, later called Champagne. At this stage he was writing and performing a great deal and his influences were diverse. In 1977 his hard work and persistence was rewarded when he signed a six-figure, long-term contract with Warner Brothers: a relationship that would prove uneasy and volatile for almost two decades. With the release of his first two albums, *For You*, and *Prince*, he set out to produce something musically new and different, which, for example, included substituting multitrack synthesiser lines for conventional horn sections, the basis for what later became known as the Minneapolis sound. What also distinguished this sound was Prince's approach to recording and getting tracks down by jamming with a reservoir of versatile musicians. Significantly, his ability to jam skilfully has always constituted a major part of his performance, an important aspect I will pick up on later.

Another distinctive quality of Prince's performativity has been the link between his music and the spectacle of his act, which has transgressed many normative forms of male expression. As with his music, the representation of his image has been full of ambiguities that can be interpreted on many different levels. It was with the release of the *Dirty Mind* album that Prince's sexual exhortations and explicit allure first shocked and delighted audiences. Through his videos, live performances, and films, crude phallic displays towards women would provoke strong reactions.

In addressing this point, Lucy O'Brien (1995) has suggested that the role of women in Prince's act have been little more than a walking fantasy with no choice, although she concedes that their glamorous portrayal might be interpreted as something more positive. Whereas, on the other hand, Scottish pop singer Sheena Easton has insisted that Prince 'has always given great respect to women – he's worked a lot with women engineers in a generally male-dominated field. He doesn't pigeon-hole and label' (O'Brien 1995: 223). While Easton's claim is indeed questionable given her position as one in a line of female protégés, Prince's relationship to women presents a useful indicator of his own identity.

From another perspective, his texts, which I will make reference to later, could also be interpreted as an alignment to women's resistance to men at least in comparison to the active and dominant roles assigned to men in rock and pop styles.[2] The reasons for this might be traced back to his childhood and to a troubled relationship with his father. In her biographical study of Prince, Liz Jones accounts for this in the following assessment:

> He is also afraid of treating women the way he saw his father treat his mother. Hence his femininity, his androgyny, his uncanny understanding of women. He wants them to adore him, and he has used every ounce of his ability to get that. His need to control, his paranoia, his inability to trust those around him, his ever-present bodyguards, all stem from the chaos and disorder that surrounded him as a child. He was shut in his room at home by one domineering man after another. He was teased at school, out-dunked on the sports field, and happiest when locked in the music room at lunchtime. [1997: 32]

Jones's account raises a number of salient points that have consequences for understanding how Prince's social awkwardness has a bearing on his popularity. Clearly, the reference to his construction of 'femininity' relates to his relationship with males and, above all, the motives behind queering his act. Within the context of a Western heterosexual male setting, we know that males often 'treat men in general suspicion despite the spaces provided for male bonding' (Segal 1997: 103). This is borne out by an absence of any intimacy (non-sexual) Prince sustains between himself and other men in his performances, something which could be interpreted as an intentional avoidance of having his own masculinity threatened.

By openly presenting himself as androgyne, he strips away many traditional notions of masculinity by a spontaneous outpouring of expression through virtuoso musical performance (see Nattiez 1993). The degree of ambiguity with which this is directed should not be underestimated, as it is the play with oppositional signifiers that operates as a principal strategy of protest. In other words, Prince's androgyneity tends to destabilise the exclusivity of masculinity. I am referring in particular to the type of masculinity found in rock exemplified by, for instance, Bruce Springsteen (see Frith 1988). Indeed, Prince's disruptions of masculinity – not least in terms of his image – are enforced through the irreducibly physical entity of his looks and mannerisms when he queers his performance. By confronting normative models of masculinity, he establishes new possibilities for experiencing eroticism and masculinity in music. Arguing this point, Robert Walser asserts that Prince entices the listener or fan into structures of desire that are '*not territorialized* by rigid patriarchal distinctions' (Walser 1994: 85, emphasis added). Drawing on Deleuze and Guattari's theorisation (1977) of pleasure, Walser suggests that Prince seeks a body 'without organs that can escape Oedipal structures' (1994: 85). But from another viewpoint, it could be said that Prince indeed symbolises the full pronouncement of a newly territorialised male figure in all its totality (with all organs clearly intact, albeit within a context of complex reconstruction). The implications of this are worth considering in terms of his stardom and musicianship. But exploring the plurality of authorship in the pop artist is a challenging task and cannot stop at gender. Rather it needs to reach into other facets of identity, not least of all the music. For all this then, a broader set of problematics is required to take into account how music functions to construct identity.

At this stage I want to suggest that another clue to Prince's identity is stored within the range of technologies attached to his musical production. As a creative tool, music technology also shapes the imaginative responses we have to pop. Indeed *how* the male artist engages with music through the changing resources of technological production is a major point for consideration when it comes to understanding social relations through gendered construction (Bradby 1990; Bayton 1998; Toynbee 2000). Moreover, experiencing music is inextricably tied to the intricacies of the storage of structures of sound.[3] In other words, the pop text is always controlled by the technological creation of its audio image.

In Prince's songs, a staggering range of emotions is channelled through the technical reflexivity of his productions. It is the degree of technological manipulation that controls the intimacy of the aural space within which his identity is positioned, whether this be in a live performance situation or in a recording. Most importantly, through the technologies of sound reproduction he administers, there is little division between Prince's skills as a performer and a composer. His sound recordings technologically blur these two traditionally separated areas of musical expression. And, as his approach to music-making through studio production reflects the aesthetic and ideological trends within the music industry, the significance of his choice of instrumentation cannot be over-emphasised. As Théberge has insisted, '[d]igital instruments have become the means for both the production of new sounds and for the reproduction of old ones – the perfect vehicle for a music industry based simultaneously in fashion and nostalgia' (Théberge 1997: 213). In this regard, the relationship between the pop artist and the technological resources of musical production become a central factor for measuring the aesthetic and formal features of musical expression.

What strikes one, in addition to the thrill of his sound and use of technology, is Prince's singing style and verbal articulations. Importantly, his lyrics, at least when compared to artists such as Morrissey and the Pet Shop Boys, are more about 'feel' than clear-cut ideas, a point Frith (1996) has emphasised when he argues how words in songs function rhetorically. Prince's lyrical delivery raises questions concerning the function of speech patterns and the *utterance*, especially as to how they occur in performance. In this respect, the effect of lyrical enunciation constitutes a prime component of reading pop songs.

A good example of this is found in the playful song, 'EMale,' from the *Emancipation* (1996) album, where Prince entices us into the cool, postmodern, technosphere of cyberlanguage. While it is apparent that the song's hook and the lyrics concern an array of messages centred around sex and fantasy, the words and sentence constructions are often obtuse and disjunct, providing us with open readings of their effect. Implied rather than stated, the lyrical impulse of 'EMale' functions as a channel through which the musical material is delivered.

Importantly, Prince's songs involve a great deal of spoken language as part of their mode of exression. To grasp this fully, it is important to consider that songs 'work with and on *spoken* language' as part of their modes of expression (Frith 1996: 166, emphases added). This observation is best exemplified by the qualities found in his vocal style, especially as it becomes intermeshed with other musical codes, in particular instrumental articulations and rhythmic gestures. Consisting of a bouncy groove – a clean-cut bass and drum idea overlaid with a tacky-synth melody – this song abounds with erotic innuendo. Beautifully sung and mixed in a type of soft-focus effect, the chorus hook, *WWW.Emale.Com.*, is air-brushed digitally into the velvety F aeolian mode, affording the listener instant gratification (Example 6.1). At the same time, the compelling sensation of the groove controls the mood of the lyrics as we are invited to participate in the filling out of its gaps through our *imagination*. Both active and passive participation in music becomes a key site for negotiating meaning.

Example 6.1   Chorus from 'Emale'

As I have suggested, the aesthetics of Prince's songs lie in the production processes, which control a build-up in textures around central rhythmic riffs through multitrack recording processes and sequencing. In 'Emale', it is the technical codes such as the brass and synth licks, vocal responses, additional percussion timbres, improvisatory interjections and rotating positions of the audio image in the mix, that pad out the audio space of the mix. Most of all, Prince's vocal style is characterised by inflections, speech rhymes and idiomatic traits of African-American music. Reminiscent of Curtis Mayfield, Al Green and Smokey Robinson, his falsetto style of singing in this song often spans a wide register, blurring any conventional divides between vocal ranges and timbres of male and female singers. Perhaps what stands out most is the high level of vocal/instrumental and technological competence. As with all of his songs, a mischievous mood in 'EMale' is articulated through the thrill of jamming around one riff. This performance tactic is evident in all his albums. For example, in *Diamonds and Pearls*, the 13 diverse commercial songs on this recording are manipulated in ways that access the current trends in pop and music technology. With a blatant borrowing and reshaping of musical styles – rock 'n' roll, blues, gospel, R&B, swing, rap, hip hop and soul – Prince's skills as a musician lie in his reworking of musical styles through an innovative approach to studio production. Expertly, the changes from one style to the next are captured by the notion of *positivity*, an attitude towards performance that is historically located in a George Clinton-type notion of people's liberation. In the song, 'Cream', many emotions capture the aura of *positivity* as they are articulated by a range of musical structures – the jumpy ascending and descending bass line, the repeated staccato organ stabs, and the straight accented kit line. The central stylistic thread of coding can be traced back to the boogie-woogie and rural blues of the late nineteenth century. Musical excursions in 'Cream' are further carried out through raunchy, grinding drum and bass rhythms and passionate vocal lines, around which the camped-up vocal hook, *cream*, is heavily accented. In a sense, this becomes a sleazy metaphor for sexual gratification and self-proclaimed success. As with other songs, such as 'Kiss', 'Sex in the Summer', 'The Human Body', 'Sexy Dancer', 'Hot Thing', 'Lovesexy' and 'Love Machine', a playful attitude towards sex is highly profiled in 'Cream'. Furthermore, in conjunction with the production, the erotics of this song and its video are teased out through the humorous gestures of sexing up the performance.

From the opening moans and sliding intervals in a vocal part that sounds like a fretless bass, the raunchiness of 'Cream' could not be more overt. Notably, it is Rosie Gaines who is privileged alongside Prince in both the music and video of 'Cream'. Only occasionally in the video are shots of the male backing musicians juxtaposed into the main visual narrative while Prince is foregrounded clasping and performing with virtuosity on his bright canary-yellow guitar. In such moments, phallic power is blatantly symbolised by instrumental virtuosity – harking back to the ideological core of heavy metal and hard rock (see Walser 1993a). As the video progresses, the guitar becomes more centralised through its colour and phallic symbolism amidst the action of the dancers. Yet, significantly, many of the mid-range shots involve Prince without his guitar, as he becomes more engaged in the task of dancing. The climactic point occurs when he lifts his instrument above the crowd around him, singing *look up in the air it's your guitar*. At this point, phallic control is relinquished as the guitar becomes the property of all. Notably the song's compositional design is characterised by a 'call and response' form, a technique derived from African and African-American performance styles. In the 'Cream' video, the group who support Prince endorse through their responses his calls for solidarity (McClary 2000: 23).

In addition to Prince's characteristic bid for elevated importance within the video, it is evident that the female participants are afforded visual priority. Significantly, the performance of 'Cream' focuses upon the black backing singer, Rosie Gaines, together with a troupe of dancers who vogue throughout. Stylistically, the music and video are funkadelic with the glam pop dimension heightened by Prince joining in as 'one of the girls' in the tightly choreographed dance sequences. Comprising an erotic shot of a female's smiling mouth as she licks her made-up lips lasciviously, this cheeky video concludes with a musical fade-out. Such an ambiguous closure seems immanent as the female has the last laugh.[4] In this video, like so many of his others, the issue of gender surfaces as a main element of spectacle, and, moreover, consideration.

From this we can see that Prince's performances clearly depend on a range of strategies,[5] all of which are underpinned by his blurring of identity constructs.[6] Perhaps the critical issue here is that Prince becomes *visually* an integral part of his musical reflexivity through his style of performance.

In recent years, gender-related issues in pop video scholarship have received much attention and debate.[7] For example, E. Anne Kaplan's groundbreaking studies of MTV have prompted a great deal of discussion around the configurations of gender, especially when situated within a postmodern discourse. For Kaplan the loss of any position from which to speak characterises the postmodern dilemma. In her opinion, MTV signals a uni-dimensional, commercialised and mass-oriented youth culture, engaged with trivialising all the subversive statements of early serious rock (Kaplan 1987: 152). At her peril, Kaplan classifies categories of consumption by setting up a typology for the analysis of videos. In addition to the numerous problems facing this approach to classification (Goodwin 1987; Walser 1993b; Shuker 1994), her attention to the function of music is insufficient. If we take her references to Prince, only fleeting comments to '1999', 'Raspberry Beret', 'Purple Rain' and 'Kiss', are made in an attempt to problematise the question of his address. By and large, the role and function of his music is glossed over.

Frequently, there is a sense that Kaplan's position on *musical expression* is avoided as she theorises the effects of the music video on gendered identity. In studying the impact of pop videos, surely the findings of any reading need to be assimilated against the subject's musical expression. After all, viewing videos cannot avoid our intimate responses to musical sound. But by over-privileging the visual construction of pop videos, Kaplan fails to acknowledge that music articulates meaning arbitrarily.[8] Let me put this another way: when I view a pop video, it is not so much the imagery that makes sense of the music as the reverse of this. Musical texts evoke responses which are based upon a combination of values linked to our personal histories and notions of musical experience. Of course these are rooted in our deepest feelings, desires and pleasures. Always connected to shifting attitudes, musical experience is ultimately wrapped up in that *imaginary circuit* which exists between performer and listener. This means that evaluating texts through the visual properties of pop expression is a task that should be predicated upon one's response to how music works on a *personal* level.

In all Kaplan's references to Prince's videos, there is an absence of this as she neglects to reference how his musical performance is aligned to the question of visual narrative.[9] This is most discernible in her references to his now legendary video, 'Kiss', directed by Rebecca Blake. Featuring Prince with Wendy Melvoin, the video is shot in a context where the nature of genderplay through musical performance is subtler than Kaplan acknowledges. I am referring here to aspects such as the miming of the male voice by the female, the effect of the high, falsetto male voice in relation to the sexualised male body, the witty dancing, or the implications of Wendy's cool, detachedness – a quality that is located in her bemused attitude to Prince's parading as she assuredly backs him on guitar. Her great strength of presence in this video cannot be overlooked.

The moment of transcendence in the 'Kiss' video occurs when Prince sings, *I want 2 be your fantasy, maybe U could be mine*. At this point, pleasure is located on multilevels, which include, for example, Wendy's indifference in response to his energy and performance pyrotechnics, Prince's affected and camped-up gestures, and the rich musical dynamics and tight control of rhythmic shapes. Above all, it is the unique stylistic redefinition of Rhythm and Blues, captured by the slow, grinding groove, which spells out the erotic charge and desires in 'Kiss'.[10]

As much as the visual display, it is the juxtaposition of musical codes, such as the wah-wah guitar fills, the dry foregrounded snare drum, and the busy bass drum figure that eroticise the video's narrative. It is the simplicity of the repetitive guitar-scratching chordal and rhythmic pattern of Wendy's riff, and its technological treatment within the mix, that provides Prince with the irresistible urge to dance. And, throughout the video, his dance movements cunningly imitate the contour and breathtaking funkiness of the groove. Dave Hill highlights the playfulness induced by this:

His dancing is a delight, his moves fluid, witty and sharp. He pursues his enigmatic partner round the floor, spinning, shuffling and daringly planting his lips
on the base of her belly. In the name of 'sickness', he leaves the miming of the
title-cum-punchline to her. The clip concludes with the pair of them framed by a
mock TV-screen, pressing forward like zoo animals, wondering whether to try
stepping out of the set. [Hill 1989: 187]

Obviously the spectacle of Prince in his tunic bra-top, and tight matching
trousers (off the *Parade* album cover), responding to his own musical gestures
through dance (rather than instrumental performance) can be read in many
ways. But there can be little doubt that he upsets traditional gender representations to the point that phallic power is exchanged at the juncture of
parody.[11] To some extent, what saves Prince from being just another male
rock cliché is the irony with which he constructs his acts *musically* and
visually. In this regard, his videos tell us much about *how* his music delineates the intricacies of performing out identity. Understanding such processes
is also helpful in questioning political charge within gendered address,[12]
especially in the case of the narcissistic pop performers of the MTV generation who present their enactments in fragments so that 'we can admire the
shape of the gesture itself' (Frith 1996: 215). For this is how measuring
identity through pop performances works. If a performer moves us, there are
always implications in bodily gestures – the pose, the mannerisms, the singing
style, the sexual innuendoes, the virtuosity of instrumental performance. So,
what role does this play in shaping the dialectics of identity for both the
musician and the spectator? As I have argued in my readings of Lennox's
'Money Can't Buy It' in Chapter 4, there can be little doubt that video
promos offer up a wealth of data for evaluating the nature of musical performance and identity. This is because videos function as critical aids in the
reading of the relationship between the performer's identity and the musical
text. To explore the signification of representation in another context, I want
to turn to the question of Prince's cultural and racial expression as a key to
understanding his musical identity.

Identity as racial commodity

Ethnocentric assumptions of racial identity always have their roots in ideological points of departure. Although this might seem an obvious comment to
start with, I feel compelled to emphasise it anyway. In the scholarly writings
on popular music, a tendency towards prescriptive categorisations of race into
white or black music has raised many debates. Everyone seems in agreement,
however, that when it comes to theorising identity in popular styles, the
question of race cannot be ignored. In fact, few areas of study provoke
as much reaction as those dealing with this issue. Discuss it to someone's

disapproval, and you can be quickly accused of being essentialist; or from another vantage point, quite the inverse, by being seen as slipping into 'political correctness' (Brackett 2000, 2nd edn). In the footsteps of the many theories already advanced by other musicologists on African-American identity,[13] I nevertheless feel the need to outline my position on this in relation to the question of Prince's biography.

Generally, it is accepted that popular music is one of the main terrains where the articulation of race systematically affects how we associate ourselves with people and institutions. Like other aspects of identity – gender, ethnicity, sexuality, class – race changes and shifts with time and space. Yet, over the past hundred years, the trajectory of changes in racial formation have certainly not eradicated racial prejudice. And, although colonialism might have ended in some of its representations, Eurocentrism continues to prevail as much as in the United States as in Europe and the rest of the world (see Bernardi 1996). Generally, in the West, the representational 'marks of Eurocentrism' are determined by the degree to which a group or individual 'counts or doesn't count as "white" ' (Bernardi 1996: 4). There can be little doubt that Western pop music has consistently constructed representational forms of Eurocentrism as the norms by which the Other either fails or conforms to. Hence, questions of stereotyping, fetishising and exhibiting exotic beauty through pop stardom require a critical engagement in order to avoid the pitfalls of strategic essentialising. In music videos, the implications of race-based scopophilia are as rife as misogyny, homophobia and sexism (Kaplan 1987). And if we rewind back to the 1920s, it was not that long ago that the African-American community was targeted by major labels of the American record industry. As Paul Oliver (1968) has described, the enormous number of record sales in the mid-1920s aimed at a black population ran into millions. Not only did this demonstrate the enthusiastic conditions of a segregated market, but also the profitable strategies behind marketing and commodifying race records. While one might conclude from this that African Americans were exploited by the majors, another angle to this is suggested by Toynbee who points out that 'the industry helped to amplify class and ethnic solidarity rather than imposing musical segregation' (2000: 119).

From whatever position one situates this debate, with the immense popularity of Rhythm and Blues following the Second World War, black audiences were targeted as consumers through specialised black radio stations. As a major contributor to rock 'n' roll, black radio soon attracted an increasing white following at the beginning of the 1950s.

Fast forwarding to the mid-1980s, 'crossover' became an established term of reference for African-American music that had moved into a commerical, predominantly white mainstream market. As a result, many debates have centred on the complexities of crossover, not least its exoticisation for a white audience. Moreover, its dilution of black ethnicity and exploitation by the mainstream market has evoked strong responses (George 1988; Ward 1998; Cashmore 1997; Toynbee 2000). In his studies, Ellis Cashmore (1997) has stressed how American blacks have been granted success within a white-based music industry for profit-making reasons. And, like numerous other scholars, Cashmore is critical of Prince's misappropriation of racial and social norms through his integrationist position: 'Was he trying to "pass" as white? Or was he effecting another definition of blackness?' (1997: 152). To be sure, Prince, like many African-American artists, has been fully aware of the exploitative nature of the recording industry, finding his way through to commercial distri- bution by means of his unique style and 'look'. Nonetheless, the extent of his crossover clearly fuels thought for further contemplation.[14]

It seems implicit within any diagnostic critique of Prince that the degree of his crossover is located in an array of musical styles, black and white, that he employs. Yet such an assumption clearly requires further clarification. Largely disputing the binary distinctions of racial identity, Philip Tagg (1989) has maintained there are no essentialist qualities in black music. Rather, there are *stylistic* features that are located in the music of people belonging to certain social groups.[15] Clearly, the stylistic origins of Prince's music are traceable to a wealth of African-American styles, as well as Euro-American, which adhere to different communities and groups.[16] Without exception, his recordings build on many traditions by redefining musical styles and often satirising the artifice of conventions. Running throughout his work, it is as if his musical gestures challenge the idea of racial segregation to the point of decolonising black and white musical styles from the racist fantasies that have historically imprisoned them.[17] I would suggest that his manner of crossing over might not only affirm a recognisable political signifier, but also a reflexive quality of musical performance. Yet, at the other end of this scale, he has fallen victim to the demands of Warner Brothers, a controversial point I will return to.

In addition to the construction of his striking image, acts of musical parody have blurred Prince's identity in countless ways. Frequently, he exercises his right to play out the many variables of his identity through the fickle disguise of the androgyne musician. His ability to be different (which is threatening to some while fascinating to others) and to manoeuvre between categories of black/white, straight/queer, male/female, might be considered as part of a general shift in political exigency. Moreover, in the disciplined control of his body – a site for pleasure as much as desire – we experience his identity as criss-crossed, time and time again. Yet, the gestures, sounds and reactions he attributes to his style cannot be overlooked in the wake of the fluidity of African-American expression. To explore the significance of this assumption, I am keen to consider further the theoretical merits of an anti-essentialist position. Cautioning us to the prescriptive perils of essentialism, Brackett has insisted that:

> The positive and negative uses of the idea of 'black music' have been available to members of many racial and ethnic groups; this tempers charges of essentialism (i.e., the idea that 'black music' is music made by black people), although some subject positions are more likely to be available to members of some groups than others. [Brackett 1995: 119]

Perhaps the key point to stress here stems from the idea that fluid connections exist due to social and historical factors. Rather than adopting a strategic oversimplification of ethnicity through musical distinction as Brackett suggests, we might concentrate on the subject positions that track music back to its original community. In other words, a critique of African-American music is required that is discursive in its formation, acknowledging the non-essentialist aspect of groupings, voices and racial differences.

Discoursing on African-American identity certainly opens a space to (re)conceptualise the implications of the popular in a context historically accustomed not only to hostility and racial prejudice, but also a kind of romanticism that sets up 'the music of black people' as a flimsy site for asserting arguments of authenticity. The suggestion outlined in the critical musicological proposal at the beginning of this book (Chapter 1), underlined a need to perceive race and ethnicity as a deep pool of meanings with countless points of intersection than as a fixed entity with clear-cut representations.

Applying this to Prince's texts, I would argue that it seems to be the sheer magnitude of his cross-referencing to musical styles and traditions that locates his performance within an African American context. In 1984, the success of the *Purple Rain* film and album that launched Prince to international stardom was a celebration of reconceptualising difference through crossover. Supported by his racially mixed band, The Revolution, he established with this autobiographical film his reputation in the pop world as a weird, glam-pop star with attitude. Occupying Number 1 position for 24 weeks, the album *Purple Rain* sold over 14 million copies, picking up the American Music Award for best Soul and Blues album. A lot less provocative in its lyrical content than the three previous albums, *Purple Rain* was notably more commercially accessible due to the dominance of its rock-based inflections. The innovative manipulation of rock idioms with a whole range of other popular styles is constantly evident through the instrumentation, arrangements and performance styles. In terms of production, the album mirrors the advances of technology in the early 1980s. This is discernible in everything from the models of drum machines used to the details of the recording techniques. For example, with a bland use of raw drum sounds, dryly mixed, and total lack of bass, the song, 'When Doves Cry,' off the *Purple Rain* album, represented for its time a radical point of departure in terms of production, style, and performance. In stark contrast to its poignancy and the restrained emotions of the R&B influenced song, the title track 'Purple Rain', with its eight-minute, self-indulgent build-up, leans clearly towards white, anthemic classic rock. In an outpouring of sentiment in the virtuosic and now legendary guitar solo, Prince clearly cross-references Jimi Hendrix by transporting the nostalgia of 'purple haze' into the mid-1980s.

For many, the image of Prince in the film was considered a shocking sign of the times: smouldering eyelined eyes, skin-tight purple cat-suits, sexy high-heeled boots, teasing, pouting, and sultry glances. In retrospect, the bold step he took into marketing such a controversial image became crucial to him negotiating his authorship and finding a niche. Significantly, the emphasis on dress and appearance in African-American culture has always had far-reaching implications in terms of musical expression, as Portia Maultsby has insisted:

> In African-American culture, the element of dress in musical performance is as important as the musical sound itself. When performers appear on stage, even before a musical sound is heard, audience members verbally and physically respond if costumes meet their aesthetic expectations. Performers establish an image, communicate a philosophy, and create an atmosphere of 'aliveness' through the colorful and flamboyant costumes they wear. [Maultsby 1990: 189]

Influenced by an array of other artists, not least of all George Clinton, James Brown and Little Richard, Prince's flamboyant image has always constituted an important part of his performative appeal and philosophical outlook. His unashamed use of make-up and dressing up offers him the opportunity to play with his look in a manner that shifts the boundaries of not only masculinity but also race. Indeed, the total effect of his androgynous image has opened up the possibilities for him to explore his fantasies by opposing the restrictions so often enforced on males.

Thus, from the outset, Prince's ability to communicate his intentions through a queering of traditions could not have been more disruptive than in its opposition to normative categories of identity. Addressing the question head-on in 1981, in the song, 'Controversy', he asked: *Am I black or white? Am I straight or gay? Do I believe in God? Do I believe in me?* By attaching notions of sexual and racial ambiguity to religious quest, the weight of songs such as this one quickly ignited a great deal of interest and fascination within a MTV youth generation and a music press bent on sensationalising quirkiness.

Of course, Prince's intentions to resist easy categorisation could not have been clearer. Instantly this fuelled the interest of a media intent on exploiting freak or gay artists who subvert traditional norms. It was as if Prince had instinctively learnt how tremendously popular the dysfunctional pop artist's role could be as he set out to blur aspects of his masculinity, race and sexuality. At the same time, it is striking how many references in his lyrics transmit verbal aggression and sexist abuse that clearly encroach, albeit with parody, on female space. Frequently, Prince imposes his sexual desires, his fantasies, through a parodic enactment of male domination through musical performance. What lurks behind this strategy is a ludic display of ironic function, a main ingredient of his seductive purpose. An example of this is found in the raunchy song 'Gett Off', from the album *Diamonds and Pearls*, where the lewd suggestion of *twenty-three positions in a one night stand* abounds with tensions that underpin the emotional dictates of 'funkadelic' bonding. From my analysis of the various representations of male identity in this and other sex-fixated songs, two features stand out: first, the erotic impulse behind Prince's performances (lyrically, sonically and visually); and, second, his ambivalent response to the female in relation to his own deconstruction of male identity. Constructed around a manipulative display of erotic teasing, a male aggressiveness belies the authority of his ironic act, as he sings: *Lay your pretty body against a parkin' meter. Slip yo dress down like I was strippin' a Peter Paul's Almond Joy . . . .*

In the recording and video of this song, the effect of competitive behaviour and playful sexual banter enhances the colourful spectacle of his performance. Yet, once again, one senses that his desire to control and dominate all those around him underlies his most deeply felt intentions. Like Madonna, Prince frequently exhibits the traits of the control freak, with a range of motives that are rooted in the discipline of polished productions and flawless performances.

Yet behind the witticism of the words in 'Gett Off' and the low register, speech-type style of singing he employs, an adulation of the Self positions Prince in full charge of his sexual games. His obsession with women could be constituted discursively by the early repression of the male's erotic bond with his mother. Nancy Chodorow's thesis (1978) holds that the male's displacement from emotional dependency, especially in terms of the mother–son bond, can result in the difficulties experienced in relationships later on. This might throw some light on why the motives of so many of Prince's songs centre on an insatiable yearning for female love. In her studies, Chodorow has argued that the ambivalence of men in their relationships with women is a result of the early repression of the bond between mother and son. This would go some way to explaining why derogatory jokes about other men's mothers, wives and girlfriends often function to highlight the fear men have of heterosexual relationships and the hostility many of them feel towards the emotional dynamics of dependency. Sexist jokes can often assert a special male bond that is defined by rule-governed aggressive behaviour. This would explain why the male bond is heightened when intimacy is separated from sexuality and women become just sex objects. However, in this case, Prince appears (in various ways) an exception to the rule.

Clearly, Prince's obsession with females problematises the dynamics of his identity, returning us to the question of his location within an African-American discourse. Seen from one perspective, he has endeavoured to fight off the cliché of the black, sexist macho man. Liz Jones has carefully investigated this and concludes: 'Prince has refused to fit the mould of the black man as ultra-macho loverman – perhaps one reason he has been so loved by black women, even if he didn't seem to love them back' (Jones 1997: 102).

Jones's observation, like Chodorow's, would suggest that underneath the brash and crude displays of male sexuality there often lies a great fear of emasculation. This would indicate that while anxieties about maleness and sexuality might be ridiculed through an ironic showdown of the ubiquitous heteronormative, Barry White-type representations, there is still a hint of a masculine ideal in Prince's texts. Deliberately ambiguous in his intentions, he sets out to forge a form of expression that addresses the serious issue of difference within his community. Clarification of this intention among artists such as Prince has been provided by Mercer and Julien who claim that: 'black male artists in music have been involved in a "struggle" around the political meanings of masculinity in their resistance to patriarchal role models. Music thus becomes a "key site" for pop stars to "reflect on their gendered and sexual identities" and make any alterations they might wish' (1988: 140).

From this perspective, the display of dancing, sports and musical performance by black males emphasises the physicality of the body as part of the 'struggle' to reinforce male identity.[18] However, in spite of the problems attached to machismo, it is interesting that black male identity can be aligned to the feminine. Lynne Segal notes that 'the assertion of Black manhood is both macho and largely homophobic, and yet at the same time, as we saw with earlier assertions of Negritude, more in tune with Western notions of the "feminine" in its claims to physicality, bodily awareness, emotional assertiveness, and a greater sense of communality' (1977: 195).

Segal's account here has relevance for working out Prince's subversion of the rigidity of normative maleness and race through a complex arrangement of physical possibilities. Importantly, the sexual inferences in his songs are celebrated in ways that contort the binarisms of male–female, black–white, gay–straight dualisms through the artifice of his masquerade, a point I return to later. As with his musical idiolects, his image flirts with a multiplicity of categories that draw out the *cultural constructedness* of his African-American identity. By scrambling a range of personal identity codes, Prince's texts display a mix of new signifiers that suggest the mobility of his cultural background. The pertinence of this observation brings into focus the varied interpretations elicited by different textual voices. Yet despite the implications of his androgynous body, Prince's derivations of musical style remain unambivalent.[19]

In effect, it is in the constant reiteration of rhythmic configurations, timbres, textures, call-response and grooves that his African-American consciousness becomes his sonic trademark. Within this context, we can begin to make sense of the role of music and its production as it functions as part of a larger, changing African American discourse.

As has already been pointed out earlier, the use of music technology in pop music not only appropriates but also reshapes and creates new styles, and this aspect is attached to the question of identity. In her studies, Tricia Rose (1994) has researched into how black cultural priorities have been developed and reworked through technological advances. Based upon a rich heritage of African-diasporic music, the styles that have emerged in recent history have provided new frontiers for the construction of cultural values. This is exemplified in the case of rap, where the connection between technology and oral utterance is most significant:

> Rap is fundamentally literate and deeply technological. To interpret rap as a direct or natural outgrowth of oral African-American forms is to romanticize and decontextualize rap as cultural form. It requires erasing rap's significant sonic presence and its role in shaping technological, cultural, and legal issues as they relate to defining and creating music. [Rose 1994: 95]

Rose's emphasis on sonic presence brings us to the question of compositional design and processes, especially in terms of repetition and non-linear musical practices of development. Dwelling on the parameter of repetition, we might say that this consists of the imitation of musical structures in a space of defined time. In contrast to much European-based art music, the use of repetition in African-American music – I am referring to the configurative reiterations of sets of harmonic and rhythmic patterns – negotiates a prime site for experiencing pleasure in most popular music (Middleton 1990). And, indeed, it is the advent of new technologies that have provided unlimited scope for exploring repetition as well as new sounds. For instance, the use of effects, such as phasing, gating and multiple delays in signal processing, has had a profound effect on the way in which rhythmic repetition is articulated. Similarly, advances in digital instruments and recording technology have led to new ways of shaping the rhythmic syntax of grooves. In this regard, the manipulation of repetition through technological editing practices, of course in conjunction with instrumental performance skills, needs to be evaluated in relation to the cultural values attached to the signifiers of African-American traditions.[20]

Always contingent upon the pulse of the beat, Prince's songs resonate with cultural and historical references. Undoubtedly, the thrill of his music is detectable in the multiple rhythmic patterns and their resulting grooves which intensify the aural excitement and pleasure of repetition. These codes are inextricably linked to the processes of sound engineering and mixing. Significantly, Prince's tracks have always embraced a wide range of techniques for manipulating the groove and getting his audiences to respond. Clearly, his choice of technological processing through performance style operates as a prime vehicle for the prioritisation of cultural and aesthetic values.

With regard to the question of instrumentation, drum machines, digital samplers and sequencers are commonplace in all his recordings. The connection between the employment of high-tech machines and acoustic instruments has a particular resonance when considering his musical identity. We know that since the 1980s many black artists have turned to sampling technology 'to articulate black approaches to sound, rhythm, timbre, motion and community' (Rose 1994: 84) as a mode of community-based expression. What seems pertinent here is the employment of new technologies as an affirmation of the power and control within musicianship.

Most importantly, it is the musical genres Prince reworks through his production techniques and performance style that can be understood as a response to the social and political realities of our time. Maultsby verifies this by explaining how in African-American music 'song lyrics and music styles of funk, disco, and rap music epitomize the changing and sometimes conflicting viewpoints about progress, which have encouraged blacks to dissipate social tensions through 'self-expression and unrestricted social interactions' (Maultsby 1990: 204). Yet, to interpret Prince's music only as a representation of African-American styles would be to disregard its sheer breadth of influences.[21] Through intricate processes of cultural syncretism, Prince's musical output indeed articulates the many new musical directions to have emerged in all complexions of Western music during the past few decades.

In other words, the musical elements found in Prince's texts can be read as a complicated representation of collective traditions and practices. The blending and blurring of styles to re-create new ones through pastiche constitutes a natural facet of his creative compositional thought. One of the focal points of this study concerns the evolution of musical styles as they provide the aural signposts within our culturescapes. In shaping our identities, musical styles pose broader questions concerning how we culturally decode meaning. Thus, with Prince, both image and sound promulgate the idea of the African-American identity in transit. In a sense, he mirrors the liberation and suppression of black people over several centuries.[22] Above all, by defining the black male through his own reconstruction and sense of blackness, Prince reveals an important historic position in the ongoing struggles for black freedom and political power. As McClary has observed, he 'reinscribes a rich history of African American music' (2000: 153) by selecting the devices that best suit his requirements.

What arises from these assumptions so far is the question of how Prince's music induces feelings and responses by way of his identity. Indeed, the processes of experiencing pleasure through his sound *somatically*, in particular in the form of dance – a dominant feature of all African-American music – is a matter of profound relevance.

Clearly, there is a need to concern ourselves with the interpretation of different types of cultural exchange that take place through our physical responses to music. Involvement with any musical text might be considered an act of desire that is cast through the ideological moorings of musical signification. Certainly the thrill of musical experience is wrapped up in the activities of everyday life. And, the manipulation of explicit sexual and racial symbols through musical performance articulate those intensified notions of desire that provide us with a great sense of pleasure. It seems then that the borders of social and political privilege, presented by artists like Prince, are omnipresent in a range of musical origins that are set against the backdrop of a wide spectrum of sexual and racial fantasies. On the general implications of this in African-American identity, Brian Ward slots Prince into a larger group of musicians who have expressed ongoing social and political struggles:

> From Michael Jackson, Whitney Houston, DeBarge and Prince, through Bobby Brown, Boyz II Men, TLC and R. Kelly, to Run DMC, Public Enemy, Snoop Doggy Dogg and the Fugees, the most popular contemporary black music has acted as a bulwark against the psychological ravages of racism, frustration, often poverty, and sometimes despair in the black community. Whether as musical creators and entrepreneurs, or as creatively participating listeners and dancers, African-Americans have continued to find in their music a vital means to express individual and collective identities, earn respect, and, in some cases, secure considerable material rewards. [Ward 1998: 451–2]

Ward's above evaluation situates the issue of racial identity alongside important issues relating to the commercialisation of culture. As a musician speaking from many subject positions, Prince not only transforms musical codes and rules into new formations and genres, but also promotes the vitalisation of difference and cultural (dis)advantage through the impact of musical performance and stylistic appropriation. Bearing this in mind, let us now turn to an analysis of examples of stylistic crossover in one of his most popular album productions.

Stylistic and technical codes in *Diamonds and Pearls*

One of the central arguments in this chapter is that musical codes and their correlation to constructs of identity form a crucial part of understanding Prince's music. In this section I want to present a few of my findings which resulted from an earlier study I carried out on the album *Diamonds and Pearls*.[23]
Through a semiotic positioning of the musical codes and idioms of the 13 songs comprising this album, I have attempted to explore the convergence and divergence of a number of stylistic routes. Implicit in this study is a curiosity to map Prince's personal expression against his employment of various music traditions and idioms. In many ways, this album, *Diamonds and Pearls*, can be considered as a celebration of inherited norms and traditional genres, a point I have laboured in earlier work: 'In the pursuit of his own identity, Prince never disguises his delight at experimenting and playing with a wide array of pop genres. It is this blatant experimentation with and articulation of familiar styles

and traditions that forms the basis of his uniquely personal musical dialect' (Hawkins 1992b: 1).

By locating a range of musical codes in each song, and, thereafter, under-taking a diagnostic analysis of all the songs in their sequential order, I have set out to examine the stylistic codification inherent in Prince's music.[24] The main purpose for this study is to explore the significance of stylistic and technical musical codes through a comparative analysis of their stylistic features.

With reference to the transcript table (Table 6.1), the data assembled charts a number of prominent features through two procedures: first, the documenta-tion of both musical and verbal descriptions of the following properties – tempo specifications, rhythmic riffs, stylistic characteristics, verbal interpreta-tive descriptions of moods and effects, studio techniques and general range of intensity levels (in terms of mood, dynamics and tension): and second, the identification of the derivation of stylistic coding that exists from one track to the next. This information serves as a starting point for assimilating the musical processes and determinants of style that Prince employs.

As I have already indicated, Prince's stylistic gestures are rooted in a rich heritage of popular idioms and styles.[25] What is most notable in *Diamonds and Pearls* are the junctures of stylistic appropriation. This is largely discernible in the qualities of vocal delivery, production techniques, performance skills and arrangements. However, what is most apparent is the level of musical variation and how this is regulated through the manipulation and creative (re)invention of style.

The levels of stylistic interchange, as illustrated in Table 6.1, can be measured through a range of specified categories. For example, some of the stylistic distinctions between the songs 'Strollin'' and 'Gett Off' are discern-ible in the following ways:

- the use of modality – G lydian in 'Strollin'' and C aeolian in 'Gett Off';
- the stylistic feel – swing, Big Band jazz feel set within a fast tempo in 'Strollin'' compared to the grinding hip-hop, funk-driven style of 'Gett Off';
- the differences of mood between performance delivery – a carefree, spon-taneity in 'Strollin'' contrasted with the dry, precise, controlled gestures in 'Gett Off';
- rhythmic expression – an innocuously simple dotted rhythmic pulse of 'Strollin'' contrasts vividly with the hard-hitting, solid riff of 'Gett Off', in which the heavily gated snare drum drives home the raw sexual desires of the lyrics. The jam-style of 'Gett Off' clearly has its roots in the P-funk world of George Clinton and James Brown.

Obviously the expressive quality of the vocals and the rhythmic impetus of the songs' grooves are attached to the diverse narratives of each song. While

Table 6.1 Semiotic transcript table: *Diamonds and Pearls*

SONGS 1-13	TEMPO	RHYTHMIC RIFFS	HARMONIC CENTRES	STYLES	VERBAL/IMAGE DESCRIPTIONS	STUDIO EFFECTS/ TECHNIQUES	INTENSITY LEVELS
Thunder	MODERATE ♩=120	*(notation)*	B minor(mel)/ aeolian (i-VI/VII-III-VI)	rock, disco, gospel,funk, 70's ballad	jubilant, big impact, american 70's, religious, spiritual feel	SAMPLED & LIVE SOUNDS GATED VOCALS EQ'D MID-RANGE	*(graph)*
Daddy Pop	MEDIUM FUNK ♩=120	*(notation)*	E aeolian/ blues (i-v7)	R & B, funk, rock, gospel, musical, soul	partytime, rockin' and rollin', happy, poppy, mischievous	UNTREATED VOCALS/ SAMPLED R.TRACK SPACIOUS MIX	
Diamonds & Pearls	SLOW BALLAD ♩=84	*(notation)*	G/Eb mixo-lydian (i-VII-I-IV-I)	rock ballad, pop, jazz, soul	smooth, warm, emotional, tuneful, radio music, orchestral Vegasy	REVERBED KIT SAMPLED SOUNDS/ DRUM MACHINE BD HIGHLY COMPRESSED/ ECHO EFFECTS	
Cream	MODERATE ♩=116	*(notation)*	Bb mixolydian/ blues (I-IV-I)	blues, classic, rock, commercial, pop, soul, boogie	humorous, chunky boogie, slick, sensual, sexy, fun-time	CLEAN, DRY MIX HIGHLY GATED BASS & KIT TRACKS/ SYNCH'SED ECHO	
Strollin'	FAST AND LIVELY ♩=133	*(notation)*	G lydian/mixo-lydian/ionian (I-II-I-IV)	swing jazz, Big Band genre	carefree, positive, pastiche, mocking, dreamy, conventional	FORECGROUN-DING KIT LINE / MIX CRISP, 'UN-AUTHENTIC' ANALOGUE SOUNDS EQ'D VOCALS FORECG'D	
Willing & Able	MODERATE ♩=132	*(notation)*	E mixolydian/ blues (I-VII-IV7)	South African township, jive, gospel-chorus	earnest, political, jiving, skipping, jumping cool	HIGH REVERB & ANALOGUE 'LIVE FEEL' ROUNDED BASS DRUM SOUND	
Gett Off	FAIRLY SLOW ♩=108	*(notation)*	C aeolian (i)	club, hip-hop, rap, house-rock, thrash	wild, erotic, sexual, subversive, thrusting James Brown, thrilling, street, clubbing, riské	HEAVILY GATED BASS & SNARE PTS. SAMPLED, EQ'D SD - OVERDRIVE CTR.	
Walk Don't Walk	STEADY ♩=96	*(notation)*	E major (I-IV-V)	70's pop style, rock ballad	easy-going urban, traffic jams, leisurely, positive, confident	MIDDLE-MIX PANNED DRMS CAR HORN SAM-PLES /CLEAN-MIX	
Jughead	MODERATE ♩=116	*(notation)*	Bb aeolian (i)	rap, dance, house, anthemic heavy-rock	aggressive, serious partying, crowded, rowdy, jackhammer, pounding, energetic, passionate	'LIVE' SOUND-EFFECTS WIDE/ 3D SPEC-TRUM	
Money Don't Matter 2 night	MODERATE ♩=120	*(notation)*	Db lydian (vii-I-III)	70's ballad song, straight pop, soul	serious-talking, emotional, relaxed, cool, nostalgic, romantic	ANALOGUE 'LIVE' KIT SOUNDS HIGH QUALITY MIX	
Push	MODERATE ♩=120	*(notation)*	Db major (I)	rap, dance, hip-hop, rock	stimulating exciting, sexual, dancing, busy, psychedelic	DENSE MIX COMPRESSED BASS TRACK	
Insatiable	SLOWLY ♩=60	*(notation)*	C lydian (I-vii-vi)	gospel, soul, soul-ballad	relaxed, spatial, sensual, intimate, gentle, innocent, naive, juvenile	SPACIOUS MIX SAMPLED SOUNDS PANNED KIT PARTS	
Live 4 Love	MODERATELY SLOW ♩=104	*(notation)*	E dorian (i-IV-I)	rap, techno-rock, funk, hard-rock	robotic, power groove, energetic, Hendrix, intense, manic, physical, authentic, erotic	DIRTY-MIX HIGH EQ'D BACK. INC VOCALS HIGHLY COMPRESSED KIT	

'Strollin'' could be interpreted as a positive and skittish stroll around the delights of easy swing, 'Gett Off' is dirty in its raunchy sound. A glance at the main rhythmic riffs in the kit and percussion parts also reveals how musical gesture plays a dominant role in articulating the moods of each song stylistically.

While it is mainly funk and rock genres that permeate *Diamonds and Pearls*, other styles are juxtaposed and woven in and out, such as rock, gospel, disco, rap, boogie, R&B, soul, jazz, township and hip hop. Of the variety of student responses I have measured concerning the influence of rock, stylistic descriptions range from straight-rock, ballad-rock, house-rock, heavy-rock, anthemic-rock, hard-rock to techno-rock. Of course such definitions highlight the fluidity of rock as a style, and how rock has been adapted throughout the 1980s and 1990s. I would argue that the extents to which rock and hip hop are modified to different styles constitute a significant part of Prince's approach to composition through pastiche.

In a general sense, the breadth of musical idioms found in *Diamonds and Pearls* highlights the processes of crossover in Prince's productions. Moreover, the unique cataloguing of stylistic and technical codes within each song from this album brings into question how one undertakes the task of categorical identification.

As I have illustrated in Table 6.1, it is more the general influences than the idea of any specific style that is most noticeable when taking the music into consideration. In the opening song, 'Thunder', for example, a collage of stylistic codes – gospel, funk, rock, disco and ballad – are mixed together by Prince who performs all the instruments on the track. Through the juxtapositioning of these stylistic references, the aesthetics of the song are vividly expressed.

In stark contrast to 'Thunder', however, the song 'Money Don't Matter 2 Night' has a distinct Steely Dan and Stevie Wonder flavour to its arrangement and production. Characterised by a slowish tempo and gentle vocal sounds, the mood of the song is captured in its smooth, spiritual ballad form. The instrumentation and chordal nuances are reminiscent of 1970s ballads, while hints of gospel and soul features are discernible in the call-and-response interrelationship between the soloist and backing vocals.

Of all the musical parameters responsible for denoting style, the one that stands out most is timbre. This parameter is one of the most neglected in music-analytic practice, especially when it comes to relating it to questions of meaning. Perhaps the most striking aspect of Prince's timbre is found in the overall quality and articulation of his sound, something that is instantly recognisable. As a rule his vocal timbre is regulated in much the same way as he controls his instrumental sounds, with an elasticity in register that is tightly controlled. This is especially evident in his instrumental solos, which often emulate the expressive gestures of his vocal lines. I am referring here to the very timbral impact of sounds as they are projected through extreme contrasts in register, that is, screams, whines and wails, long sustained notes, large intervallic slides and leaps, and heavy use of vibrato. In terms of the music's overall expression, there is always an emphasis on the control of dynamics, through an almost exaggerated sense of volume fluctuation and variable textural shadings.[26] Generally, the technical codes of the production are complex and polished to the smallest detail as Prince exerts pressure on the scope of his timbral quality through technological innovation.

What I am leading towards here is that the stylistic diversity in *Diamonds and Pearls* is contingent upon the details of its timbral control as much as the parameters of rhythmic, melodic, production and harmonic nuances. In a sense the regulation of timbre is shaped and controlled through the technical employment of EQ (equalisation), reverb, compressors, noise gates and enhancers. In Table 6.1 the high-intensity levels (4/5) in the song, 'Push', for example, are experienced as a direct result of the overall mix compression and its high threshold. For example, the pumped-up effect of the bass line in this song results from its control by a 'fast release' in compression and low band-width in the enhancer control. Moreover, the regulation between *dry* and *wet* signal processing[27] profoundly increases the contrasts in effect of timbre.[28]

What conclusions then can be drawn from this survey of the music in *Diamonds and Pearls*? Significantly, Prince's music demonstrates how the utilisation of musical codes in different stylistic ways can add up to a profusion of exciting events. In a general sense, his music delineates notions of difference or, for some, *originality* (although I am weary of the implications of this term), in terms of the heterogeneous quality of his sound-box. We might say that *Diamonds and Pearls* exemplifies how Prince's compositional thought is characterised by the effect of its diverse integration of styles and idioms. Clearly, the indefatigable absorption of styles has its direct parallels in the constitution of Prince's African-American identity, which is constructed out of the vast array of the materials of his cultural heritage. In this sense, his musical idiom, like his identity, is based upon the tensions and contradictions of his polysemic texts. There is always this sense that the handling of musical ideas through processes of appropriation is distinctly Princean. But most of all, it is the composite set of dialogic components that add up to the total effect of his musical style, and it is to the implications of this that we will now turn.

Sexing and 'spinning' gender in musical expression

In a Barthesian sense, Prince's music can be read as *referential*, with the principal referent being that of the body. One could further argue that his physicality is displayed as a multifaceted phenomenon in which the suppressed

Subject in one instance becomes the oppressor in another. Here, tension between these two states is regulated through the provocation of his spectacle. As sexuality and religion have emerged as a focus of media attention more and more in mainstream politics of the 1980s and 1990s, changing values and their meanings have continued to confront the grand narratives of morality and religious orders (see Lyotard 1984).

Evidence of these changes and social movements are catalogued in the representations of the music of their time. Clearly, pop scores from this period offer us a way of experiencing the prevailing attitudes and cultural shifts through various forms of musical representation. In this respect, pop music chronicles historical, cultural and political events, while engaging us with questions relating to ethics and taste. Mainly, it is through performance that we can gain insight into how the politics of representation offer a way for disseminating meaning. In the case of Prince, it is how his gendered body responds and communicates *musically* that calls into question the issues that deal with social attitudes. Given this, the main question I will consider in this section concerns the function and idealisation of the body in the context of the late twentieth and early twenty-first century. How do pop performers approach sexual and gendered response through musical performance? And how does performance inflect the changes, ambivalences, and political exigencies of human behaviour at specific points in time?

In the mid-1980s, it was the impact of AIDS during the Reagan and Thatcher administrations that led to serious political and moral debates concerning the individual's responsibility and social attitude towards sex. For instance, the AIDS era signalled the biggest shake-up in progressive sexual politics in the West. Yet, in the desperate campaign against AIDS, fierce struggles against misogyny, homophobia and the breakdown of rigid gender binarisms have continued on many levels. Like many artists of the AIDS generation, Prince's reckless flaunting of risqué sexual desires has been regarded by many as dangerous, provoking outrage and condemnation from the more conservative sectors of society (with many of his record sleeves carrying the 'Parental Advisory Explicit Lyrics' warning). One might argue that his performances, for their time, offered daring critiques on a range of sexual potentialities through performances of erotic display. From the outset, his texts signified an eroticisation of a unique blend of gender that could celebrate sexuality without inhibition.

Now whatever approach one takes to studying Prince, there is no escaping the erotic link between his musical output and his organisation of sexual roles. There can be little doubt that the combination of these two elements largely accounts for his huge popularity.[29] But, the key organising agent of sexual identity is gender. As Michael S. Kimmel puts it, 'gender informs sexuality, sexuality confirms gender' (1987: 19). Through Prince's performances, the display of sexuality becomes a main mechanism in constructing new displays of gender and confounding old ones. It is from this position that his gender-bending constitutes the primary part of an act that stylises his performance around different experiences and pleasures. For the most part, his decentred, subverted representations of masculinity chart a range of differences from one song to the next. McClary describes the kinds of sexual activity Prince exposes us to as 'anything but natural – [rather they are] bizarrely erotic' (2000: 156). This assumption inevitably opens up the discussion of 'naturalness' within any discourse on sexuality, something I have already raised in Chapter 2 and 3. Yet, obviously the construction of a 'natural' or freak mode of expression when it comes to gender is never determining in any absolute sense.

A basis for exploring territories of gender and sexuality has been suggested by the musicologist, Lawrence Kramer (1993). The analytical objective in his article, '*Carnaval*, Cross-Dressing, and the Woman in the Mirror', is to discover how the *mobility of gender* raises a number of issues concerning the unrestricted crossing of gender boundaries. Primarily, Kramer contests a musicological approach to Robert Schumann's *Carnaval* by Dahlhaus and Rosen, who, according to Kramer, deny the work's cultural agency. As with the bulk of scholarly work on Western art composers, we learn through Kramer that Dahlhaus and Rosen's analyses of Schumann are separated from issues of gender and sexuality to the point that '... by scanting the question of gender, they write a phallocentric criticism' (Kramer 1993: 324). Underlying their approach are the tenets of the Western canon and the ideologies and practices attached to it:

> The 'classical' canon, even a canon no longer limited to the works of white males, is sure to become increasingly marginal unless we can link it to our most vital interests. We can no longer do that as formalists at a time when ideologies of unity are collapsing and the demands of difference and diversity are rightly being heard on all sides. We must learn to *spin*. [Kramer 1993: 325, emphasis added]

Expanding on Kramer's metaphor of spinning a little further and considering the traditions that adhere to the classical canon in the light of pop texts, we might consider how musical expression, in a general sense, articulates its own discourses of power through gender and sexuality. In rejecting the formalist approach to textual analysis, Kramer's suggestion to *spin* arises from a notion of the formalisation of the spinning wheel as a mode of repression. Camille Saint-Saëns's dubious comments on female creativity in his interpretation of the French poem, *Omphale's Spinning Wheel* (*Le Rouet d'Omphale*, 1871–72) provide the source for Kramer's idea on spinning within a musicological critique. I see this as helpful in problematising the workings of power in musical expression and the materiality of discourse. Indeed, it would seem to make sense that a general discourse within musicology needs to account for how representations of identity often serve to objectify the sound. In particular, questions relating to how music is fetishised and empowered are connectable to working out how constructions of difference function as desire.[30] In opposition to the mutually exclusive categories for male and female subjects, the idea of a mobility of gender through musical expression is well suited to a further exploration of male identity through Prince's texts.

As I have noted so far in my studies of the Pet Shop Boys and Morrissey, the male in the 1980s and 1990s became increasingly sexualised and objectified through the hype of advertising and patterns of consumption. While feminists in the 1980s argued that the male as sex object could not withstand the weight of sexual objectification, this has not been the case in popular culture with the packaging of male pop icons. Tailoring his look and sound according to his need, Prince's strategy is to appeal to a type of polysemic gazing. Walser addresses this in his analysis of Prince when he insists that '[Prince] invites men to imagine different modes of eroticism and relations, and invites women to imagine men who could imagine such things' (1994: 85). If we go along with Walser's claim, then it stands that Prince's texts are received through a wide variety of subject-positions as he exercises his claim to power through commodification. In other words, the dissemination of pop texts must be understood in relation to the sexual construction of meaning at the moment of reception (Cubitt 2000: 153).[31] My main point here is that Prince's songs mobilise codes of gender by positioning the listener in dialectical relationship to himself.

Quite conscious of this, Prince works at constructing an image that arouses intrigue, and, at times suspends belief on a variety of levels. Of course, at the basis of his appeal is his showmanship and the versatility of his performance style. This constitutes his authorship, something that is characterised by a flamboyancy of physical expression that is articulated through the visual and sonic energy of dancing, strutting, jumping, jamming, improvising and running, which quickly takes a grip on one's imagination.

In terms of spectatorship, Prince's performances signify a set of political representations that survive by being deceptively elusive. In most of his songs, there is an element of ambivalence and, arguably, denial. This is manifested in a strategy of genderbending that is constantly revitalised through tactics of queering. To pick up on the range of debates I have already entered into in Chapters 2, 4 and 5, queering in performance has significant political and ideological ramifications, and, yet, should not be viewed as utopian in its liberating function: 'the term [queer] has come to mean a representation that is not necessarily right on. Queer representations may not always be positive; they are frequently ambiguous, slippery, and in total don't add up to a coherent whole. They often leave the spectator/viewer questioning' (Evans and Gamman 1995: 47).

From this, it follows that identfying Prince's strategy of queering can only relate to its reception within in a transpersonal context – a site where masquerade can destabilise the coherent whole. Indeed, masquerade can be understood as a form of masking that intends to resolve gendered identification within a presumed context of heteronormativity. One might read Prince's motives as based round a fear of his own phallicism – the phallic identity he flaunts yet shys away from. In this sense, Prince's masquerading highlights his femininity as a reflection of the Phallus in order to expose the bisexual possibilities that commonly disrupt and challenge heteronormativity. Of course, interpreting his queer antics leads to a rethinking of sexual politics beyond the historic dogma of essentialist spectatorship. Yet the question still remains: what then is masked by masquerade and queering, and how might we rethink the very reflexive notions of masculinity that encompass the performing out of sexual difference?

Often depicted through a somewhat comical portrayal of sex and religion, Prince parodies his role as an object of desire for everyone to identify with.[32] An interesting corollary to his androgyny is the humorous display of cross-dressing. Clearly, by refuting conventional male dress codes through, for example, a blending of tight-fitting catsuits with high-heel stilettos, make-up and tacky jewellery, he strips away at the seriousness of austere tailoring of traditional male clothing.[33] It is as if the image he plays with heightens the distinction between his anatomy and the categories of gender he decides to reject and construct. Often with Prince one has this sense that within the midst of the contingent dimensions of corporeality we are presented with, there lies a falsely coherent sense of unity. Indeed, if read as parodic, it is this strategy which converts into a great amount of pleasure as we recognise the dramatic potential of relations between gender parody and musical expression. To be more precise, what Prince's performance constitutes is an enactment of the very performativity of gender itself.

Often there is a sense that Prince's stylised musical sound can be likened to the verbal emphases on words in 'quotation' marks, where certain ironic prerequisites are always attached to musical structures. In this sense, a ludic irony exposes the full potential of his act, as his identity emerges from a range of conflicting meanings by implying repressed alternatives. As much as with his dress codes and his panache for fashion is an implicit musical camping-up of traditional musical styles, such as funk, rock, rap, hip hop and metal. Prince constantly reinvents himself musically. His colourful, Clinton-carnivalesque displays are illustrative of the ways in which his musical performance delineates meaning. Such forms of showing off verify the theatrical dimension of pop music as something seen as much as heard. But what counts most here is Prince's unique sense of theatricality, which is executed through a campness that radiates the glamour of virtuosic showmanship.

Generally, the polymorphous identities of pop stars, especially among the generation of MTV superstars, are presented to us via the fragmented and spliced-up body parts of their iconography (Kaplan 1987). Yet the conditions of fragmentation in pop aesthetics seldom detract from the star's own sense of authenticity. Again this raises the question of 'realness' within a postmodern critique (Kellner 1995; Frith 1996; Toynbee 2000). Prince, like Madonna, has constantly referred to himself as an artist, most notably, from 1993 to 2000, when he replaced his name, Prince, with a symbol denoting his androgyny.

To return to a similar point raised in my readings of Madonna in Chapter 2, we need to ask to what degree the artist's notion of their self-authentication evokes levels of anxiety through the implosion of their politics of representation (see Baudrillard 1983a, 1983b). Thus, another way of approaching the question of the artist-in-performance is to consider the psychoanalytic work that I have referred to on spectatorship. As we have already seen, studies undertaken in this field have exposed how reflexivity on the part of the individual functions in shifting ways. The effect of this, as Laplanche and Pontalis (1986) have argued, is to destabilise normative readings on the part of the spectator. In this sense, theoretical positions that insist on closed readings of texts might be considered in opposition to the advances of plurality and difference.

According to Jacques Lacan (1977b), the idea of reflection directly concerns the dialect of one's self-recognition. Notably, the image-in-the-mirror metaphor functions to disrupt notions of fixed identity that suggests that the evaluation of personality can never translate into reality. Prince presents himself and (re)defines himself through the multiple voices that emphasise the potential of his polysemic construction.

The main point I am emphasising here is that Prince's authorship is inscripted in a calculated control of ambiguity. In contrast to the male performer locked into dominant roles of representation (Cubitt 2000), Prince demands a less rigid position on the part of the spectator. In a sense, it is the mobility of his gender that characterises his phallic parading and spells out his playfulness. This is manifested through masquerade as he fools around with masks, which, from a Lacanian perspective, distances him from himself and his image.[34] As Lacan (1977a, 1977b) has demonstrated, the individual is defined as *lacking* in terms of sexual differentiation in the womb. Throughout life the search for the lost component of the Subject is directed through a narcissistic object-directed love. This implies that the Subject's identity is located within the ideal of the Other – subjectivity only functions through a set of relationships based on difference. While Lacanian theory might be read as phallocentric and sexist (feminist writers have argued that he reinforces Freudian theory by simply transferring privilege from the penis to the phallus), his model of individuality goes some way in opening up the debates concerning difference at least in terms of symbolic signification.

At the heart of Lacan's theory, language is situated in a way that connects social realities with the unconscious. And so, within a male-dominated setting, indifferent to any historical process, Lacan's concepts work at a level which deny the relationship of power to sexual identity by the prioritisation of language as the prime site of focus. Meaning here becomes part of a complex phallocentric linguistic determinism that avoids the fluid structures of gender within different social contexts.

For the purpose of this study, the value of a Lacanian approach lies in its clarification of how the Subject's identity is assembled through an array of symbols and signifiers that relate to language. Importantly, this is connected to the phallic function of gazing that has traditionally asserted male dominance. As Richard Dyer's film studies (1982) stress in their application of Lacanian theory, it is the male gaze that exerts *staring* as a form of active dominance. In this respect, Prince frequently stares into the camera while being portrayed *in an active state* – dancing, playing musical instruments, simulating sex, or executing James Brown spins. Yet, notably, he often flirts with passivity in performance as he shares his performance space with active women who assume dominant positions (see McClary 2000). In such moments, the unified signification of phallic posturing parodies the limitations of male expression. I will now link this to the problematic distinction between eroticism and sex.

Interpretations of sexual display are always predicated on variable predispositions, especially when we move from the classification of pornography to eroticism. In his studies, Robert Stam has emphasised that 'porn has no single audience' (1989: 168) and therefore can never be perceived as a monolithic entity. Clearly, there are contexts in which definitions of pornography can be substituted as eroticism for some and not for others. In pop texts, especially videos and films, we need to be aware of the existence of an extensive range of erotic-pornographic taxonomies. By the same token, the explicit content of Prince's performances is quite removed from the autolectic dimension of mainstream phallocentric porn, which generally sets out to generate a loss of aura. In many ways, his texts succeed in exposing eroticism as a discursive construct. From his first hits in the late 1970s, Prince has always turned to sexual fascination and its lure. One way to analyse the nature of Prince's erotic depictions is to measure them against a general consideration of his musical performance. Through the erotics of his performances, his sexuality is constantly pushed forward as a focal point.[35] Always exhibited with acrobatic panache, the sexiness of his performances might be read as a demonstration of his propensity for living out erotic fantasies to their full.

In exploring the polarities of sexual identity in Prince's work, it is worth noting that his references to phallic power often strain between resistance and compliance. His masculinity is reconstructed to the point that the more he appropriates clichés of phallocentricity, the more his gestures are called into question by himself. Above all, Prince demonstrates that masculinity is always in a state of flux, although its bizarre representation is inevitably tied up within power and control. So, through a calculated construction of his image, he parodies the myths of male dominance by satirising the restrictive roles that have traditionally repressed men from expressing themselves emotionally. Especially, the erotic fantasies surrounding black male sexuality are teased out through the politics of his performance. This, in turn, raises questions concerning how signs of sexuality and race are destabilised or reinforced through music. Effectively, features of musical expression draw our attention to the cultural constructedness and artifice of our gendered environments (Mercer 1988).

Meanwhile to return to an earlier point, there would appear to be a price here as black performers often have to compromise their identity in order to reduce their sexual threat (see Segal 1991). Seen in this light, the political strategy of Prince also needs to be interrogated within a commodity-driven cultural context where the play on ambiguity and pretence too easily becomes the norm. For we know that in pop performances, androgyneity and difference have become fashionable in a media-driven cultural climate which thrives on the slightest variation in sexual orientation while still adhering to the male/female dichotomy of gender.

In considering the full extent of the construction of playfulness in the context of pop, we need to carefully approach the question of motive. Here, I would suggest that the gratification and fun derived from the flaunting of the queered body through different representations of gender can signify one of the most complicated components of the pop aesthetic. In a sense, the reappropriation of the body occurs through a direct transference of the fulfilment of desire onto the musical code. This would imply that the exploitation of the musical code in this context is realised through the body in a narcissistic fashion. And when appearing liberated through dance, the body becomes charged with a Baudrillardian sense of *synthetic narcissism* (see Baudrillard 1983a). Thus, deconstructed through signs of seduction, the body in pop performance emerges rearranged by the subject as an object of totalisation. And so, in Prince's case, there emerges a subversive thrill in the pastiche effect of his set of practices. The sheer impact of this is to open up self-parodic manifestations of himself as a strategy to expose the illusion of gender norms.

What seems at issue here is how the body-as-pop-commodity becomes the idealised consummation of the narcissistic Subject. In Prince's case, his idiolect is shaped by the ambivalence of the symbolic male/female model whose *sign* results in his own metamorphosis and name substitution. From this, it would seem that Prince has set out to demonstrate that gender does not refer to a substantive being but rather a relative point of convergence among culturally and politically constituted formulations.

Carnivalesque musical display: Signs of the times?

What emerges from the discussion so far is the idea that the pop text is a series of positioned utterances rather than a unitary text. In this respect, the task of reading the text, at least within a music-theoretical discourse, lies in exposing various features of musical representation. To pursue this further, we might consider Prince's texts as regressive *and* progressive in that they are tied to the constraints of corporate support and political strategy. In the music industry we know that the corporates have the manipulative power to control both the artist and audience: hence Prince's resort to changing his name and inscribing 'SLAVE' on his face prior to severing his ties with Warner Brothers in 1995.

Within this context, a master and slave analogy seems obvious. Given that both these categories never denote innate entities, the idea of the master/slave opposition, at least in a Hegelian sense,[36] could be interpreted as a motivic object of the historical process by which the character of the master is negated dialectically by the slave. By transcending himself through gruelling labour and an obsession for perfection, Prince liberates himself from the adversity of the master's control by undergoing change *dialectically* through sublimation and survival. But, in another sense, Prince becomes both master and slave. Here the master re-emerges as the slave's own conscience, thus signifying a transmutation into psychic reality. This represents a form of empowerment that not only turns back on itself, but also on itself. Notably, in the poignant song, 'Slave', from the album *Emancipation*, he makes this clear as he cries *everybody keeps trying to break my heart*, pleading for his (and others') release from Warner Brothers. Helping to exploit the force of this message, every musical code is united in the pounding-out of his political sentiments. Foregrounded in the mix of 'Slave', the highly compressed snare-shots (placed on the second and fourth beats of each bar) beat up the passion of the frenzied lyrics with striking ferocity.

When contemplating the signification of a song such as 'Slave', it becomes clear that the link between production and performance is critical in determining what delineates meaning. Within the slickly produced settings of his videos and live performances, Prince's style of jamming, a central part of his compositional approach, often appears utopian. Yet, situated amidst gleeful multi-ethnic crowds – dancing, parading or partying on streets and stage-sets – the locations of his performance jams also represent the commercial aerobics of a fiercely competitive industry. In a Bakhtinian sense, this frames the political strategies and ironic intentions of the pop star whose texts encapsulate an intended pluralism. I am referring here to a pluralism in which the syncretic nature of diverse utterances flow effortlessly into a deceptive pool of utopia.

Often teasing and confusing, it is the surprise tactics inherent in masquerade that guarantee the delight of subversive pleasures.[37] Almost all Prince's texts contain some element of this in one way or another. The cover alone of the *Lovesexy* album (1988), depicting Prince bashfully posing naked, attracted enormous attention with certain chain record stores in the US declining to stock it.[38]

Figure 6.1 Prince on the *Lovesexy* album cover

   Stylistically, the music on this album stretches funk to its utmost limitations
through dense and complex full-band arrangements, extended polymodal
passages of harmonic intricacy, spiritual melodies, kicking rhythmic riffs juxtaposed with cheeky, discordant horn stabs. Notably, this album signifies a
period when Prince's personality peaked at a point of self-revelation, as he
declared his spiritual and religious beliefs. Delivered with the most intense
sexual and religious fervour ever witnessed, the *Lovesexy* world tour balanced
carnal lust alongside extreme erotic flirtations with Sheila E and Cat on a set
no one will ever forget. In the dramatic closing part of the first set, part of
the act included Prince being 'shot' while singing the song 'Bob George', only
to rise out of a cloud of smoke on a hydraulic heart-shaped set, resurrected,
singing the most cathartic of all his songs, 'Anna Stesia'. Representing one of
his most poignant songs, 'Anna Stesia' signified an ecstatic unleashing of all

his sins as he acquired spiritual attainment through liberation (Hawkins 1992a).

Like *Emancipation* and *Diamonds and Pearls*, the album *Sign O' the Times,* released in 1987, contains a wide breadth of musical styles and is inventive in its production.[39] Within the songs of this album, Prince redefines R&B and rock into an orgiastic display of new musical ideas. In one of his most seriously political statements, the prophetic song, 'Sign O' The Times', heightens the impact of the word as symbol with a range of compelling musical gestures.

In the video of this song we are once again reminded how identity is constructed through language in one of the most daring visual productions of its time, which completely omits Prince from its visual content. Here, the striking array of visual fonts centres on a dramatisation of the song's lyrics, as the words are juxtaposed into a brilliant spectrum of different sizes and colours. Like the multitrack production of the musical material, the visual tracks are composited in a minimal and effective manner. Their dramatic rhetoric is heightened through the extreme fluctuations in speed, which is aligned to the tightly edited speech rhythms in the musical text. In particular, the single visual code, 'TIME', functions as a riveting hook for the song, moving slowly and persistently in time to the slow, dotted, C minor rhythmic bass riff (Example 6.2). At the same time, the bleak political spirit of the 1980s, captured menacingly by the groove, refers to drug abuse, AIDS, space-ship disasters, impending nuclear war and discriminatory social policies.[40] Only the shortest moment of respite occurs when the pedal-chord Cm, briefly resolves (Fm11 and Gm7) as Prince pleads, *Oh why, oh why?* Most of all, it is the level of technological virtuosity captured in the sound recording and video that provides this rhetorical question with its carnivalesque charge. Importantly, this dark and sinister song (at least for its time) functions as a sign that Prince's texts do not just resonate with sexual desire and self-narcissism.

In quite a different song, 'If I Was Your Girlfriend', off the *Sign O' the Times* album, controversy has surrounded both the title and lyrical content. Here, the vocal parts are laced with an erotic, affected passion with exaggerated

Example 6.2   Synth-bass line from 'Sign O' the Times'

falsetto and camped-up delivery. Throughout the song we wonder whether this
is directed towards a man or woman, boy or girl. What form of genderplay is
Prince taking on?[41] In a song where the male artist situates himself in the
unlikely role of a girlfriend and says such intimate things to the listener,
irrespective of gender, there is bound to be intrigue.[42] Liz Jones throws an
interesting light on this song:

> The song is so detailed and so observant, trying so hard to please ('Baby can I
> dress U, I mean help U pick out your clothes before we go out, I ain't saying
> you're helpless...') and so touching that it revealed a new and complex side to
> Prince, the lyricist. He sobs. He begs. Most women can't believe a man would
> be able to say those things. [Jones 1997: 115]

Jones's description highlights Prince's eagerness to access the female through
carnivalesque display. In reconstructing his masculinity, it seems that he offers
up the notion of a world where normative gender roles vanish through a
release from their binary imprisonment. Seductively, Prince entertains a free
play on self-identification that resignifies his masculinity in a destabilised
manner. The perception of normative male identity is juxtaposed on the
desire to be the female figure, which, in turn, creates exchanges of various
sorts. For Prince, it is as if the task is not necessarily to prefer the feminine
side of the binary, but rather to *displace* the binary through a disintegration
of its heteronormativity. In quite another reaction to the song 'If I Was Your
Girlfriend', the feminist scholar Suzanne Moore considers the issue of
gender tourism: 'The dark continent that he wants to visit is naturally the
world of the feminine. There lies the key to the perfect union – with himself,
with another. But in sensing the possibilities of this kind of gender travel
Prince both recognises the limitations of masculinity whilst clinging to them'
(1988: 166).

If we go along with Moore's critique, Prince's position is by no means
unique. Often appearing liberated from traditional binary divides, the sexual
politics of pop artists impinge on the domain of the feminine. However, there
would seem little doubt that dissolving male identity at one level is bound to
reconfirm it at another. By creating a social space where oppositions cease to
exist and where notions of difference become desirable, we might ask *whose*
desire is being addressed. Again, I turn to Moore's interpretation: 'For whether
it's Barthes writing about desire or Prince singing about it, the desire in
question is, in all its confusion, still *his* desire, *their* desire, *male* desire. So
what I want to know is this – if Prince wants to be his girlfriend's girlfriend,
what does *she* want to be?' (1998: 169).

From the above account it seems the fragility of male identity as an ideological construction is obvious, especially when the pleasure derived from the
mobility of the Subject's position becomes a key factor in determining
popularity and musical trend. Aware of the strong implications of his motives,

Prince manages to shape and retain a personality that relies largely on seduction, not least through the sound of his voice as much as through his image. This again returns us to a critique of authenticity. As Frith puts it, '[f]or the pop star the "real me" is a promise that lies in the way we hear the voice, just as for a film star the "real" person is to be found in the secret of their look' (Frith 1996: 199). Indeed the 'voice' and the 'look' are regulated by a seductive rhetoric that oscillates between active and passive states.

So, for the tens of thousands of fans who turned out for the *Symbol* tour[43] at Wembley in 1993 to see The Artist Formerly Known As Prince, there seemed to be little doubt of their sentiments of adulation, as they sang along to the chorus of one of his cheekiest songs, 'Sexy M.F'. Written together with Levi Seacer and Tony M, this song is a stirring tribute to funk in the 1990s.

Triggered off by a whacking hard, compressed snare up-beat, the song imitates James Brown chord stabs and horn voicings, pounding bass lines, intricate rhythmic licks and variations in vocal style. In the introduction of 'Sexy M.F', the highly syncopated string of A7#9 chords establish the modal riff for the entire song (Example 6.3). With its quivering, throaty glissandi, the opening organ riff constitutes the main groove over which the spoken, rap-like lyrics are delivered by Prince and Tony M. The style of vocal performance clearly has its roots firmly in the fantasy world of George Clinton P-funk. At the end of the melodic phrases tension is dissolved in the cadential shifts from the tonic (A7#9) to the subdominant (D9), then chromatically through D♭9 to resolve on C9, the flattened mediant of the home key. In stark contrast to the whirring Hammond sounds, the brass and horns take up the chromatic cadential punctuation. Following only a beat's pause, the hook phrase, *U sexy motherfucker*, enters on its own without any backing (see Example 6.3). This two-bar phrase then steers us back to the tonic through the cunning interplay of tension between perfect and flattened fifth intervals. The end of this melodic hook resolves to a C natural, which fits (as the sharpened 9th) neatly into the tonic chord as the groove revs up again.

Intensified by a guitar solo by Leavi Seacer Jr and Tony M's rap in the refrain, the energetic drive of 'Sexy M.F', with its impudently chauvinistic lyrics – *sexy motherfucker shakin' that ass* – becomes a compelling gesture of satirical cheekiness. The funk style of this song provides the main point of impact, while the trivial narrative – a love story set in a villa on the Riviera – simply serves as an accompaniment to the heated musical passion. Spoken lines, in quasi-rap style, are experienced on the basis of their speech patterns and rhythmic organisation. Ultimately, the impact of the words lie in their manner of delivery which, with a range of idioms, is most reminiscent of a George Clinton jam session.

Once again, this song illustrates the important distinction between words as speech and words as sounds as Prince's sexist and denigrating hook, *U sexy*

Example 6.3 **Main organ and brass riffs in 'Sexy M.F.' and vocal
'Usexymotherfucker' riff**

motherfucker, parodies black machismo. This is so self-parodic, deprecating
and wimpish that in such moments, Prince's desire can be read as mockingly
predatory as he perpetuates the rituals of the male pop star through a notion of
gender parody that is multitracked in its purpose.

Conclusion

As with many of the pop stars of the MTV generation, Prince sets out to
manipulate all aspects of his identity. This is not just restricted to his promo
videos. In the film, *Under the Cherry Moon*, he privileges his identity in a
curious way through his relationship with Kristin Scott Thomas and Francesca
Annis, both light-skinned women. His rudeness towards a black woman is
discernible in one of the scenes as he impudently shuns her on the basis of
race (Jones 1997). There is little doubt that the script of *Under Cherry Moon*
is deliberately littered with derogatory verbal exchanges and poor jokes which
are intended to 'turn on the disrepute whites associate with black-American
mores: in sexuality, musical taste, and most of all in language' (Hill 1989:
179). Similarly in the film *Purple Rain*, one can only question the strategy
behind how women are portrayed. Yet in her deconstruction of Prince's blackness, the feminist scholar, bell hooks, is not prepared to view this in essentialist terms:

Prince wouldn't have been able to say, I'll have all black women behind me ...
His journey is a lesson in what happens when a black artist crosses over and is
rewarded by whites as not being black-identified, when in fact he was always
black-identified, except they didn't know it. Look at the Fugees, relegated to the
black music divisions until they are a success, then they're everybody's success.
[hooks in Jones 1997: 183]

Of course, as hooks argues, appealing to a mass audience cannot avoid selling-
out and compromising at many levels. The pressure of crossover in the music
industry of the 1980s cannot be underestimated. To a large extent, black artists
have had to modify their style at a cost. But, just a glance at trends in the
1990s shows that black youth audiences want to identify with black stars more
than ever before (George 1988, 1992; Jones 1997).[44]
   While Prince might not be the first preference for a new generation of black
kids, or indeed black enough for them, we cannot rule out his position as a
leading proponent of African-American pop music, not least in the ways in
which he has fooled about with and challenged codes of identity through
musical performance.
   Importantly though, he still bridges over generations through his musical
diversity and versatility. Significantly, his personal development and changes
in style have outlived most of his contemporaries from the 1980s, with his
music in recent years encapsulating the revival that is taking place in hip hop
and dance music. Most of all I see his musical texts as an embodiment of
creative intertextuality whereby everyday speech and music genres are subdi-
vided into more sub-styles. Often the genres he references are subverted and
manipulated into a startling display of new idioms as he *re-invoices* (as
Bakhtin terms it) the sounds of his cultural heritage. As a result, the subversive
pleasures found in Prince's music arise from the intertexts that privilege
musical performance. But, more than mere festivity, these texts signify the
multiple voices of the oppressed in their mockery of political, musical and
sexual repression. In this sense, Prince's carnivalesque play becomes dialogically inscribed within a changing world of erotic and political aspirations.
   Launched in 1996, his *Emancipation* album signified yet another 'sign of the
times' as Prince went out of his way to celebrate his release from Warner
Brothers. Questions relating to his identity throughout this album continue to
arise from the inventiveness of his musical expression.[45] Prince still teases out
notions of desire and uncertainties of gender in the construction of his own
unique identity in a way that affirms his authority. In the songs off *Emancipation* we are reminded once again that identity can never be fixed in its manifestation, and, more importantly, that the strategies for survival are often feminine
ones. Musically, it is in his additive approach to creating ideas, with layer upon
layer, through recording technology, that Prince discloses his identity.[46] In this
way, the processes of production affirm the unique quality of his persona
through the *éclat* of his sound.

As we have seen, Prince's performances exploit familiar genres of pop texts through an innovative technological treatment of compositional design. The narcissistic self-representation of the pop star indeed raises questions concerning what pop music is about. In particular, the urge to romanticise sexual difference in pop stars of the post-1980s generation as the utopian apotheosis of a radical identity ought to be rejected. While always in control of himself and his entourage, Prince satirises the plight of the modern Subject, as his skills as a musician are linked to his aesthetic of excess that always moves beyond the limits of established practice. But most importantly, his identity is the result of a predominance of African-American traditions and styles alongside a range of other musical influences, extending from the Beatles to Joni Mitchell. Ultimately, it is his own ideas of difference that are responsible for both his production and consumption.

Finally, when listening to Prince's music, watching his videos, experiencing him perform live, there is always the telling realisation that musical experiences in pop are enormously pleasurable because of a special commonality in the sharing process across the barriers of race, nationality, politics, sexuality and class. It is these components then that invigorate the critical attributes of musical expression, and, in so doing, contribute to the formation and understanding of ours and others' identities through pop texts.

Notes

1   Notably, this period was witness to the rise of white superstars who directly attributed their sound and musical style to African-American music – Madonna, George Michael, Peter Gabriel, Robert Palmer, Phil Collins.

2   It is interesting that those close to Prince have described his intense concern from an early age that women might find him not desirable (see Jones 1997). This might help explain the abundance of songs that deal with his obsession for being 'desired'.

3   Here I do not intend to enter into the debates on technological determinism that have been undertaken in Cultural Studies since the 1970s. Rather, my approach is to treat technology as a site for an emerging aesthetic in pop music and a means for compositional production. The arguments revolving around gender in music production are closely related to the politics controlling social and cultural change. This domain has been addressed thoroughly by Mavis Bayton (1998) and others.

4   Interestingly, the effect of this has direct parallels in the ending of Madonna's 'Justify Our Love' video, in which the closing scene portrays her walking away smiling and chuckling. Also see McClary 1991 and Whiteley 1997a.

5   In my many discussions with music students and fans of Prince, I have observed that their accounts of pleasure – and understanding of Prince's act – centre primarily on the spectacle of the star within the context of the virtuosity of his musical performance.

6   This claim is based on the numerous observations I have noted by both male and female fans.

7   See for example, Abt 1987; Mercer 1988; Fiske 1987; Goodwin 1993a, 1993b; Björnberg 1993, 1994; Drukman 1995; Hawkins 1996; Cook 1998; Whiteley 1997a, 2000.

8   For similar perspectives on this see Ruud 1997a, 1997b; Green 1988, 1997.

9   Note that Robert Walser has emphasised how the importance of the music in a video can be 'overlooked' due to it being seen as a representation of a live performance. Because the frame 'is more arbitrary' it is presumed to be more significant (Walser 1993a: 126).

10 Short chorus interjections in 'Kiss', together with such high camp delivery, have their origins in 1960s hits, such as the Brenda Lee song 'Sweet Nuthins' from 1960.

11 Even the guitar that Wendy plays, as Walser has explained, 'is the least phallic of all possible electric guitars, a hollow-body that looks more like an acoustic guitar than the flashy electrics played by most rock and funk musicians' (1993a, p. 86).

12 Note that Frith (1996) picks up on this point when he evaluates the dynamics of true and false gestures in stylised performances.

13 For important discussions on this point, see Tagg 1989; Maultsby 1990; Middleton 1990; Walser 1993a; Brackett 1995.

14 For a more extensive range of debates on the historical, sociological and musicological debates surrounding African American music, also see Keil 1966; Gates 1988; Floyd 1991; Cashmore 1997.

15 See Philip Tagg (1989) for one of the most succinct problematisations of essentialisation of racial identity. His sociomusicological position sets the precedent for many of the critical musicological perspectives advocated by Scott and myself (1994). Cf. Frith (1983) for a more essentialist-based interpretation of black music that addresses the issue of performance in terms of spontaneous music-making.

16 In particular, artists such as Jimi Hendrix, Sly and the Family Stone, James Brown, Nat Cole, Stevie Wonder, George Clinton, Aretha Franklin, Miles Davis and Little Richard.

17 For an account of self-definition through the playing around with boundaries of freakishness, see bell hooks (1992) for an excellent analysis of Prince's identity.

18 Brackett raises a similar point in his analysis of James Brown when he addresses the homology between African-American social values and musical expression (1995: 115–24).

19 The traditions he draws on are unmistakably rooted in the legacies of Hendrix, Sly and the Family Stone, George Clinton and Little Richard. This is not to say that his songs do not draw on a wealth of sources outside the African-American diaspora. It is also important to reiterate a point made earlier, that the issue of Prince's blackness has raised much concern by numerous black scholars who feel he has denied his racial heritage by opting out to a predominantly white-based music industry (Cashmore 1997).

20 For further detailed discussion on the theorisation of technology as a prominent feature in the recognition of musical genres, see Paul Théberge (1997).

21 Importantly, Prince has also acknowledged the references in his music (and interviews) to artists such as the white fusion-folk artist Joni Mitchell and the Latin rock guitarist Carlos Santana. While working within a distinctly black music tradition, he would be the first to admit that his musical style is also linked to countless other influences.

22 See Gates (1988) for one of the best discourses on race. He demonstrates in his research how black people have inscribed their culture through the breaking-down of racial hierarchies.

23 This formed part of a research project I conducted at Oslo University in May 1992.

24 Part of my research methodology involved a generalised task of measuring the reactions and responses of musicians to issues of style and gesture. To this end, I am indebted to the cooperation and enthusiasm of large cohorts of music students at undergraduate and postgraduate level at my former place of work, Salford University, and Oslo University.

25 For the majority of listeners questioned in this study, each song appeared to be self-contained within its own idiomatic identity, thus functioning in stark contrast to the next.

26 For an illuminating discussion on how instrumental sounds in African-derived music emulate vocal timbres, see Bebey (1975).

27 These terms differentiate between the raw untreated signal and the same signal once it has undergone effect processing. In much of Prince's music I would suggest that the tracks are recorded *dry* in order to keep open the options for the mixdown stage. This enables the producer to make decisions based on the overall impression of the mix.

28 See Anne Danielsen (1997), who has described the overall effect of the control of sound in 'Push' as fragmented. Through the role of the sampler and MIDI technology she explains how different elements are positioned 'in their right positions along the time and space axis' (Danielsen 1997: 283).

29 See Gilroy (1987) for a detailed account of the popularity of black music amongst white audiences, which is positioned within the context of an anti-essentialistic political discourse.

30 On the problematisation of difference within a challenging framework of male feminism, see Stephen Heath (1987).

31 What I am suggesting here is that the feminine position which is marginalised is also open to both women and men. Thus the assumption of feminine and masculine positions cannot be reduced to the binary constructs of biological determinism.

32 However, as I have pointed out earlier, his blatant displays of sexuality can smack of the traditional masculine oppression he so often appears to resist.

33 In fact, Prince's appropriation of ornamental, narcissistic dress codes, has its associations in male dress of earlier centuries and periods when both the female and male were permitted to celebrate such flamboyancy of clothing in the name of pleasure.

34 I should emphasise here that the use of the term 'spectator' in this context is derived from the way it is employed within psychoanalytic film theory. My use of this term is associated with the concentration on subject positions created by the musical text.

35 Displayed through sound, lyrics, and imagery, his preoccupation with sex is parti-cularly complex and multidimensional. His film, *Under The Cherry Moon*, from 1986, is no better example for advancing the notion that it is a wealth of utterances that mould Prince's erotic position. If one considers his range of resources for erotic and sexual exchange, and the potentialities of exhibiting power and desire in this film, the question of sexual expression creeps into almost every scene. Centred on the pianist gigolo, Christopher Tracey (played by Prince), the narrative of *Under the Cherry Moon* is a love story involving a whole set of complex inter-personal relationships. In the film, Prince wallows in the spectacle of soft-porn sequences accompanied by a series of songs which articulate a vivid erotic sensi-bility that often collide in climax.

36 Here I am referring to Hegel's *Phenomenology of Spirit*, which concerns questions relating to how the Subject is constructed through subordination. Hegel follows the

slave's approach to freedom and his lapse into a state of dissatisfied consciousness. Also see Butler (1997) for an account of how the Subject's own self-identity can be characterised by a process of becoming subordinated by power that can then turn on itself.

37   For example, throughout the exhausting *Lovesexy* tour in 1988, which started at the Palais Omnisport in Paris and finished five months later at Reunion Arena in Dallas, Prince's performances were probably at their most sexually explicit and musically compelling. The sheer innovative dimension of the *Lovesexy* performance video and album from a musical and visual perspective left critics in little doubt of his ranking as musically extraordinary. His 32-date European tour, seen live by almost 500,000 spectators, confirmed his megastar status in Europe with a popularity comparable to the *Purple Rain* period in the US. See Per Nilsen (1993) for one of the best chronologies of Prince and his career.

38   Often I have observed how it is the lack of any ironic sensibility towards pop culture that leads to contempt and scorn especially when debating authenticity. Walser (1993a) makes this point in his analysis of glam metal's gender constructions.

39   Released in March 1987, his ninth album *Sign O' the Times* was not a commercial success although a number of music reviews were full of praise, comparing it to the Beatles' *White Album*. Yet, market sales only tell part of the story. Liz Jones has claimed that if 'David Bowie had produced an album like this, music critics the world over would have spontaneously combusted' (1997: 117).

40   Prince would have hardly escaped noting the decline of living conditions for black Americans under the Reagan administration in the 1980s, a period when the cutbacks in welfare programmes resulted in extreme hardship. The bleak prospects for finding employment led to an increase in crime in inner-city ghettos. Black styles, such as rap (which greatly influenced Prince) became the music of political protest, exemplified by artists and groups such as Queen Latifah, Ice-T, Public Enemy, NWA, Ice Cube and Sister Souljah.

41   Interestingly, the song 'If I Was Your Girlfriend' did not do well in the US, reaching only 67 in the Hot 100 charts. It was more popular in the UK where it reached number 13. This raises questions concerning differences in preference according to audiences and nationality.

42   Most likely this song was written for the Californian girl, Susannah Melvoin, twin sister of Wendy, with whom Prince had a serious relationship based on infatuation, heartache, torment and passion. Envious of the closeness Susannah had with Wendy, Prince promises profusely in the song to do anything and everything in order to keep her.

43   Released in October 1992, his fourteenth album featuring the New Power Generation was available in record stores with astonishing speed only a few weeks following the European *Diamonds and Pearls* tour. Notably the songs on this album were recorded live with very little technological processing during a period when the New Power Generation were at their peak and gaining critical acclaim everywhere.

44   In a North American context, this is hardly surprising where statistically young black males are far more disadvantaged than their white counterparts, and where the probability of them being murdered is eight times higher than whites.

45   The song 'Slave,' off the *Emancipation* album, which I have already made mention to, is clearly a 1990s song in terms of its production, its sounds and its conglomeration of influences. The poignancy of the text captures a stark reality as Prince articulates his sentiments regarding captivity through the nature of one's

circumstances. A chant-like sorrowful chorus runs through this song, functioning as a reminder that music is ultimately a result of our personal experiences.

46 For a detailed discussion of multitrack sound recording and approaches to 'additive' approaches to composition in Eno's work, see Théberge (1997: 215–22).

Bibliography

Abt, Dean (1987), 'Music Video: Impact of the Visual Dimension', in Lull, J. (ed.), *Popular Music and Communication*, London: Sage.

Allemann, B. (1956), *Ironie und Dichtung*, Pfullingen: G. Neske.

Bakhtin, M.M. (1981), *The Dialogic Imagination*, M. Holquist (ed.), C. Emerson and M. Holquist (trans.), Texas: University of Texas Press.

Bakhtin, M.M. (1986), *Speech Genres and Other Late Essays*, in Emerson, C. and Holquist, M. (eds) V.W. McGee transl., Texas: University of Texas Press.

Balfour, Ian (1991), 'Revolutions per Minute or The Pet Shop Boys Forever', in J.C. Credon and Bill (eds), *Readings Surfaces*, 1.2 Folio 1, Montreal.

Barthes, Roland (1977), *Image-Music-Text*, S. Heath ed., London: Fontana/Collins.

Barthes, Roland (1988), *S/Z*, New York: Noonday Press.

Baudrillard, Jean (1983a), *Simulations*, New York: Semiotext(e).

Baudrillard, Jean (1983b), *In the Shadow of the Silent Majorities*, New York: Semiotext(e).

Bayton, Mavis (1997), 'Women and the electric guitar', in Whiteley, Sheila (ed.), *Sexing the Groove*, London: Routledge.

Bayton, Mavis (1999), *Frock Rock: Women Performing Popular Music.* Oxford: Oxford University Press.

Beadle, Jeremy (1993), *Will Pop Eat Itself?* London: Faber and Faber.

Bebey, Francis (1975), *African Music: A People's Art*, Josephine Bennett trans., New York: Lawrence Hill.

Bennett, Andy (1997), 'Representations of "Britishness" in Britpop', paper presented at the Britpop Conference, Department of Music, University of Leeds, April.

Bennett, Andy (2000), *Popular Music and Youth Culture: Music, Identity and Place, London:* Macmillan.

Berland, Jody (1993), 'Sound, Image and Social Space: Music Video and Media Reconstruction', in S. Frith, A. Goodwin and L. Grossberg (eds), *Sound and Vision: The Music Video Reader*, London: Routledge.

Bernardi, Daniel (ed.) (1996), *The Birth of Whiteness: Race and the Emergence of U.S. Cinema*, New Jersey: Rutgers University Press.

Björnberg, Alf (1985), 'On aeolian harmony in contemporary popular music', paper presented to the Third International Conference of IASPM, Montreal.

Björnberg, Alf (1993), 'Structural relationships of music and images in music video', *Skriftserie 1993: 3*, University of Oslo.

Björnberg, Alf (1994),'Structural relationships of music and images in music video', *Popular Music*, 13/1, pp. 51–74.

Blacking, John (1976), *How Musical Is Man?*, London: Faber and Faber.

Blacking, John (1995), *Music, Culture, & Experience: Selected Papers of John Blacking*, R. Byron ed., London: University of Chicago Press.

Bourdieu, Pierre (1984), *Distinction*, London: Routledge.

Bourdieu, Pierre (1990), 'The uses of the "people"', in P. Bourdieu (ed.), Matthew Adamsen (trans.), *In Other Words*, Cambridge: Polity Press.

Bracewell, Michael (1998), *England is Mine: Pop Life in Albion from Wilde to Goldie,* London: Flamingo.

Brackett, David (1992), 'James Brown's "Superbad" and the double-voiced utterance', *Popular Music*, 11/3, pp. 309–24.

Brackett, David (1995) (2nd edn 2000, California: California University Press), *Interpreting Popular Music*, Cambridge: Cambridge University Press.

Bradby, Barbara (1990), 'Do-talk and don't talk: the division of the subject in girl-group music', in S. Frith and A. Goodwin (eds), in *On Record: Rock, Pop and the Written Word*, London: Routledge.

Bradby, Barbara (1992), 'Like a virgin-mother?: Materialism and maternalism in the songs of Madonna', *Cultural Studies*, 6/1, pp. 73–96.

Bret, David (1994), *Morrissey: Landscapes of the Mind*, London: Robson.

Brett, Philip (1994), 'Musicality, Essentialism, and the Closet', in P. Brett, E. Wood and G.C. Thomas (eds), *Queering the Pitch*, London: Routledge.

Burnett, Robert (1996), *The Global Jukebox: The International Music Industry*, London: Routledge.

Burns, Lori (2000), 'Analytical Methodologies for Rock Music: Harmonic and Voice-Leading Strategies in Tori Amos's "Crucify", in W. Everett (ed.), *Expression in Pop Rock Music: A Collection of Critical and Analytical Essays*, London: Garland Publishing.

Burston, Paul and Richardson, Colin (eds) (1995), 'Introduction', in *A Queer Romance: Lesbians, gay men and popular culture*, London: Routledge.

Butler, Judith (1990, 2nd edn 2000), *Gender Trouble: Feminism and the Subversion of Identity* London: Routledge.

Butler, Judith (1995), 'Melancholy gender/Refused Identification', in M. Berger, B. Wallis and S. Watson (eds), *Constructing Masculinity*, London: Routledge.

Case, Sue-Ellen (1991), 'Tracking the Vampire', *Differences* 3/2.

Case, Sue-Ellen (1993), 'Toward a Butch-Femme Aesthetic', in H. Abelove, M.A. Barale and D.M. Halperin (eds), *The Lesbian and Gay Studies Reader*, London: Routledge.

Cashmore, Ellis (1997), *The Black Culture Industry*, London: Routledge.

Chapman, Rowena (1988), 'The Great Pretender: Variations on the New Man Theme', in R. Chapman and J. Rutherford (eds), *Male Order: Unwrapping Masculinity*, London: Lawrence & Wishart.

Chester, Andrew (1970), 'Second thoughts on a rock aesthetic: The band', *New Left Review*, 62, pp. 75–82.

Chodorow, Nancy (1978), *The Reproduction of Mothering*, Berkeley: University of California Press.

Citron, Marcia J. (1993), *Gender and the Musical Canon*, Cambridge: Cambridge University Press.

Cook, Nicholas (1990), *Music, Imagination, and Culture*, Oxford: Oxford University Press.

Cook, Nicholas (1994), 'Music and Meaning in the Commercials', *Popular Music*, 13/2, pp. 27–40.

Cook, Nicholas (1998), *Analysing Musical Multimedia*, Oxford: Oxford University Press.

Cook, Nicholas and Everist, Mark eds. (1999), *Rethinking Music,* Oxford: Oxford University Press.

Covach, John (2000), 'Jazz-Rock? Rock-Jazz? Stylistic Crossover in late-1970s American Progressive Rock', in W. Everett (ed.), *Expression in Pop-Rock Music: A Collection of Critical and Analytical Essays,* London: Garland Publishing.

Covach, John and Boone, G. (eds), Understanding Rock: Essays in Musical Analysis, New York: Oxford University Press.

Cubitt, Sean (2000), ' "Maybellene": Meaning and the Listening Subject', in R. Middleton (ed.), *Reading Pop: Approaches to Textual Analysis in Popular Music,* Oxford: Oxford University Press.

Culler, Jonathan (1988), *Framing the Sign: Criticism and its Institutions,* Oxford: Blackwell.

Dame, Joke (1994), 'Unveiled Voices: Sexual Difference and the Castrato', in P. Brett, E. Wood and G.C. Thomas, (eds), *Queering the Pitch,* London: Routledge.

Danielsen, Anne (1997), 'His name was Prince: a study of *Diamonds and Pearls*', *Popular Music,* 16/3, pp. 275–91.

De Lauretis, Teresa (ed.) (1986), *Feminist Studies/Critical Studies,* Bloomington: Indiana University Press.

De Lauretis, Teresa (1987), *Technologies of Gender,* Bloomington: Indiana University Press.

Deleuze, Gilles and Guattari, Felix (1977), *Anti-Oedipus.* New York: Viking.

Derrida, Jacques (1981, 1st edn 1972), *Positions,* A. Bass (trans.), Chicago: University of Chicago Press.

Doty, Alexander (1993), *Making Things Perfectly Queer,* Minneapolis: University of Minnesota Press.

Drukman, Steve (1995), 'The gay Gaze, Or Why I Want My MTV', in P. Burston and C. Richardson (eds), *A Queer Romance,* London: Routledge, pp. 81–95.

Dyer, Richard (1982), 'Don't Look Now – The Male Pin-Up', in *Screen,* 23/3–4, Sept./Oct.

Edwards, Tim (1994), *Erotics & Politics: Gay Male Sexuality, Masculinity and Feminism,* London: Routledge.

Ellen, Barbara (1995), 'Meanwhile, Back at the Raunch' in *New Musical Express,* 2 December.

Evans, David T. (1993), *Sexual Citizenship: The Material Construction of Sexualities,* London: Routledge.

Evans, C. and Gamman, L. (1995), 'The Gaze Revisited, or Reviewing Queer Viewing', in P. Burston and C. Richardson (eds), *A Queer Romance,* London: Routledge, pp. 13–56.

Everett, Walter (ed.) (2000), *Expression in Pop-Rock Music: A Collection of Critical and Analytical Essays,* London: Garland Publishing.

Fiske, J. (1987), *Television Culture,* London: Methuen.

Fiske, J. (1989), *Reading the Popular,* London: Routledge.

Floyd, Samuel A., Jr. (1991), 'Ring Shout! Literary Studies, Historical Studies, and Black Music Inquiry', *Black Music Research Journal,* 11/2 (Fall), pp. 265–88.

Frith, Simon (1981), *Sound Effects,* New York: Pantheon Books.

Frith, Simon (1983), *Sound Effects: Youth, Leisure and the Politics of Rock 'n' Roll,* London: Constable.

Frith, Simon (1987), 'Towards an Aesthetic of Popular Music', in R. Leppert and S. McClary (eds), *Music and Society: The Politics of Composition, Performance and Reception*, Cambridge: Cambridge University Press.

Frith, Simon (1988), *Music for Pleasure*, Cambridge: Polity Press.

Frith, Simon (1992), 'From the Beatles to Bros: Twenty-Five Years of British Pop', in N. Abercrombie and A. Warde (eds), *Social Change in Contemporary Britain*, Cambridge: Polity.

Frith, Simon (1993), 'The Sound of *Erotica*: Pain, Power, and Pop', in L. Frank and P. Smith (eds), *Madonnarama: Essays on Sex and Popular Culture*, Pennsylvania: Cleis Press.

Frith, Simon (1996), *Performing Rites*, Oxford: Oxford University Press.

Frith, Simon (1997), 'Værdispørgsmålet inden for popularmusik. The Pet Shop Boys som eksempel', in C. Madsen and B.M. Thomsen (eds), *Tidens Former*, Aarhus University Press.

Frith, Simon and McRobbie, Angela (1978/9), 'Rock and Sexuality', *Screen Education*, 29, pp. 3–19.

Frith, Simon and Savage, Jon (1997), 'Pearls and Swine: Intellectuals and the Mass Media', in S. Redhead with D. Wynne and J. O'Connor (eds), *The Club Cultures Reader: Readings in Popular Cultural Studies*, Oxford: Blackwell.

Gaar, Gillian G. (1993), *She's A Rebel: The History of Women in Rock & Roll*, London: Blandford.

Gates, Henry Louis, Jr. *The Signifying Monkey: A Theory of African-American Literary Criticism*, New York: Oxford University Press.

Gay, Leslie C. (1998), 'Acting Up, Talking Tech: New York Rock Musicians and Their Metaphors of Technology', *Ethnomusicology*, 42/1.

George, Nelson (1988), *The Death of Rhythm & Blues*, New York: Pantheon.

George, Nelson (1992), *Buppies, B-Boys, Baps & Bohos: Notes on Post-Soul Black Culture*, New York: Harper Collins.

Geyrhalter, Thomas (1996), 'Effeminacy, camp and sexual subversion in rock: the Cure and Suede', *Popular Music*, 15/2, pp. 217–24.

Gibbs, R.W. (1984), 'Literal meaning and psychological theory', *Cognitive Science*, 8, pp. 275–304.

Gill, John (1995), *Queer Noises*, London: Cassell.

Gilroy, Paul (1987), *There Ain't No Black in the Union Jack*, London: Hutchinson.

Godoy, Rolf-Inge (1997), *Formalization and Epistemology*, Oslo: Scandinavian University Press.

Goodwin, Andrew (1987), 'Music Video in the (Post) Modern World', *Screen*, 28/3, pp. 36–55.

Goodwin, Andrew (1993a), *Dancing in the Distraction Factory: music television and popular culture*, London: Routledge.

Goodwin, Andrew (1993b), 'Fatal Distractions: MTV Meets Postmodern Theory', in S. Frith, A. Goodwin, and L. Grossberg (eds), *Sound and Vision: The Music Video Reader*, London: Routledge.

Goodwin, Andrew (1997), 'On Being a Professor of Pop', *Popular Music and Society*, 21/1, pp. 43–52.

Green, Lucy (1988), *Music on Deaf Ears*, Manchester: Manchester University Press.

Green, Lucy (1997), *Music, Gender, Education*, Cambridge: Cambridge University Press.

Greig, Charlotte (1989), *Will You Still Love Me Tomorrow? Girl Groups from the 50s on . . .*, London: Virago.

Groß, Thomas (2000), 'Berühmtheit als Kunst form', *Die Zeit*, 2000/39.

Grossberg, Lawrence (1987), 'Rock and Roll in search of an Audience', in J. Lull (ed.), *Popular Music and Communication*, London: Sage.

Grossberg, Lawrence (1992), *We Gotta Get Out of This Place: Popular Conservatism and Postmodern Culture*, London: Routledge.

Grossberg, Lawrence (1993), 'The Media Economy of Rock Culture: Cinema, Post-modernity and Authenticity', in S. Frith, A. Goodwin and L. Grossberg (eds), *Sound and Vision*, London: Routledge.

Hamm, Charles (1982), 'Some thoughts on the measurement of popularity in music', ed. D. Horn and P. Tagg (eds), in *Popular Music Perspectives* (Gothenburg and Exeter), pp. 3–15.

Hamm, Charles (1995), *Putting Popular Music In Its Place*, Cambridge: Cambridge Univesrity Press.

Hawkins, Stan (1992a), 'Prince: Harmonic Analysis of "Anna Stesia" ', *Popular Music*, 11/3, pp. 325–336.

Hawkins, Stan (1992b), 'Stylistic Diversification in Prince of the Nineties: An analysis of "Diamonds and Pearls" ', *Skriftserie 1992:4*, University of Oslo.

Hawkins, Stan (1994), 'Lost in Music – Problems facing Musicologists', *Popular Musicology*, Vol. 1.

Hawkins, Stan (1996), 'Perspectives in popular musicology: music, Lennox, and meaning in 1990s pop', *Popular Music*, 15/1, pp. 17–36.

Hawkins, Stan (1997a), ' "I'll Never Be An Angel": Stories of Deception in Madonna's Music', *Critical Musicology Journal* (Leeds) <http://www.leeds.ac.uk/music/Info/CMJ/cmj.html>.

Hawkins, Stan (1997b), 'The Pet Shop Boys: Musicology, masculinity, and banality', in S. Whiteley (ed.), *Sexing the Groove*, London: Routledge.

Heath, Stephen (1987), 'Male Feminism', in A. Jardine and P. Smith (eds), *Men in Feminism*, London: Methuen.

Hebdige, Dick (1985), *Subculture*, London: Methuen.

Hill, Dave (1989), *Prince: A Pop Life*, London: Faber and Faber.

hooks, bell (1992), *Black Looks: Race and Representation*, London: South End Press.

Hughes, Walter (1994), 'In the Empire of the Beat: Discipline and Disco', in A. Ross and T. Rose (eds), *Microphone Fiends: Youth Music and Youth Culture*, London: Routledge.

Hutcheon, Linda (1994), *Irony's Edge: The Theory and Politics of Irony*, London: Routledge.

Irigaray, L. (1985), *Speculum of the Other Woman*, G.C. Gill (trans.), Ithaca, NY: Cornell University Press.

Jameson, Frederic (1983), 'Postmodernism and Consumer Society', in *The Anti-Aesthetic: Essays on Postmodern Culture*, Hal Roster (ed.), Port Townshend: Bay Press, pp. 111–25.

Jones, Liz (1997), *Slave To The Rhythm: The Artist Formerly Known As Prince*, London: Little, Brown and Company.

Kaplan, E. Ann (1987), *Rocking Around the Clock: music television, postmodernism, and consumer culture*, London: Routledge.

Kaplan, E. Ann (1993), 'Madonna Politics: Perversion, repression, or Subversion? Or Masks and/as master-y', in C. Scwichtenberg (ed.), *The Madonna Connection*, Oxford: Westview Press.

Keil, Charles (1966), *Urban Blues*, Chicago: Chicago University Press.

Keil, Charles and Feld, Steven (1994), *Music Grooves*, Chicago: Chicago University Press.

Kellner, Douglas (1995), *Media Culture: Cultural Studies, identity and politics between the modern and the postmodern*, London: Routledge.

Kempster, Chris (ed.) (1996), *History of House*. London: Sanctuary Publishing.

Kerman, Joseph (1980), 'How We Got into Analysis and How to Get Out', *Critical Inquiry* 7/2, pp. 311–31.

Kimmel, Michael S. (1987), *Changing Men: New Directions in Research on Men and Masculinity*, London: Sage.

Koskoff, Ellen (1987), 'An Introduction to Women, Music, and Culture', in E. Koskoff (ed.), *Women and Music in Cross-Cultural Perspective*, New York: Greenwood Press, pp. 1–23.

Kramer, Lawrence (1993), '*Carnaval*, Cross-Dressing, and the Woman in the Mirror', in Ruth A. Solie (ed.), *Musicology and Difference: Gender and Sexuality in Music Scholarship*, London: University of California Press.

Kristeva, Julia (1980), *Desire in Language: A Semiotic Approach to Literature and Art*, New York: Columbia University Press.

Kristeva, Julia (1984), *Revolution in Poetic Language*, New York: Columbia University Press.

Kristeva, Julia (1989), *Language the Unknown: An Initiation into Linguistics*, Anne M. Menke (transl.), New York: Columbia University Press.

Lacan, Jacques (1977a), *Ecrits: A Selection*, London: Tavistock.

Lacan, Jacques (1977b), *The Four Fundamental Concepts of Psycho-Analysis*, London: Penguin.

Laing, David (1969), *The Sound of Our Time*, Oxford: Oxford University Press.

Laing, David (1985), *One Chord Wonders. Powers and Meaning in Punk Rock*, Milton Keynes: Open University Press.

Langer, S.K. (1941), *Philosophy in a New Key*, Cambridge, MA: Harvard University Press.

Langlois, Tony (1992), 'Can you feel it? DJs and House Music culture in the UK', *Popular Music*, 11/2, pp. 229–38.

Laplanche, Jean and Pontalis, Jean-Bertrand (1986), 'Fantasy and the Origins of Sexuality', in V. Burgin, J. Donald and C. Kaplan (eds), *Formations of Fantasy*, London: Routledge.

Lewis, Lisa A. (1990), *Gender Politics and MTV: Voicing the Difference*, Philadelphia: Temple University Press.

Lewis, Lisa A. (1993), 'Emergence of Female Address on MTV', in S. Frith, A. Goodwin and L. Grossberg (eds), *Sound and Vision*, London: Routledge.

Livingston, Paisley (1996), 'Characterization and Fictional Truth in the Cinema', in D. Bordwell and N. Carroll (eds), *Post-Theory: Reconstructing Film Studies*, Wisconsin: University of Wisconsin Press.

Longhurst, Brian (1995), *Popular Music & Society*, Cambridge: Polity.

Lyotard, Jean-Francois (1984), *The Postmodern Condition: A Report on Knowledge*, Manchester: Manchester University Press.

McClary, Susan (1987), 'The Blasphemy of Talking Politics during Bach Year', in R. Lepppert and S. McClary (eds), *Music and Society: The Politics of Composition, Performance, and Reception*, Cambridge: Cambridge University Press, pp. 13–62.

McClary, Susan (1991), *Feminine Endings*, Minnesota: University of Minnesota.

McClary, Susan (1994a), 'Same As It Ever Was: Youth Culture and Music', in A. Ross and T. Rose (eds), *Microphone Fields*, London: Routledge.

McClary, Susan (1994b), 'Constructions of Subjectivity in Schubert's Music', in P. Brett, E. Wood and G.C. Thomas (eds), *Queering the Pitch*, London: Routledge.

McClary, Susan (2000), *Conventional Wisdom: The Content of Musical Form*, London: University of California Press.

McRobbie, Angela (1994), *Postmodernism and Popular Culture*, London: Routledge.

Maultsby, Portia K. (1990), 'Africanisms in African-American Music', in J.E. Holloway (ed.), *Africanisms in American Culture*, Indiana University Press, pp. 185–210.

Mercer, K. (1988), 'Monster Metaphors: Notes on Michael Jackson's *Thriller*', in A. McRobbie (ed.), *Zoot Suits and Second Hand Dresses: An Anthology of Fashion and Music*, Boston: Unwin Hyman.

Mercer, K. and Julien, I. (1988), 'Race, Sexual Politics and Black Masculinity: A Dossier', in R. Chapman and J. Rutherford (eds), *Male Order: Unwrapping Masculinity*, London: Lawrence & Wishart.

Middleton, Richard (1990), *Studying Popular Music*, Milton Keynes: Open University Press.

Middleton, Richard (1993), 'Popular Music Analysis and Musicology: bridging the gap', *Popular Music*, 12, pp. 177–90.

Middleton, Richard (ed) (2000), *Reading Pop: Approaches to Textual Analysis in Popular Music*, Oxford: Oxford University Press.

Mitchell, Tony (1996), *Popular Music and Local Identity: Rock, Pop and Rap in Europe and Oceania*, London: Leicester University Press.

Moody, Paul (1998), 'Tipping the Light Fantastic', *New Musical Express*, 28 February.

Moore, Allan F. (1992), 'Patterns of harmony', *Popular Music*, 11/1, pp. 73-106.

Moore, Allan F. (1993), *Rock: The Primary Text*, Buckingham: Open University Press.

Moore, Allan F. (2001), *Rock: The Primary Text*, Aldershot: Ashgate.

Moore, Suzanne (1988), 'Getting a Bit of the Other: The Pimps of Postmodernism', in R. Chapman and J. Rutherford (eds), *Male Order: Unwrapping Masculinity*, London: Lawrence & Wishart.

Mort, Frank (1988), 'Boys Own? Masculinity, Style and Popular Culture', in R. Chapman and J. Rutherford (eds), *Male Order: Unwrapping Masculinity*, Lawrence & Wishart.

Mort, Frank (1996), *Cultures of Consumption: Masculinities and Social Space in Late Twentieth-Century Britain*, London: Routledge.

Mulvey, Laura (1975), 'Visual Pleasure and Narrative Cinema', *Screen*, 16/3, Autumn.

Nattiez, Jean-Jacques (1990), *Music and Discourse: Toward a Semiology of Music*, Princeton: Princeton University Press.

Nattiez, Jean-Jacques (1993), *Wagner Androgyne: A Study in Interpretation*, S. Spencer (transl.), Princeton: Princeton University Press.

Negus, Keith (1992), *Producing Pop: culture and conflict in the popular music industry*, London: Edward.

Nehring, Neil (1997), *Popular Music, Gender, and Postmodernism: Anger Is an Energy*, London: Sage.

Neill, Alex (1996), 'Empathy and (Film) Fiction', in D. Bordwell and N. Carroll (eds), *Post-Theory: Reconstructing Film Studies*, Wisconsin: University of Wisconsin Press.

Nilsen, Per (1993), *Prince: A Documentary*, London: Omnibus Press.

O'Brien, Lucy (1995), *She Bop: The Definitive History of Women in Rock, Pop and Soul*, London: Penguin Books.

Oliver, Paul (1968), *Screening the Blues: Aspects of the Blues Tradition*, London: Cassell.

Reynolds, S. and Press, J. (1995), *The Sex Revolts*, Cambridge, MA: Harvard University Press.

Richardson, John (1999), *Singing Archaeology: Philip Glass's Akhnaten*, Hanover: Wesleyan University Press.

Rietveld, Hillegonda (1968), *This is Our House: House music, cultural spaces and technologies*, Aldershot: Ashgate/Arena.

Rietveld, Hillegonda (1995), 'Pure Bliss – Intertextuality in House Music, *Popular Musicology*, 2.

Robertson, Pamela (1996), *Guilty Pleasures: Feminist Camp from Mae West to Madonna*, Durham, North Carolna and London: Duke University Press.

Rogan, Johnny (1992), *Morrissey and Marr: The Severed Alliance*, London: Omnibus Press.

Rose, Tricia (1994), *Black Noise: Rap Music and Black Culture in Contemporary America*, Hanover: Wesleyan University Press.

Ross, Andrew (1993), 'This Bridge Called My Pussy', in L. Frank and P. Smith (eds), *Madonnarama: Essays on Sex and Popular Culture*, Pennsylvania: Cleis Press.

Rutherford, Jonathan (1988), 'Who's That Man', in R.Chapman and J. Rutherford (eds), *Male Order: Unwrapping Masculinity*, London: Lawrence & Wishart.

Ruud, Even (1997a), *Musikk og identitet*, Oslo: Universitetsforlaget.

Ruud, Even (1997b), 'Music and Identity', *Nordic Journal for Music Therapy*, 6/2.

Savage, Jon (1990), 'The Enemy Within: Sex, Rock, and Identity', in S. Frith (ed.), *Facing the Music*, London: Mandarin.

Savage, Jon (1996), *Time Travel: Pop, Media and Sexuality 1976–96*, London: Chatto & Windus.

Scott, Derek (1989), *The Singing Bourgeois: Songs of The Victorian Drawing Room and Parlour*, Milton Keynes: Open University Press.

Scott, Derek (1990), 'Music and Sociology for the 1990s: A Changing Critical Perspective', *The Music Quarterly*, 74/3, pp. 385–410.

Scott, Derek (ed.) (2000), *Music, Culture, and Society: A Reader*, Oxford: Oxford University Press.

Scott, D. and Hawkins, S. (1994), 'Critical Musicology: A Rationale', *Popular Musicology*, Vol. 1, p. 3.

Segal, Lynne (1977), *Slow Motion: Changing Masculinities*, Changing Men, London: Virago.

Seidler, Victor J. (1987), 'Reason, desire, and male sexuality', in P. Caplan (ed.), *The Cultural Construction of Sexuality*, London: Routledge.

Seidler, Victor J. (1994), *Unreasonable Men: Masculinity and Social Theory*, London: Routledge.

Shepherd, John (1977), 'The Musical Codings of Ideologies', in J. Shepherd, P. Virden, G. Vulliamy and T. Wishart (eds), *Whose Music? A Sociology of Musical Languages*, London and New Brunswick, NJ: Rutger University Press.

Shepherd, John (1982), 'A theoretical model for the sociomusicological analysis of popular musics, *Popular Music*, 2, pp. 145–77.

Shepherd, John (1987), 'Music and Male hegemony', in R. Leppert and S. McClary (eds), *Music and Society: the Politics of Composition, Performance, and Reception*, Cambridge: Cambridge University Press, pp. 151-72.

Shepherd, John (1991), *Music as Social Text*, Cambridge: Polity Press.

Shepherd, John (1993), 'Difference and Power in Music', in Ruth A. Solie (ed.), *Musicology and Difference: Gender and Sexuality in Music Scholarship*, London: University of California.

Shepherd, John (1994), 'Music, culture and interdisciplinarity: reflections on relationships', *Popular Music*, 13/2, pp. 127–141.

Shepherd, John and Wicke, Peter (1997), *Music and Cultural Theory*, Cambridge: Polity.

Shuker, Roy (1994), *Understanding Popular Music,* London: Routledge.

Simon, William (1996), *Postmodern Sexualities*, London: Routledge.

Small, Christopher (1987), *Music of the Common Tongue*, London: John Calder.

Solie, Ruth A. (1993), 'Introduction: On "Difference", in Ruth A. Solie (ed.), *Musicology and Difference: Gender and Sexuality in Music Scholarship*, London: University of California.

Sontag, S. (1964), 'Notes on Camp', in *Against Interpretation*, New York: Farrar, Strauss and Giroux.

Stam, Robert (1989), *Subversive Pleasures: Bakhtin, Cultural Criticism and Film*, London: The John Hopkins University Press.

Stefani, Gino (1984), 'An interview with Gino Stefani', by U. Fiori, IASPM Newsletter, 5, pp. 18–19.

Stefani, Gino (1987a), 'A Theory of musical competence', *Semiotic*, 66, 7–22.

Stefani, Gino (1987b), 'Melody: A popular perspective', *Popular Music*, 6/1, pp. 21–35.

Stokes, Martin (ed.) (1997), *Ethnicity, Identity and Music: The Musical Construction of Place,* Oxford: Berg Publishers.

Storry, M. and Childs, P. (1997), *British Cultural Identities*, London: Routledge.

Straw, Will (1993), 'Popular Music and Postmodernism in the 1980s', in S. Frith, A. Goodwin and L. Grossberg (eds), *Sound and Vision: The Music Video Reader*, London: Routledge, pp. 3–24.

Stringer, Julian (1992), 'The Smiths: repressed (but remarkably dressed)', *Popular Music*, 11, pp. 15–26.

Subotnick, Rose Rosengard (1991), *Developing Variations – Style and Ideology in Western Music*, Minnesota: University of Minnesota.

Sweeney Turner, Steve (1994), 'Trivial Pursuits', *Musical Times*, April 1994.

Sweeney Turner, Steve (1996), 'Björk and the Figure of the Machine', paper delivered to the Centre for Cultural Studies, University of Leeds.

Sweeney Turner (1998), Review of *Sexing the Groove*, S. Whiteley (ed.), *Popular Musicology* Vol. 3.

Tagg, Philip (1979), *Kojak – 50 Seconds of Television Music: Towards the Analysis of Affekt in Popular Music*, Department of Musicology, University of Gothenburg.

Tagg, Philip (1982), 'Analysing popular music: theory, method and practice', *Popular Music*, 2, pp. 37–67.

Tagg, Philip (1987), 'Musicology and the Semiotics of Popular Music', *Semiotica*, 66-1/3, pp. 37–67.

Tagg, Philip (1989), ' "Black music", "Afro-American music" and "European music," ' *Popular Music*, 8/3, pp. 285–98.

Tagg, Philip (1991), Fernando the Flute, unpublished conference paper, University of Liverpool.

Tagg, Philip (1992), *Towards a Sign Typology of Music*, UK IASPM conference paper presented at University College, Salford.

Théberge, Paul (1997), *Any Sound You Can Imagine: Making Music/Consuming Technology*, Hanover: Wesleyan University Press.

Toorn, Pieter C. van den (1995), *Music, Politics, and the Academy*, Los Angeles: University of California.

Toynbee, Jason (2000), *Making Popular Music: Musicians, Creativity and Institutions*, London: Arnold.

Treitler, Leo (1993), 'Gender and Other Dualities of Music History', in Ruth A. Solie (ed.) *Musicology and Difference: Gender and Sexuality in Music Scholarship*, University of California.

Uhelski, Jan (2001), interview with Morrissey, *Mojo*, April.

Walser, Robert (1992), 'Eruptions: heavy metal appropriations of classical virtuosity', *Popular Music*, 11/3, pp. 263–308

Walser, Robert (1993a), *Running with the Devil: power, gender, and madness in heavy metal music*, Hanover: Wesleyan University Press.

Walser, Robert (1993b), 'Forging Masculinity: Heavy-Metal Sounds and Images of Gender', in S. Frith, A. Goodwin and L. Grossberg (eds), *Sound and Vision*, London: Routledge.

Walser, Robert (1994), 'Prince as Queer Poststructuralist', *Popular Music and Society*, 18/2, pp. 79–89.

Ward, Brian (1998), *Just my soul responding: Rhythm and Blues, black consciousness and race relations*, London: University College London Press.

Warning, R. (1982), 'Irony and the "Order of Discourse" in Flaubert', M. Watson (trans.), *New Literary History* 13/2, pp. 253–86.

Whiteley, Sheila (1992a), *The Space between the Notes*, London: Routledge.

Whiteley, Sheila (1997), 'Seduced by the Sign: An analysis of the textual links between sound and image in pop videos', in S. Whiteley (ed.), *Sexing the Groove*, London: Routledge, pp. 259–276.

Whiteley, Sheila (1997b), 'Introduction', in S. Whiteley (ed.), *Sexing the Groove*, London: Routledge.

Whiteley, Sheila (1998), 'Repressive Representations: Patriarchy and Femininities in Rock Music of the Counterculture', in T. Swiss, J. Sloop and A. Herman (eds), *Mapping the Beat*, Oxford: Blackwell.

Whiteley, Sheila (2000), *Women and Popular Music: Sexuality, Identity and Subjectivity*, London: Routledge.

Wicke, Peter (1990), Rock Music: Culture, Aesthetics and Sociology, R. Fogg (trans.), Cambridge University Press.

Wishart, Trevor (1977), 'Musical Writing, Musical Speaking', in J. Shepherd, P. Virden, G. Vulliamy and T. Wishart (eds), *Whose Music? A Sociology of Musical Languages*, London: Latimer.

Wood, Elizabeth (1994), 'Sapphonics', in P. Brett, E. Wood and G.C. Thomas (eds), *Queering the Pitch: The New Gay and Lesbian Musicology*, London: Routledge.

Discography

Madonna

The First Album, Sire (1983)
Like A Virgin, Sire (1984)
True Blue, Sire (1986)
Who's That Girl, Sire (1987)
You Can Dance, Sire (1987)
Like A Prayer, Sire (1989)
I'm Breathless, Sire (1990)
The Immaculate Collection, Sire (1990)
Erotica, Sire (1992)
Bedtime Stories, Maverick (1994)
Something To Remember, Maverick (1995)
Ray of Light, Maverick (1998)
Music, Warner (2000)

Morrissey (including The Smiths)

Hatful of Hollow, Rough Trade (1984)
Meat Is Murder, Rough Trade (1985)
The Queen Is Dead, Rough Trade (1986)
World Won't Listen, Rough Trade (1987)
Louder Than Bombs, Rough Trade (1987)
Strangeways Here We Come, Rough Trade (1987)
Viva Hate, HMV (1988)
Bona Drag, HMV (1990)
Kill Uncle, HMV (1991)
Your Arsenal, HMV (1992)
Beethoven Was Deaf, HMV (1993)
Vauxhall and I, Parlophone (1994)
Southpaw Grammar, RCA (1995)
Maladjusted, Island (1997)

Annie Lennox (including Eurythmics)

In the Garden, RCA (1981)
Sweet Dreams (Are Made Of This), RCA (1983)
Touch, RCA (1983)

Touch Dance, RCA (1984)
Be Yourself Tonight, RCA (1985)
Revenge, RCA (1986)
Savage, RCA (1987)
We Too Are One, RCA (1989)
Diva, RCA (1992)
Medusa, RCA (1995)

Pet Shop Boys

Please, Parlophone (1986)
Disco, Remixes, Parlophone (1986)
Actually, Parlophone (1987)
Introspective, Parlophone (1988)
Behaviour, Parlophone (1990)
Discography, Collection, Parlophone (1991)
Very, Parlophone (1993)
Relentless, Parlophone (1993)
Disco 2, Remixes, Parlophone (1994)
Alternative, Parlophone (1995)
Bilingual, Parlophone (1996)
Originals, Parlophone (1997)
Bilingual Special Edition, Parlophone (1997)

Prince

For You, Warner (1978)
Prince, Warner (1979)
Dirty Mind, Warner (1980)
Controversy, Warner (1981)
1999, Warner (1982)
Purple Rain, Warner (1984)
Around The World In A Day, Warner (1985)
Parade, Paisley Park (1986)
Sign O' The Times, Paisley Park (1987)
Lovesexy, Paisley Park (1988)
Batman, Warner (1989)
Graffiti Bridge, Paisley Park (1990)
Diamonds And Pearls, Paisley Park (1991)
Symbol, Paisley Park (1992)
Prince: The Hits Collection, Paisley Park (1993)
The Black Album, Warner (1994)
Come, Warner (1994)
The Gold Experience, Warner (1995)

Chaos and Disorder, Warner (1996)
Emancipation, NPG (1996)
Crystal Ball, NPG (1998)
Newpower Soul, NPG (1998)

Index